THE
EVERYTHING

PARENT'S GUIDE TO

CHILDREN
WITH
ASTHMA

Professional advice to help
your child manage symptoms,
be more active, and breathe better

Janice C. Simmons

Technical Review by Marijo A. Miller Ratcliffe, A.R.N.P., M.N.

A adamsmedia

Avon, Massachusetts

To Jim, Alexander, and Margaret, thanks for your guidance.

• • •

An Everything® Series Book.
Everything® and everything.com® are registered trademarks of F+W Publications, Inc.

Published by Adams Media, an F+W Publications Company
57 Littlefield Street, Avon, MA 02322 U.S.A.
www.adamsmedia.com

ISBN 10: 1-59869-430-8
ISBN 13: 978-1-59869-430-7

Printed in Canada.

J I H G F E D C B A

Library of Congress Cataloging-in-Publication Data
is available from the publisher.

*This book is available at quantity discounts for bulk purchases.
For information, please call 1-800-289-0963.*

*All the examples and dialogues used in this book are fictional, and have
been created by the author to illustrate disciplinary situations.*

THE EVERYTHING®

PARENT'S GUIDE TO

CHILDREN WITH ASTHMA

Dear Reader,

Years ago, being a child with asthma meant sitting on the side-lines. Now, it means being in the game—literally. It's great seeing several of my son's friends, who have had asthma since they were young, playing alongside him in football, baseball, soccer, and basketball. They're not going to let a chronic condition such as asthma penalize them as they charge through life.

That's the way it should be.

They've had great support from their families and their health care providers to help them manage their asthma. They've learned what medications work for them, what triggers to avoid, and how to manage their symptoms better—before an emergency occurs.

Sometimes, children with asthma have difficulties reaching those goals for a variety of reasons. While the information is out there, it's difficult during our busy days as parents to wade through the volumes of news and reports to find what works—at home, at school, and in the community—for children with asthma.

I hope this book can provide new, informative, and practical ideas to assist your home team.

Janice C. Simmons

Welcome to

THE

EVERYTHING

PARENT'S GUIDES

As a parent, you're swamped with conflicting advice and parenting techniques that tell you what is best for your child. THE EVERYTHING® PARENT'S GUIDES get right to the point about specific issues. They give you the most recent, up-to-date information on parenting trends, behavior issues, and health concerns—providing you with a detailed resource to help you ease your parenting anxieties.

THE EVERYTHING® PARENT'S GUIDES are an extension of the bestselling Everything® series in the parenting category. These family-friendly books are designed to be a one-stop guide for parents. If you want authoritative information on specific topics not fully covered in other books, THE EVERYTHING® PARENT'S GUIDES are the perfect resource to ensure that you raise a healthy, confident child.

When you're done reading, you can finally say you know **EVERYTHING**®!

DIRECTOR OF INNOVATION Paula Munier

EDITORIAL DIRECTOR Laura M. Daly

EXECUTIVE EDITOR, SERIES BOOKS Brielle K. Matson

ASSOCIATE COPY CHIEF Sheila Zwiebel

ACQUISITIONS EDITOR Kerry Smith

DEVELOPMENT EDITOR Brett Palana-Shanahan

PRODUCTION EDITOR Casey Ebert

Visit the entire Everything® series at *www.everything.com*

▶**Asthma** n. **1.** A chronic inflammatory condition of the airways that can cause—without appropriate treatment—varying levels of breathing difficulties.

Contents

Introduction

BREATHE. JUST BREATHE. Today, many children with asthma can deeply inhale and release their breaths slowly to create soap bubbles or scatter milky white dandelions seeds or cool their hot soups. They don't cough, nor do they wheeze. With new medications and new knowledge that sheds light on how to control asthma, they almost take for granted what even a generation or two before them couldn't fully imagine: Safely controlling their asthma—by reducing constriction and inflammation of their airways—to do almost anything they want.

But there's a flip side to this picture. Many other children with asthma—perhaps even friends of those children who are controlling their asthma symptoms well—find themselves excusing themselves from gym class for fear of triggering their asthma symptoms. Or, maybe they have become regulars at the local hospital's emergency room for when they have one of their frequent asthma flare-ups.

Today in the United States, an estimated 6.5 million children under age eighteen (almost 9 percent of the population) are now diagnosed with asthma. This rate has more than doubled since 1980, according to the Centers for Disease Control and Prevention. It's now the most common chronic childhood disease in the country.

But, despite the medical inroads that have been made in asthma treatment and control, many children in this growing population are still finding it hard to breathe. They're continuing to cough and wheeze during the day, and sleep uncomfortably through the night. Many don't have an asthma action plan or they're not sure how to use a peak flow meter or inhaler correctly. These children are letting asthma symptoms manage them—instead of them managing it.

Parents know that it's a tough job getting on top of asthma—trying to monitor symptoms or figure out if those prescribed medications are doing their jobs. Oftentimes, it means working with a reluctant child who hates being different from friends or siblings.

There's no easy answer—especially working with a health care system that can be fragmented and short of time when it comes to communicating effectively. But you don't have to let that control you—you can control it by asking physicians and health care providers to partner with you and answer your questions about how to best manage your children's asthma. Guidelines exist about getting the best outcomes for asthma. You should know about them.

You also can take control of your indoor environment—eliminating tobacco smoke and eradicating molds and dust mites from your home, and taking aim at air quality and chemical use in the schools. And, you can take control of your outdoor environment—monitoring the air quality in your neighborhood.

As a community, we have to take control as well. In particular, people need more understanding of why the pediatric population with asthma is expanding so quickly. Aside from looking at genetic relationships, many theories are now being explored regarding exposure to viruses, environmental pollutants, or even lifestyle behaviors.

As you are seeing, medical science has moved along quickly to find better ways to treat and manage asthma symptoms. But sometimes science gets ahead of what you can practically do every day to help your children understand what asthma is and how they can live with it and control it.

The aim of *The Everything® Parent's Guide to Children with Asthma* is to let you know that children with asthma can learn to confidently manage their condition—with you—and enjoy everything life has in store for them. Just remember, there's an easier way to breathe—today and every day.

Acknowledgments

With the current trend, soon one in ten children in this country will have asthma. It's a chronic condition that knows no boundaries. I want to thank those families that talked to me about what it is like to live with asthma. I heard your concerns and expectations, and I hope they are reflected in these pages.

CHAPTER 1

Asthma Defined

To understand asthma, it helps to understand the word "asthma" itself, which comes from the Greek word meaning to pant. While the disease has ancient roots, it's still very active today. New treatments and new approaches toward asthma have changed the way people view asthma. But when your child is diagnosed with asthma, you worry—which is normal. But now that you have more information at your fingertips, are you doing all that you can to help the child understand what asthma is—and how he can better manage it?

How Does Asthma Occur?

Ask your child what he least likes about asthma, and he'll likely respond that it's when it seems hard for him to breathe sometimes— maybe like trying to suck air from a straw. Or maybe he will complain that his chest hurts or that he can't catch his breath. It may seem scary for him—and you.

Asthma affects the bronchial tubes, which are also called airways. As your child probably knows, when he breathes normally, air is pulled into his nose and mouth. It then goes into the windpipe or trachea, through the airways, and into the lungs. In the lungs, oxygen is delivered that goes through the blood stream and out to the rest of the body. Meanwhile, carbon dioxide is removed and then exhaled through the airways back out again.

 **Fact**

Individuals with asthma have airways that become inflamed. In addition to producing a thick layer of mucus, they swell and become sensitive to certain stimuli, called triggers, such as viruses that cause colds, mold, pollen, household dust, exercise, fragrances, air pollutants, secondhand tobacco smoke, or wood smoke. This reaction causes the smooth muscles that line the airways to constrict—making it difficult for air to move in and out of the lungs.

With asthma, breathing difficulties can happen periodically. When this occurs, your child is having what can be referred to as an asthma attack, flare-up, or episode. Without a short-term quick-relief medication, these attacks can last for several hours.

Between the attacks, your child's breathing can seem normal. Other times, though, it may be accompanied by various symptoms such as coughing, wheezing, or nasal congestion. Sometimes, it may only appear when doing physical exercise or, more commonly, it can appear during the night—disrupting your child's sleep.

Many daily long-term control medications have been introduced in recent years to help prevent the swelling and inflammation of those airways and stop the occurrence of asthma flare-ups.

The Asthma Impact

For your child, asthma symptoms could interfere with his day at school or with his favorite activities. Perhaps you might notice on some days that he may have less stamina during play than other children, or he may be trying to limit or avoid various sports or physical activities to prevent coughing or wheezing.

This could be the story for millions of other children as well. According to the Centers for Disease Control and Prevention (CDC), nearly 9 percent of all children—6.5 million children under the age eighteen—were reported to have asthma in the United States in 2005. This was almost double the rate since 1980, when 3.6 percent of children reportedly had asthma. These numbers currently make it one of the top chronic conditions among children in the country.

Numbers Snapshot

The CDC numbers show that asthma, as a significant health problem, is making an impact on many children's lives:

- Children with at least one asthma attack in the previous year (nearly 4 million children) missed a cumulative total of 12.8 million school days due to asthma in 2003.
- Over 5 percent of all children (3.8 million) had at least one asthma attack in the past year.
- Asthma-related emergency department visits for children remained fairly stable from 1992 to 2004—103 visits per 10,000 children in 2004—compared to 98 visits per 10,000 in 1992.
- Twenty-seven hospitalizations for asthma per 10,000 children were reported in 2004 for a total of 198,000 hospitalizations nationwide—or the third leading cause of hospitalization in the country for children.
- After increasing steadily between 1980 and 1998, asthma death rates among children have declined since 1999 from 3.2 deaths per one million children under age 18 in 1999 to 2.5 deaths per one million (or 186 children) in 2004.

The number of asthma-related visits to physician offices have increased sharply since the early 1990s, from less than forty visits per 1,000 children under age eighteen in 1990 to eighty-nine visits per 1,000 in 2004. This rise continued while the rate of visits to physician offices by children for any reason did not increase.

This may not be bad news, though, according to the CDC. While part of this spike in office visits might be related to an increase in severe asthma symptoms, this also might reflect increased health care use to improve asthma control.

Disparities

Behind the numbers, though, are faces—and disparities. The numbers show that some population groups are being disproportionately affected by asthma.

Among racial and ethnic groups, Puerto Rican and non-Hispanic African American children were reported to have the highest percentages of asthma (19 percent and 13 percent respectively).

In 2005, American Indian and Alaska Native children had asthma rates 25 percent higher and African American children had rates 60 percent higher than white children. Puerto Rican children had a rate 140 percent higher than non-Hispanic white children. The rates for Asian American and Mexican American children, though, were low.

The statistics show that African American children are visiting physician offices far less than white children. This disparity may be reflected in other outcomes: African American children had a 260 percent higher emergency department visit rate, a 250 percent higher hospitalization rate, and a 500 percent higher death rate.

The State Picture

Among the thirty-seven states for which data were available, the states with the highest percentage of children with asthma in 2005 were Massachusetts, Hawaii, Oklahoma, Maryland, and Rhode Island. The states with the lowest percentage of children with asthma were Utah, California, Iowa, Tennessee, and Washington.

Overall, the highest asthma rates among children were found in the Northeastern states and the least in the West Coast states.

Why More Asthma Cases?

As the number of children with asthma continues to increase, a natural question you might have is why? The answer, though, may not be clear and has been the cause of much discussion inside and outside the medical and scientific communities.

Younger Patients

One part of the increase may be related to the number of infants and toddlers being diagnosed with asthma. For many years, the medical community believed that children younger than three years could not have asthma. Instead, their providers would diagnose them, for instance, with conditions such as wheezy bronchitis or an upper respiratory infection.

Today, it is known that even infants may exhibit repetitive symptoms that suggest an asthma diagnosis. And, the sooner they are treated, the sooner they can feel better and avoid possible lung damage in the future.

Also, through medical technology, more babies born at lower birth weights are surviving. However, studies have shown that a lower birth weight may be associated with more respiratory symptoms and asthma during the child's younger years.

Also, other studies have linked frequent respiratory infections during a child's early years with the development of asthma, especially if that child has a history of eczema and/or allergies or parents with asthma or allergies.

A Too-Clean Environment?

One theory proposed to explain the increased prevalence of asthma is sometimes called the "hygiene hypothesis." This idea suggests that because personal and public hygiene have improved in recent years, children now get fewer infectious diseases during early childhood and are treated with antibiotics more frequently than many years ago.

Essential

The hygiene hypothesis suggests that as a child's immune system develops, his body responds to allergens and pollutants rather than bacteria and viruses. As a result, the immune system becomes "biased" toward allergic responses.

In turn, this leads to an increased incidence of asthma—particularly among individuals who have family histories of asthma and allergies. On the other side, if a child is exposed to infections earlier in life, he may have a reduced risk of asthma or allergic diseases. While the hypothesis continues to be studied, this may explain the association between large family size, later birth order, daycare attendance, and reduced asthma risks.

Pollutants in the Environment

Conversely, some have pointed to increases in outdoor air pollutants. The National Institute of Environmental Health Sciences (NIEHS), a part of the National Institutes of Health (NIH), found in a study of air pollution levels of ten Southern California cities that the closer children live to a freeway or major highway, the greater their chances of being diagnosed with asthma.

The researchers reported that they saw a relationship between higher levels of asthma and certain pollutants that come from the burning of fossil fuels—such as the exhaust of cars or trucks—as well as from emissions from industrial plants.

Smoking

The rise in cigarette use by adults during the past century may explain the asthma epidemic in children, according to some researchers. Secondhand tobacco smoke that is inhaled by nonsmokers has a higher concentration of some toxic substances than the smoke inhaled by smokers.

Alert!

Others have looked at the effect of global warming—saying it could impact individuals with asthma because of more carbon dioxide in the air and longer plant growing seasons. These longer growing seasons can mean more pollen in the air, which in turn can trigger more asthma symptoms throughout the year.

Children breathe more air than adults relative to their size and have narrower airways, so secondhand smoke becomes a greater risk factor of asthma in children—and it can increase the severity of their asthma symptoms, the researchers note. In various developing countries where more people are beginning to smoke, a similar pattern of increased cases of childhood asthma is emerging, one study has observed.

Is There a Cure for Asthma?

Taking prescribed medicines such as inhaled corticosteroids have been found to benefit young children with frequent wheezing and breathing problems by reducing the number of days and nights with asthma symptoms and allowing the child to be more active. However, ongoing research from the NIH has found that this daily treatment will not prevent the development of persistent asthma when the medications are stopped, which is defined as symptoms occurring at least two days a week (but not daily).

 **Essential**

While many factors come into play, various studies have suggested that many children's symptoms will improve through their teen years; up to half are likely to be wheeze-free by the time they turn into adults. However, they may not be entirely out of the woods: Up to 80 percent of those symptom-free adults could experience various bronchial problems or even redevelop asthma.

What Is Asthma Control?

According to the National Asthma Education and Prevention Program guidelines, the goals of therapy for asthma control are: minimal or no chronic symptoms day or night; minimal or no flare-ups; no limitations on activities; no school or parents' work missed; minimal use of quick-relief medication (such as albuterol) with minimal or no adverse effects from medications; and pulmonary (or lung) function as close to normal as possible.

Getting your child to those goals requires a few key steps.

Diagnosing

A detailed medical history and physical examination is performed by a physician or other health care provider in order to help identify symptoms that may indicate asthma. Those symptoms include wheezing, coughing, shortness of breath, or continuing chest tightness; symptoms that occur or become worse in the presence of asthma triggers such as exercise, viral infections, dust mites, pollen, or weather changes; or symptoms that occur or worsen at night—disturbing a child while he sleeps. When those symptoms repetitively occur after exposure to triggers, and improve when given albuterol or other quick-relief asthma medications, a young child may be diagnosed with asthma.

However, in a child over six years of age, a health care provider's assessment will be greatly enhanced, and findings may be affirmed, when diagnosing asthma through "objective assessments" such as through a machine called a spirometer that measures airflow from the lungs. In addition, many health care centers are able to measure exhaled nitric oxide, a gas that is exhaled and indicates the presence of inflammation in airways.

To get everyone on the same page, your health care provider should develop an asthma action plan or self-management plan customized for your child. The asthma action plan gives you, your child, and your family—and anyone else who interacts with your child—information about when and how to use daily medications, emergency medications, and her peak flow meter. It also helps indicate when to seek emergency medical care.

Medicating

Except for very mild cases of asthma, your child likely will be prescribed both a quick-relief medication to treat his symptoms and one of a variety of longer-acting control medications taken daily to help stop inflammation.

But remind your child that for the medications to work, he has to take them. The quick-relief medication may make him feel fine now—it relaxes the muscles around his airways. But, what he doesn't realize is that inflammation in his airways—which daily control medicines help—may be getting worse without them.

Avoiding Triggers

Asthma triggers can be divided into two categories: those related to allergies and those that are not. Asthma can be triggered by such allergens as mold spores, animal dander, foods, or contents found in household dust. An estimated 75 percent of children in the U.S. have this type of asthma.

Asthma also can be caused by irritants that aggravate the nose, throat, or airways. These include cigarette smoke, strong odors or smells, wood smoke, household cleaners, or environmental pollutants.

Asthma symptoms also are triggered through infections such as colds or pneumonia, or exercise, and may be triggered by other physical conditions such gastroesophageal reflux disease, medications, and emotional anxiety. Some children have been found to have several triggers, and addressing them all can improve their health.

The Asthma Disconnect

While many know how to control asthma symptoms, it is often not being done by all asthmatics—including children—for a variety of reasons.

According to 2003 CDC statistics, only 39 percent of children with asthma received an asthma management plan from their health care providers; 57 percent reported being taught how to monitor peak flow; and 52 percent reported being advised how to change things at home or school to improve asthma management.

A national survey of asthma patients and parents of asthma patients released in 2007 by the National Consumers League also found that:

- Sixty-three percent of parents said they understood their children's condition very or extremely well (compared with 57 percent of adults), but only 17 percent reported that their child currently used a peak flow meter to monitor their breathing.
- Ninety percent of parents reported their child's asthma as mild or moderate, but nearly 20 percent said their child had very severe or extremely severe coughing (20 percent), difficulty breathing (19 percent), wheezing (18 percent), tightness in chest (18 percent), and difficulty falling or staying asleep (19 percent).

- The perception of mild symptoms may translate into under-dosing: 67 percent of parents said they permitted under-dosing—or permitting their children to take less than the prescribed dose of their quick-relief inhalers—because they felt their flare-ups were not severe enough.

Parents of asthmatic children, though, did reveal a greater level of involvement, concern, and anxiety than adult asthmatics: 34 percent of parents said they were more likely to contact their physician than adults (compared to 11 percent) when they had questions between doctor visits.

Asthma in the Future

More than fifty years ago, the metered-dose inhaler was introduced as a popular way to easily carry quick-relief medication anywhere you went. Since that time, new devices, new medications, and new ways of diagnosing asthma have been introduced to the market. But other ideas are continually springing up—maybe bringing asthma symptom management to a new level. Perhaps, even finding a way to cure asthma may not be far off.

 Essential

New emphasis could shift to the prenatal level. Research has been ongoing into what mothers do before an infant is born—such as smoking or eating foods with antioxidants or omega-3 fatty acids—and how that can impact their children's chances of developing or not developing asthma in the future.

Interest is always high for creating new medications that work quickly, have fewer side effects, and are more potent, or for improving devices or delivery systems that can make current medications work even better.

There are a few other areas where the treatment of asthma could be changing as well.

Thermoplasty

A process called bronchial thermoplasty singes away smooth muscle from the bronchial airways in an effort to significantly reduce symptoms in people with moderate to severe asthma. Bronchial thermoplasty involves moving a flexible catheter with an expandable wire basket at the tip through the mouth and down the major airways that lead to the lungs.

The basket is expanded so it fits against an airway wall and sends a ten-second jolt of thermal energy to remove tissue and reduce smooth muscle. These are the muscles that contribute to asthma by contracting and narrowing the airway during an attack.

Target Genes

Research already has shown that asthma runs in families. When one or both parents have asthma, a child is more likely to develop it, too. This process is known as genetic susceptibility.

Researchers at NIEHS are taking this further to learn more about which genes make people susceptible to developing asthma when they encounter various asthma triggers in a process called gene expression profiling. They are currently screening thousands of genes at once to identify which genes are activated when a patient's airways become obstructed or inflamed.

And, science appears to be taking this in another direction as well. In Scotland, for example, researchers have identified a gene that could lead to a new treatment for asthma. This gene has been studied by teams working on diabetes, cancer, and heart disease. Their studies revealed that a certain gene makes young asthmatics two to three times more likely to have acute asthma attacks. They are hoping to replace inhaled corticosteroid therapies with tablets that are similar to those used to treat diabetes.

Remodeling

Remodeling refers to the presence of early structural changes in tissue lining the airways leading to a thicker airway wall, which creates a smaller caliber airway and makes it harder to breathe. Researchers have expressed an interest in identifying airway remodeling in young children with asthma as a way to detect and possibly prevent inflammation that may lead to reduced function later on in their lives.

Researchers have noted that cellular and biochemical changes have been detected in the airways of children with asthma and in children with respiratory symptoms or allergies even before a diagnosis of asthma has been made. Understanding the processes at work could lead in the future to new therapies and the modification of asthma's natural history, the researchers said.

New Detectors

Science may be moving beyond the traditional spirometer to detect if a child has asthma. Some medical facilities already are using devices that record and analyze exhaled nitrous oxide levels to find if asthma is present.

Under study is an "electronic nose" that uses sensors to determine if volatile organic compounds (VOCs) are present in an individual's breath. The nose, already in use in the wine and perfume industries, develops a "smell print" to compare the breath of an asthmatic with standardized readings.

CHAPTER 2

Raising the Asthmatic Child

I f your child has asthma—one of the most common chronic diseases among children in the country today—you may be worried that you have your work cut out for you. In a way, you do. Asthma, especially with more severe cases, is not something you take lightly. But, you're not alone. Guidance from health care providers, use of effective medications, better identification of asthma triggers, and more can make that work a little easier and help you address asthma in a way that is smarter—not harder—for you and your child.

Taking It Day by Day

When you heard that your child was first diagnosed with asthma, what first ran through your mind? Days lost at school for your child or at work for you because of symptoms related to asthma? Repeated trips to the hospital emergency room when severe attacks occurred? Your child sitting on the sidelines while her friends enjoy themselves on the playground or soccer field?

Could these scenarios happen? Yes, they could—if your child's asthma is ignored or left untreated. But does it have to happen? Absolutely not. Today, working with your "team"—including you and your child, your health care provider, your child's school staff, your child's sports coach, your child's caregiver, and even your health plan—you can erase these troubling scenes from you mind.

Instead, you and your child can become knowledgeable about what asthma is—and the best way to manage it. Whether it will be easy or difficult is not easy to predict. There are so many variables: the age of your child, the locale where you live, the availability of health insurance, the sensitivity and communication skills of your health care provider, and even the environment inside and outside of your home.

 Essential

> With a better understanding of what causes your child's symptoms—plus use of appropriate medications and various lifestyle changes—your child can grow up with her family and friends being healthy, happy, and active.

For some children, their asthma symptoms will disappear as they grow older. But, there's no guarantee that will happen. For now, it's important to find out how you and your family can help your child manage her condition—each day as it comes.

Communicating with Your Child

How you talk with your child about his asthma and related symptoms is very important. Communications, of course, will vary with the age of a child, and the messages will evolve as well as he grows older. But, it is important that as a parent you anticipate what to expect, and help guide your child toward appropriate asthma management and daily activity decisions. As your child's understanding of asthma grows and develops, he will need to take more—and eventually all—responsibility for his care. Allow your child to participate in care as his age permits, and teach him appropriate words and terms for communicating symptoms, as well as the names and appropriate use of medications and equipment.

Setting the Tone

The key to communicating with your child is to first understand your own reaction to the diagnosis of asthma. Initially, learning that your child has asthma can be confusing and upsetting. You may wonder: "Why my child?" Or, you may feel angry with yourself that you didn't recognize that symptoms—such as coughing or wheezing—were actually related to asthma. Those feelings are natural among parents and families.

Alert!

If your messages to your child are continuously fearful and anxious about his asthma, you may not be helping your child. Keep in mind that while anxiety by itself does not cause asthma, constant worry and stress could actually lead to worsening asthma symptoms.

Children may internalize that worry—afraid to run, exercise, or play with other children. This could lead to other problems in the long run for them, such as poor physical conditioning and lack of socialization skills. Increasingly, it appears that obesity may even be another factor that can make asthma worse.

If you find yourself extremely anxious about your child's condition, talk to your health care provider about your feelings, or find other parents of asthmatic children in local support groups. While it's understandable for you to be cautious when it comes to asthma symptoms, you also want your child to feel confident that she can manage her condition in a variety of situations.

Empower Through Knowledge

Children, even as young as preschoolers, should have an understanding of what their condition is and how severe it could be. Talk with him about what signs and symptoms make him uncomfortable, and when he should mention them, for instance, to you, a caretaker, a teacher, or a coach.

These are symptoms—maybe a feeling of tightness in the chest or breathing problems while playing a sport—that might not be immediately apparent to those watching over him but may signal an asthma problem.

He should be familiar with what his green zone (doing well), yellow zone (getting worse), and red zone (medical alert) mean on his asthma action plan or daily management plan prepared by his health care provider. This should be on file with his daycare provider and/or school. And, he should be aware of the potential "triggers"—such as dust mites, pollen, or air pollution—that could affect his asthma symptoms.

Dissolving the Myths

Aside from talking to your child about what asthma is, you need to emphasize what it is not:

- Asthma cannot be cured. However, its symptoms can be controlled with medication and management. Among some children, symptoms—such as wheezing or coughing—may improve as a child gets older.
- While asthma is a common chronic condition, it is not an infectious or contagious disease. While this may be an obvious point to adults, it may not be to children who today are constantly bombarded by news headlines about outbreaks and diseases. Let her know how asthma is related to heredity (possibly other family members have it) or to various triggers. (See Chapter 4.)
- Asthma is not a condition to be ignored—even when your child feels better. When she feels healthy and free of her

symptoms, daily medications should not be stopped. Just remind her of why she is feeling better in the first place—with her medications.

- Asthma is not another word for inactivity. In years past, children were persuaded not to be active—lest they trigger an asthma episode. Today, the opposite is true: the asthmatic child should be encouraged to be as active as possible— providing her asthma is under control.

- Use of inhaled steroids to treat asthma will not harm your child physically, will not become addictive, or will not make her appearance "puffy." Part of those concerns may be based on the confusion between inhaled asthma steroids and anabolic steroids, which have been used and abused by some athletes to become stronger. These are two different compounds.

- Going to the emergency room or being hospitalized is not a regular part of having asthma. While it can happen, the goal should be for your child to control her asthma through proper management every day.

- You do not need to buy lots of expensive retail products and equipment to control your child's asthma symptoms at home. While many products are on the market (see Chapter 16) to reduce indoor triggers that are related to asthma, reducing symptoms starts with basic activities such as vacuuming, eliminating molds, and reducing exposure to tobacco smoke (see Chapter 15).

Be a Part of Life

Help your child realize that asthma is not a condition that automatically places him on the sidelines and prevents him from participating in many activities with his family and friends.

If your child feels disconnected from those around him at times because of his asthma, encourage him to talk about it. Maybe he might be embarrassed or self-conscious about his condition or frustrated with continuing use of medications. Keep an open mind about suggestions—such as using a smaller inhaler that can be used without notice during the day.

If your child is using asthma as a reason why he needs to skip activities in school, such as recess or physical education class, additional questions may need to be answered to determine if his asthma is being adequately managed. In fact, 10 to 15 percent of Olympic athletes have learned to manage their asthma and compete at that elite level. This indicates that asthma can be controlled and should not be a reason to prevent a child from actively playing with friends.

When it comes to household chores, keep in mind that some asthmatic children probably should avoid various chores such as vacuuming floors and carpets, dry dusting, raking leaves, mowing grass, or brushing or bathing pets because they might trigger asthma symptoms.

But on the other hand, they can do many other chores around the house such as washing dishes, folding laundry, cooking most foods (except for fried foods), running errands, washing cars, food shopping, or even babysitting.

Talking with Your Family

While it's important to talk to your child about her asthma, also remember to talk to family members about her condition—both about what she needs and also what they need in terms of monitoring and understanding it. Talking openly with everyone in the family is important in successfully managing asthma.

Feelings of jealousy or resentment could be triggered among siblings if they perceive the asthmatic child is getting special treatment or extra attention from you. Think of it: the asthmatic child may get out of vacuuming her room or she automatically gets the top bunk so she can avoid allergens while she sleeps. Or, a trip or family event may be delayed or postponed if an asthmatic episode occurs.

Essential

Rather than let resentments related to the asthmatic child build up among family members, make sure everyone meets together once a week—like a team—to discuss the current situation. Have them speak together about what their concerns are and why they feel the way they do.

Talk to all the children honestly, and explain how they all have to work together to help support asthma management in the household. In particular, they may need to find ways to keep down triggers such as dust, mold, or animal danders in your home.

This may sometimes involve difficult decisions such as removing a family pet or no longer eating snacks in the family room on the sofa. However, all family members should feel they have some input in reaching goals.

When Families Separate

When parents separate or divorce, it can be a traumatic time for a family. When at least one of the children in that family has a chronic illness such as asthma, new challenges can be thrown into the situation —such as who will pay for various aspects of care.

This is one of those times that differences should be put aside— for the sake of your child with asthma. This means committing yourselves to maintaining a smoke-free environment at home and in vehicles, and removing sources of possible asthma triggers such as pets. It also means not arguing in front of the child about her asthma and its treatment.

To help, work with your child's physician on drawing up a plan incorporating what is needed to treat and control his asthma every day. It will help your child to know that his parents are both on the same page when it comes to managing his asthma symptoms.

Talking with Your Health Care Provider

One of the critical members of your asthma "team" is your health care provider. In raising your asthmatic child, the health care provider should be there to provide guidance and advice, note changes in symptoms, adjust medications when necessary, keep up to date with the latest science and guidelines, and answer your questions.

But, the type of communication you have with this health care provider—be it a pediatrician, a family health care provider, or a specialist—will differ somewhat from visits with other health care providers. Each time your child sees this provider—whether it's a follow-up visit or a visit related to an asthma event—the health care provider should wear not only the hat of a prescriber but that of an educator, consultant, and even good listener. At least two or three times a year, your child should be re-evaluated to see if her treatment plan is adequate.

 **Fact**

Asthma is not a static condition: it can change with each visit. Children can develop new triggers or change responses to medications. Sometimes children aren't even using the medications as required. The health care provider needs to work with the other members of your team—you and your child—to see what adjustments are needed to best manage your child's condition and prevent symptoms.

Unfortunately, many children with asthma do not appear to be getting the adjustments—or the education and advice—that they need. In a study of children with persistent asthma in Alabama, California, Illinois, and Texas, four out of five children were found not to be keeping their symptoms under control.

The reasons were numerous: nearly half had medications but failed to use their inhalers daily as required, and a third failed to obtain the medications that were prescribed.

In addition, about three out of four children with asthma symptoms were found to live with sources of asthma triggers in their homes including: a fireplace or wood stove, a kerosene heater, an unvented gas stove, cockroach infestation, dust mites, visible mold, and indoor pets. Almost one in six were exposed to secondhand tobacco smoke.

Also, poor office-based management was common among those children who were failing to control their asthma: more than half had not received an asthma management plan from a health care provider; more than a third had not been taught to use a peak flow meter; and one in six had never been taught to recognize their symptoms.

 Essential

To help your child better manage her condition, first consider finding a health care provider who can work with you and your child. This provider should be familiar with updated asthma guidelines for children—which look at issues of asthma severity and control—released by the National Asthma Education and Prevention Program of the National Institutes of Health (NIH) in 2007.

The objective of good asthma management is to establish treatment goals that not only prevent asthma symptoms from occurring today but to ensure better outcomes and quality of life down the road. Next, put those goals in writing by developing an action management plan that is easy to understand and effective in monitoring asthma symptoms day to day.

Tailoring Treatment Goals

To set asthma goals, you need a baseline. A challenge for any provider in treating a patient is tailoring a treatment plan to fit his level of asthma. Is it intermittent, mild persistent, moderate persistent, or severe persistent? To do this, your health care provider needs to ask specific questions regarding your child's medical history: Does your family have a history of asthma; how often does he wheeze; how does he react to certain asthma triggers; how is he sleeping; is he having problems breathing while in school; how often does he use a quick-relief medication; how does he react to exercise?

Then there are the objective measures of how is he really breathing. A child generally above the age of four or five will be asked during a physician visit to breathe into the hose of a spirometer, a machine that measures the speed and volume of air flowing in and out of his lungs. For younger children, signs and symptoms will be evaluated.

Assessing Severity

From these questions and testing, the severity of the child's underlying asthma can be determined, which will aid in the creation of an asthma action plan that provides medical directions. This level of severity looks at risk (i.e., reports of a flare-up requiring oral corticosteroids) and impairment (i.e., specific symptoms in the past two weeks or nighttime awakenings). Under the 2007 NIH guidelines, the classifications of asthma severity are separated into three age categories: 0 to 4 years, 5 to 11 years, and 12 years to adult. The severity classifications are:

- Intermittent—Asthma symptoms are mild and do not last for long, and quick-relief medications are needed infrequently. Generally, these children do not need hospital or emergency room care. However, severe flare-ups still could occur that might require additional medication.

- Mild Persistent—Brief but recurrent episodes may occur that are usually treated with quick-relief medications. Everyday medications, though, might be suggested. Symptoms such as coughing or wheezing may occur no more than twice a week.
- Moderate Persistent—Asthma symptoms appear daily, and quick-relief medications usually are needed daily. Daily inhaled corticosteroids probably will be needed. Risk for flare-ups exist that may point to a need for hospitalization or an emergency room visit.
- Severe Persistent—Symptoms appear daily, and quick-relief medications are quickly used up. Stronger inhaled cortico-steroids are needed. Asthma specialists may be needed in providing treatment.

Determining the level of severity usually depends on the frequency and intensity of asthma flare-ups, according to the guidelines. (See Appendix C.) Also, children who are determined to have intermittent symptoms still could encounter severe flare-ups.

Assessing Control

The current NIH asthma guidelines also encourage health care providers to assess how well a child's asthma is being controlled with treatment. The assessments, which review daily impairment and flare-up risks, are divided into three age categories: 0–4 years, 5–11 years, and 12 years to adult. The levels of control are:

- Well Controlled—Symptoms appear less than twice a week and no interference is reported with daily activities.
- Not Well Controlled—Symptoms appear more than twice a week and some limitation is reported with daily activities.
- Very Poorly Controlled—Symptoms occur throughout the day and normal activities are extremely limited.

A child receiving treatment who has no asthma flare-ups—or only one asthma flare-up that requires an oral corticosteroid—during a one-year period may be considered to have her condition well-controlled. A child with flare-ups more than three times a year that require oral corticosteroids may be considered to have very poorly controlled asthma. However, the guidelines note that not only the frequency but the intensity of the flare-ups needs to be taken into consideration as well when considering the level of asthma control.

In the long run, the goal is to develop a treatment plan and strategies that are targeted just for your child's asthma (Also see Chapters 3 and 6). And, it should be a plan that she is comfortable following every day—whether it's at home, school, a friend's house, an athletic field, or a nearby shopping mall.

Developing an Asthma Action Plan

To get on board with better control of asthma symptoms, a health care provider can help your child develop a written asthma action plan, which is also called a self-management plan. Keep in mind that the action plan is a way to provide direction—for you, a caretaker, a teacher, a coach, or anyone else who works with your child—to improve daily care and prevent asthma attacks. It also provides a guide to your child, and lets him know if he needs additional help.

The asthma action plan does not replace visiting your health care provider or imply that you and your child are left to manage his asthma alone. But, it gives you and your child points of reference to help you decide when asthma symptoms might be problematic—and what you can do to immediately address them before they become more serious. It also lets you follow a plan and identify when those symptoms indicate a need for emergency help.

Not all asthma episodes or attacks are the same, and some are worse than others. When severe, your child's airways can constrict to the point that they prevent adequate oxygen from getting to the rest of his body. But, by monitoring your child's asthma, most asthma episodes can be handled at home by following your asthma management plan.

Early Warning with Peak Flow Meters

One of the items listed on an asthma action plan is peak flow meter readings. To determine if your child's asthma is about to flare up, you could monitor her symptoms to see if her airways are narrowing—leading to troubled breathing or coughing. However, a quicker—and somewhat more reliable method—is to use a peak flow meter, a relatively inexpensive device that can measure lung function when your child blows into it.

Children can start using peak flow meters around the age of five years. With the peak flow meter, the more air the child can blow, the higher the numerical reading.

 **Fact**

If your child's airways are tightening, the peak flow meter readings become lower. Peak flow readings may be able to detect a possible asthma flare-up long before reduced breathing or other symptoms in your child become apparent.

To get the most from the peak flow meter, it's important to get a "personal best" reading when your child's airways are normal. This reading should appear near the top of the asthma action plan. The packaged inserts with the meter usually provide lists of normal values for their meters. Keep in mind, though, that your child's readings can be above or below these levels.

For infants and toddlers who, of course, are too young for peak flow meters, you should be alert for symptoms that could indicate an asthma attack such as agitated behavior, decreased feeding, rapid breathing rate (see chart below), inability to say more than a few words at a time without taking a breath, bluish discoloration of fingers or lips, and sucking in of the chest around the ribs or collarbone.

Normal respiratory rates change for children as they grow. The following is a guideline for normal breathing rates at rest in children:

AGE (Years)	RESPIRATORY RATE
0–1	30–40 breaths per minute
1–2	22–30 breaths per minute
2–4	20–26 breaths per minute
5–10	18–22 breaths per minute
10–18	16–20 breaths per minute

In the Action Plan Zones

These peak flow readings, plus information from the child's medical history, become pivotal in developing three zones to be used in the action plan:

- The green zone means the child is doing well in terms of breathing and his asthma appears well controlled. There is no coughing or wheezing, and he can play or sleep well. He could need some quick-relief medication—maybe before exercising or going outside when high pollen levels are present.
- The yellow zone means his symptoms are getting worse or caution is needed. In this zone, his airways may have begun to constrict (showing about 50 to 80 percent of his personal best reading). Some quick-relief medication may be needed every several hours, or possibly some longer-term medications might be needed.
- The red zone means your child's breathing is significantly impaired and the red zone plan for medications must be started to prevent an emergency from occurring. The peak flow reading may be between 0 to 50 percent of his personal best reading. If he has trouble walking or talking and

medicines do not appear to be helping, a call to his health care provider is needed. If that person is not available or you cannot contact someone from the child's health care provider's office right away, then a trip to the hospital or call for emergency help may be necessary. If your child is not responding to you or has severe difficulties breathing, blue lips or fingernail beds, or mucus membranes, call 911 right away.

Each child's plan will vary depending on several variables such as severity classifications (intermittent, mild persistent, moderate persistent, and severe persistent). Triggers should be indicated on the action plan, as well as your child's common asthma symptoms.

In addition to keeping your own asthma action plans, these should be distributed to your child's school, sports or physical fitness programs, and daycare program. But this document should not be considered static: It should be updated every few months—reflecting any changes in your child's triggers or medications.

Where You Live: The Indoor Environment

One survey found out that more than half of parents questioned thought only asthma symptoms—and not their underlying causes—could be treated. More studies have shown that when many triggers inside the home and even schools—ranging from dust mites to cockroaches to molds—are removed, asthma symptoms can be drastically reduced. (See Chapters 4 and 12.)

Sometimes these triggers may be in the most unexpected places such as in upholstery or bedding. Therefore, removing triggers may mean more than just laundering or cleaning, but taking new steps to make lifestyle changes: For instance, you could have your child place dirty clothes into a hamper in another room or avoid use of products with fragrances such as scented candles.

Where You Live: The Outdoor Environment

Where you raise your child could be influencing her symptoms. Auto exhaust, smog and ozone, particle pollution, or the lack of smoking bans could mean less than optimum, breathable air in the community where she lives and goes to school. It also could mean greater use of asthma medications, higher rates of school absenteeism, or increased emergency room visits or hospital admissions.

 Essential

While it's probably not practical to just move from an area because of poor air quality—and its impact on asthmatics—it does make sense to work with medical professionals to draw up asthma action plans to help children when they are outdoors, especially on days with high levels of air pollution.

To reduce risks on bad air days, make sure that your child:

- Limits the amount of time she spends outdoors playing.
- Keeps her outdoor activities as far as possible from busy roads, highways, and other sources of air pollution.
- Avoids congested streets and rush hour traffic.
- Has teachers, camp directors, and coaches with policies in place to protect her when air quality is poor.
- Has her inhaler and her spacer with her on bad air days to provide emergency relief.

Roadway Pollution

If you reside close to—or your child attends school near—a major highway or roadway, she may be breathing in air with pollutants from traffic that could be harming her lung development. For children without asthma, the pollution may be irritating their lungs and making them more susceptible to asthma.

In one study, children who lived within a third of a mile from major highways were found to be more likely to develop asthma or other respiratory diseases than children living about a mile away, according to researchers.

In the Children's Health Study, which followed a group of 3,600 children from the ages of ten through eighteen in Southern California, even healthy children who were not asthmatic showed decreases in their lung function from traffic pollution—if they lived near those roads. The researchers noted that someone having poor lung function as a child could face risks for respiratory and cardiovascular diseases later in life.

CHAPTER 3

Asthma Signs and Symptoms

You observe your child's symptoms—maybe sneezing, wheezing, coughing, or a runny nose. The questions begin: Is it related to a respiratory infection or an allergy—or is it asthma? Is another medical condition involved? Is a call to your health care provider or a trip to the emergency room necessary? These are all good questions—with a variety of answers. If it is asthma, different triggers and levels of severity should be considered. But one thing is certain: You want answers now.

The Asthma Diagnosis

You think your child might have asthma, but you're not sure. The signs and symptoms are there, but then again it could be something else. Since 1997, the National Asthma Education and Prevention Program of the National Institutes of Health has published guidelines for health care providers that suggest how to diagnose and manage asthma based on the latest research. The latest guidelines were published in 2007. The guidelines can give you insight on what a health care provider will be looking for during a medical visit.

The Key Indicators

A detailed medical history and physical examination is recommended that can help identify symptoms—or key indicators—that are likely to be related to asthma. Eczema, hay fever, or a family history of asthma or allergic diseases often are associated with asthma, but they are not considered key indicators by themselves. Combining them, though, with other multiple indicators could increase the possibility of the diagnosis of asthma:

- Wheezing or high-pitched whistle sounds that occur when breathing out. (Lack of wheezing and a chest exam will not rule out asthma.)
- History of any of the following: cough that is worse—particularly at night; continuing wheeze; recurrent difficulty in breathing; and continuing chest tightness.
- Symptoms that occur or become worse in the presence of asthma triggers such as exercise; viral infections; furry animals; dust mites in bedding, carpeting, and furniture; mold; tobacco and wood smoke; pollen; weather changes; strong emotional expressions; airborne chemicals or dust.
- Symptoms that occur or worsen at night—disturbing a child's sleep.
- Symptoms that improve when asthma medicines, such as albuterol, are given.

In the physical examination, the focus is on the chest, upper respiratory tract, and skin.

 **Fact**

Asthma is considered a "variable disease" or a condition that can change throughout the day. Any sign of airflow blockage, which occurs during an asthma attack, may not be evident at the time of the physical exam.

However, other physical symptoms may exist that can assist with the diagnosis of asthma. They include: appearance of hunched shoulders, some chest wall deformity; increased nasal secretions or nasal polyps; and eczema or other allergic skin conditions. Sounds of wheezing during normal breathing also will be examined.

Pulmonary Function Test

A health care provider's assessment to diagnose asthma will benefit from "objective assessments" that are obtained with a machine called a spirometer, which measures airflow from the lungs.

If your child is older than six years, he can breathe into the hose of the spirometer, which will calculate the volume of air exhaled. After having your child use a quick-relief inhaler, he will try about fifteen minutes later. The higher the volume of air he breathes out, the better his lungs are functioning.

For younger children, observation and review of symptoms and/or responses to asthma therapy are used. A newer technology, using impulse oscillometry, is now being used on a limited basis to observe airway resistance among children as young as two years. This would permit treatment to start earlier. (Also see Chapter 7.)

 Essential

As studies have revealed, these pulmonary function tests may discover more about a child's asthma than was initially assumed. Sometimes when combined with symptoms, some children were found to have asthma that was more severe than initially thought. At other times, some had less severe asthma—which meant that less medication was needed.

For diagnostic purposes, the spirometer—and not the peak flow meter—is recommended in a provider's office. Instead, the peak flow meter can be used for monitoring symptoms at home or school.

Swelling Airways

The terms allergies and asthma often are linked together. In reality, they are two different medical conditions although the cause of both conditions is closely related. Some children have allergies without asthma, and some have asthma without allergies, but most children have both. The medical community, though, is taking closer looks at how treatment of allergies can impact the management of asthma symptoms.

Asthma symptoms occur when inflamed airways overreact to a variety of stimuli including physical activity, upper respiratory viral infections, allergens (such as pollen or molds), and irritants (such as tobacco smoke). Exposure to these stimuli—often called triggers—can create more swelling and blocking of the airways. (Also see Chapter 4.)

On the other hand, allergies are diseases of the immune system that cause an overreaction to allergens. Allergies generally are grouped together by the kind of trigger, time of year they occur, or where symptoms appear on the body. Allergens can be inhaled into the lungs, ingested by mouth, injected through needles (medications) or insect stings, or absorbed through skin.

 *Fact*

> Not all children with allergies will develop asthma. However, approximately 80 percent of children with asthma also have allergic asthma, a type of asthma caused by allergens. This makes allergens the most common asthma trigger.

The connection between allergies and asthma, though, is gaining more attention—especially in light of the fact that treatment of underlying allergies has been found to often improve asthma symptoms.

Signs of Asthma and Allergies

While every child is different, you may detect a few distinct signs along the way that might indicate asthma. While a health care provider can suggest tests to help diagnose asthma, a few clues might be right in front of you to indicate that your child might have more than just allergies.

For example, the lowly, microscopic dust mite—one of the most common asthma triggers in homes—is found everywhere. Dust mites create their homes in upholstery, carpeting, and bedding, and their remains often make up a substantial amount of dust found indoors.

A child with a dust mite allergy may show signs and symptoms similar to hay fever. These allergic symptoms can include sneezing, runny nose, itchy and watery eyes, nasal congestion, itchy nose, swollen mouth or throat, swollen or bluish-tinted skin under the eyes, postnasal drip, cough, irritability, or facial pain or pressure.

But the child with asthma also may show signs and symptoms such as lung congestion, wheezing, and shortness of breath. She may be more likely to have these symptoms at night while in a bed filled with dust mites.

A dust mite allergy can range from mild to severe. With a mild case of asthma, a dust mite allergy might consist of an occasional runny nose, watery eyes, and sneezing. For severe cases, the child might have symptoms such as persistent wheezing, sneezing, facial pressure, and congestion.

Sensitization

During a process called sensitization, your child's immune system could mistakenly identify an inhaled dust mite residue as an invader. His body then produces an antibody against it called immunoglobulin E (IgE). These antibodies often are the prime culprits in children who develop asthma after the age of three.

Then, the next time he's exposed to the dust mite residue, his immune system begins an allergic reaction. The IgE antibodies will trigger the release of histamine, an inflammatory chemical that causes swelling of the mucous membranes in his lungs, nose, sinuses, and eyes. This results in wheezing, runny nose, sneezing, watery eyes, and increased mucus production.

Since IgE is involved in the early stages of a body's response to an allergen, ongoing research has emphasized that reducing IgE may help prevent asthma symptoms and attacks before they even begin. A child's IgE level can be determined by a blood test.

Allergy Connection

Since many children with asthma have allergies, consider checking with your health care provider to see if an allergy evaluation will be part of her treatment.

 ## Essential

> Ongoing research has found that allergy testing can help a health care provider tailor a child's allergy and asthma care. This should be accompanied by individual instruction that provides children and parents with information that assists them in identifying—and removing—allergens or triggers that could cause problems.

Allergy Testing

The use of allergy testing—whether done through either a blood test or a skin test (performed by an allergy specialist)—is still often overlooked by many health care providers. With the blood test, a blood sample is collected to test for specific antibodies for allergens (such as IgE). With skin testing, small amounts of allergens are applied to the skin, and any local reactions are observed. For the earlier example of dust mites, you would develop a temporary red, itchy bump where the dust mite extract is scratched onto the skin.

In particular, many of those providing care to children with asthma in the past under the age of five years have not used the tests—citing too many false positives. However, more evidence is emerging that testing could be valuable in treating these patients.

In one study, allergies often were found to be underdiagnosed in a study of more than 5,000 children living in urban settings. Less than half of the children had received allergy diagnoses, and only 40 percent of those children had received allergy testing. Those who had undergone testing were more likely to be taking allergy medication (in addition to their asthma medication) and to be exposed to fewer environmental triggers in the home.

Researchers noted the strong overlap between the management of allergies and better asthma outcomes in terms of such factors as fewer days missed from school.

Immunotherapy

If your child's symptoms are difficult to control or are producing bothersome nose, eye, or asthma symptoms, your health care provider may suggest allergy shots (immunotherapy) to desensitize her to dust mites.

In immunotherapy, your child would receive injections, for instance, of dust mite extract (if she was allergic to dust mites). The doses would be increased once or twice a week. Once a maintenance dose has been reached, injections would be needed every four weeks.

Allergy testing can be helpful in identifying what your child may be allergic to. However, it will not be helpful in identifying *if* your child has asthma.

Rhinitis and Asthma

One particular allergy that has attracted attention for its reported tie to asthma is allergic rhinitis, which is better known as hay fever. For years, both have been treated as separate medical conditions. Allergic rhinitis can be caused by outdoor allergens (pollens, molds) and indoor allergens (animal dander, indoor molds, dust mites).

The treatment of allergic rhinitis includes use of antihistamines, decongestants, and anti-inflammatory nose sprays that are similar to medications used for asthma patients.

An estimated 10 to 20 percent of young school children and 15 to 30 percent of teenagers worldwide have rhinitis. This condition usually starts at three to five years of age, but it is commonly found years later in childhood and adolescence, when severe forms could be more frequent.

 *Fact*

> Ongoing research has cited evidence that allergic rhinitis and asthma are linked—suggesting the idea of "one airway, one disease." This means that management of one disease was found to improve when the other condition was taken into account.

One recent study found that one in three allergic rhinitis patients may go on to develop asthma within ten years—further increasing the number of children with asthma.

Wheezing

Another common asthma trigger among children—particularly younger children—is viral respiratory tract infections. These infections often are associated with wheezing. Wheezing by itself is not necessarily an indicator of asthma among the younger set—especially if it occurs only once or twice.

In addition, ongoing research has found that infants who have viral infections with wheezing during infancy will have a higher risk of developing asthma in the future. The researchers said that protecting infants from viral infections now may prevent the development of asthma late in childhood.

 **Alert!**

Viral infections such as bronchiolitis, caused by the respiratory syncyial virus (RSV), is a common cause of wheezing in younger children. But, if you notice that it occurs repetitively, or at least three times in a year, asthma is suspected, and generally treatment for asthma should begin.

Cough-Variant Asthma

Chronic coughing is often defined as a cough that endures longer than three weeks. Chronic coughing in children can have several causes such as reaction to secondhand tobacco smoke, postnasal drip, pneumonia, or bronchitis.

Sometimes asthma can cause chronic coughing—existing without other asthma symptoms such as wheezing or nasal congestion. This is called hidden or cough-variant asthma. Some studies have indicated that between 30 to 50 percent of individuals with a chronic cough may actually have undiagnosed asthma.

The cough may first surface following a cold or upper respiratory tract infection. It could begin as a small "tickle" in your child's throat, and it is nonproductive, meaning that no sputum or mucus is produced with the cough. Other times coughing could be triggered by a variety of activities including laughing, exercise, or even cold weather.

According to the American Academy of Pediatrics, a persistent cough is usually secondary to a condition such as asthma, an allergy, an infection, or environmental irritants such as tobacco smoke or dust. Therefore, therapy should be directed at the underlying condition for the maximum benefit. Also, coughing can be helpful by loosening secretions and clearing them from the airways.

 ## Essential

Coughing that is related to asthma will not respond to antibiotics or over-the-counter cough remedies such as cough medicine or cough drops. Only prescribed medications used to treat asthma symptoms will work.

If you see your child coughing, for instance, while playing sports or involved in other strenuous activities, consider an asthma evaluation. A health care provider should be prepared to evaluate any cough that does not stop within three to six weeks.

Nocturnal Asthma

More than 90 percent of patients with asthma, including children, do experience symptoms of wheezing and coughing during the night. With the lack of sleep, children can begin to feel groggy during daylight hours, which can often affect their school attendance and performance.

Symptoms of asthma are common between midnight and 8 A.M.—especially between 3 A.M. and 5 A.M. when those with uncontrolled asthma may wake up coughing and wheezing.

 *Question?*

Why do asthma symptoms sometimes act up at night?
This may be related to your child's daily natural circadian rhythms and changes in his body's hormones. Repeated disturbances in his sleep patterns usually mean that his asthma might be inadequately controlled and may require a visit to the health care provider to reevaluate his current treatment.

Sometimes the function of a patient's lungs with asthma can decline by up to 50 percent between evening and morning when nocturnal asthma occurs. The causes are not totally understood, but several explanations include:

- Exposure at night to allergens such as dust mites or animal dander in the bedroom and on bed linens
- Movement of stomach acid into the esophagus because of gastroesophageal reflux disease
- Nighttime changes in the nervous system's control of airways
- Sinusitis and postnasal drip
- Sleep apnea or sleep-disordered breathing

Research is continuing to determine if one of these factors—or a combination of them—can cause airways to react and wake the asthmatic child. Also, ongoing research has shown that airway inflammation could be more severe in an individual who was lying flat or prone on a bed instead of resting in a more upright position.

Testing for Nocturnal Asthma
To determine if your child may have signs of nocturnal asthma, have him use the peak flow meter in the evening and then again

in the morning when he wakes up. If the morning reading shows a greater than 20 percent drop from the night before, nocturnal asthma could be present indicating the need for better asthma control medications during the day.

Research has shown that nocturnal asthma attacks can be more severe and dangerous than those attacks that might occur during the day. A majority of almost-fatal and fatal attacks occur during the midnight to 8 A.M. period.

Impact of Nocturnal Asthma

Nocturnal asthma can cause impaired breathing and restless nights. The parents of a child that experiences nocturnal asthma may be impacted as well—finding it difficult to get to work or sometimes missing work because of these nighttime episodes.

Working with the child, a health care provider should determine if treatment should be tailored to address the nighttime symptoms. First, any child waking up with asthma-related symptoms during the night at least two to three times a month should already be taking an inhaled anti-inflammatory or asthma-controlling medication daily. Also, a quick-relief medication, such as albuterol, should be nearby.

 **Fact**

The impact of nocturnal asthma can transfer into the daylight hours when children who wake up the night before because of their asthma symptoms may miss school or perform poorly in school, feel sleepy, and be noncompliant during the day.

A provider may consider adding a long-acting beta2-agonist drug or a leukotriene modifier (which both need to be used with an inhaled steroid drug). (See Chapter 6 for detailed information on asthma medications.) The provider also may look at changing the daily timing of a child's asthma medication—maybe to later in the day—so it coincides better with the times that nocturnal asthma occurs.

Also, consider allergy testing in order to appropriately make environmental changes such as prohibiting furry or feathered pets from sleeping in your child's bedroom or taking precautions to eliminate the majority of dust mites that are making a home in your child's bed. (Also see Chapter 15.)

Other Asthma-Related Conditions

While your child's provider may suggest ways to treat her asthma through medication, another route her provider might take is looking for underlying conditions that can cause asthma symptoms to increase. In addition to allergies mentioned earlier in this chapter, other medical conditions exist that could prevent your child's asthma from getting better.

Gastroesophageal Reflux Disease

Gastroesophageal reflux disease—better known as GERD, acid reflux disease, or heartburn—is a major asthma trigger for children and adults. Studies have show that the presence of GERD symptoms may be higher among children and adolescents who have asthma. Research is ongoing, though, on whether reflux can cause asthma, or whether asthma can cause reflux.

With GERD, stomach acid and undigested food can wash back into the esophagus from the stomach when a valve (called a lower esophageal sphincter) fails to hold it back.

Sometimes this acid can travel back up the esophagus and then down the airways, causing them to contract. This may cause wheezing, hoarseness, congestion, sore throat, and coughing that does not respond to asthma medications. Sometimes, a child may complain of a sour taste in her mouth or you may notice frequent burping. Other times, no symptoms seem to be apparent.

 **Fact**

> GERD usually occurs after meals or when lying down—which means it is more likely to occur at night. Preventing GERD includes elevating the head of your child's bed, encouraging her to avoid spicy food, restricting caffeine use, eating smaller meals, and not eating snacks before bedtime.

Medications such as antacids, antihistamines that block stomach acid release, and medications (proton pump inhibitors) that lower stomach acid production are prescribed for older asthma patients.

Since GERD is hard to diagnose, check with your health care provider about what to do if you suspect that your child may have GERD that is triggering her asthma. Also check before you use any over-the-counter medications designed to help heartburn since they may not be for use by children.

Sinusitis

Another often overlooked but common childhood condition that may aggravate asthma is sinusitis. Sometimes it may be acute (occurring once) or chronic (continues to occur). Up until recently, sinusitis —or inflammation of the sinuses—usually was not considered by health care providers when examining young children.

Symptoms of sinusitis are: pressure in the area of the affected sinus behind the top of the nose in children who are older than six years, nasal congestion, postnasal drip, cough, sore throat, and thick and often green nasal discharge. She may sleep poorly at night and also have bad breath.

Diagnosing sinusitis in a child can pose some challenges— particularly if it is not clear whether it is related to an infection (caused by bacteria), or if it is related to a common cold (caused by a virus), or allergies causing congestion.

Several theories have been raised regarding why untreated sinus-itis aggravates asthma. One is that children tend to breathe through their mouths when their noses are stuffed up. This means the air moving into their chests has not been warmed up through their noses, which could trigger asthma symptoms when crossing a child's inflamed airways. Another theory is that mucus in the sinuses may back up and spread down through already inflamed airways.

 Essential

Studies have shown that sinusitis can exist among children as young as one year. The common cold or viral upper respira-tory illnesses, allergies, and factors in the environment (such as tobacco smoke or mold sensitivities) are common triggers for the development of sinusitis.

When diagnosed, sinusitis may be treated in one of several ways, using nasal washes, steroidal nasal sprays, or antibiotics (when nec-essary for bacterial infections).

Signs of an Attack

It can happen to all children: an asthma attack. Also called an asthma flare-up or an asthma episode, an attack is a worsening of asthma symptoms caused when muscles tighten around your child's airways, which are already swollen.

Milder attacks are usually more likely to occur, with airways opening up within several minutes to a few hours following treat-ment. Severe attacks can occur, but they happen less often. They could last longer and require prompt medical care.

But, it's important to identify and immediately treat even these attacks with milder symptoms to help stop severe episodes from occurring and keep asthma under control.

 ## Alert!

During the impending attack, the airway lining becomes further inflamed or swollen, and a thick layer of mucus is produced. This causes symptoms such as labored breathing, wheezing, coughing, and shortness of breath. Other symptoms include a pale and sweaty face; chest pressure; harsh wheezing when inhaling or exhaling; repeat coughing; tightened chest and neck muscles; chest pains; blue lips or fingernails; and trouble talking.

Failure to Treat

Sometime, individuals interpret the cessation of the wheezing as a sign that asthma symptoms have improved and fail to get immediate treatment. This could mean trouble ahead for your child: His breathing could become more strained, whether or not you can hear audible wheezing.

If your child uses a peak flow meter, his readings could drop—when compared with his personal best reading—into the "yellow zone" (caution) or "red zone" (danger) signs on his asthma action plan.

As his lungs continue to tighten, he will be unable to use his peak flow meter. His lungs could begin to shut off air movement to the point that wheezing stops. This is a dangerous sign that means he must be sent to the hospital at once. A bluish color will appear around the lips, indicating less oxygen in the blood. Without immediate treatment, he could become less responsive, more listless, and eventually, if not treated, possibly die.

Early Warning

Your child, though, may have early symptoms that indicate an asthma problem may be on its way. While they often won't stop your child from doing her day-to-day activities, they may be helpful in flagging that an asthma attack may occur if she doesn't take precautions now.

These early warning signs for your child include frequent throat clearing; coughing (particularly at night); shortness of breath; difficulty resting or sleeping; fatigue or weakness when exercising; constant feelings of tiredness; or signs of cold or allergies (sneezing, runny nose, cough, sore throat, and headache).

Signs also may include declining peak flow meter readings (as indicated by the asthma action plan) among children old enough to use it. By detecting these asthma signs, it's possible to stop an asthma attack or prevent one from getting worse.

In Case of Attack

Use your child's asthma action plan if she is experiencing an asthma attack and her symptoms fail to improve. If she falls into the plan's "red zone," follow the emergency instructions regarding prompt medical attention. This may include calling your health care provider for more medication, such as oral steroids, going to the hospital, or calling an ambulance.

 **Essential**

When an emergency occurs, you can set the tone for your child and prevent increased anxiety or panic. During an asthma attack, it's important that you remain calm and talk to him in a soothing, reassuring voice. While an attack can seem anxious and scary, your child is more likely to remain calm if you maintain your composure.

If your child is coughing or wheezing, your agitated or panicked voice could make her breathing even worse. Try to talk your child in a cool and collected manner. Tell her that you are there, and you're going to work through this with her step by step.

First, get her to use her quick-relief inhaler, and reassure her that the medicine will help. Urge her to physically relax—so her medicine will do its work. Consider holding her or using several massage techniques to calm her. (See Chapter 5.)

Bring up some other pleasant topics that will keep her mind off the attack. Offer her some water or juice, if possible, since fluids help keep the mucus moist and loose. Avoid cold liquids, though, since some children could become more symptomatic with them.

Also, consider using some video or audio recordings or books that she enjoys to redirect the stress she feels from the asthma attack. Soothing music can be helpful as can trying to control breathing by inhaling as slowly as tolerable and exhaling slowly through pursed lips.

If the quick-relief inhaler is not effective or does not last up to three or four hours before being needed again, consult your health care provider as other medication or treatments may be needed. Most importantly, have an asthma action plan ready to go before your child becomes ill so no time is wasted.

CHAPTER 4

Asthma Triggers

Triggers are what cause your child's asthma symptoms to flare up. They can be found everywhere—in your home, in your car, on the playground, in his classroom, in his bed. Each child's trigger is different. Some may be visible (pollen, mold), while others may seem hidden (cold viruses, ozone). The first step is to work with your child's health care provider to determine what his triggers are and spell them out in his action plan. Then, you have a course to follow—to avoid those triggers so that your child can better control his asthma.

Know Your Child's Triggers

When trying to identify triggers, it may seem easier to divide those triggers into two categories: those related to allergies and those that are not.

Asthma that is accompanied by allergies is often referred to as atopic or extrinsic asthma. Reactions are triggered by such allergens as mold spores, animal dander, or contents found in household dust. These allergens may cause your child's airways to swell—triggering her asthma. With continued inflammation, her airways may become even more sensitive to triggers. An estimated 75 percent of children in the United States have atopic asthma.

Asthma not caused by allergens is referred to as nonallergic, nonatopic, or instrinsic asthma. It can include irritants that aggravate the nose, throat, or airways. These irritants include cigarette smoke, strong odors or smells, wood smoke, household cleaners, or environmental pollutants.

Asthma symptoms also may be triggered through infections such as colds or pneumonia, exercise, other physical conditions such as gastroesophageal reflux disease, medications, food, and emotional anxiety.

 ## Essential

Studies have found that children often have several triggers, and that tackling all of those triggers together can improve a child's health. In one inner-city study, researchers found that using multiple measures to reduce several indoor triggers at once resulted in substantially fewer asthma symptoms and sick days related to asthma when compared with a control group.

But ongoing studies also have found that triggers such as air pollutants may be aggravating the health of childrens' lungs—reducing their lung function and making them more susceptible to other triggers.

You have an important role as a researcher yourself: Observe your child when she plays, studies, exercises, eats, or sleeps. Also, observe her a few hours after an activity has happened or if symptoms are occurring after your child has returned from a different location. Do you notice asthma symptoms—such as coughing, wheezing, or difficulty breathing—at specific times or locations? Remember that triggers can constantly change and can vary by time of year. Let your health care provider know so your child's action plan can be updated to help your child manage her asthma.

Common Indoor Allergens

You may not necessarily see them, but indoor allergens are all around you and could be triggering your child's asthma at home, school, and other indoor environments. While it may be difficult to completely eradicate these allergens, you can take steps to pinpoint and reduce them in your child's environment. (See Chapters 11 and 15.)

Dust Mites

You might be astonished to know that your child could be sharing his bed with anywhere from 100,000 to 10 million dust mites every night. These tiny organisms, which are invisible to the naked eye, are related to spiders and live in all homes—including in upholstered furniture, carpeting, and bedding in your home. These dust mites thrive in warm, humid environments—eating dead skin cells from humans and their pets.

 **Fact**

The dust mites leave behind residue in the form of their excrement—at about 200 times its weight—and decaying bodies. These blend in with household dust and become airborne. While this dust mite residue is harmless to those not allergic to it, it could be problematic for your asthmatic child, especially if she is already sensitive to it.

Your child could be especially prone to asthma attacks at night if he's lounging on a mite-infested sofa or sleeping in a mite-infested bed.

From 1998 to 2002, the federal government conducted an extensive survey, called the National Survey of Lead and Allergens in Housing, to assess how widespread these indoor allergens were in American homes. The researchers found that more than 46 percent of the homes surveyed had levels of dust mite allergens high enough to produce allergic reactions, and nearly a fourth had levels high enough to trigger asthma symptoms in individuals who were genetically susceptible.

Taking measures to decrease the number of dust mites in your home—through cleaning, storing, vacuuming, and reevaluating furnishings—could improve control of your child's asthma, along with use of prescribed medications.

If your child's symptoms are difficult to control, your health care provider may recommend allergy shots or immunotherapy to provide desensitization to the dust mites.

Cockroaches

Allergies related to cockroaches also are common among children. Cockroach allergens come from several sources such as their saliva, fecal material, secretions, cast skins, and dead bodies.

The National Survey of Lead and Allergens in Housing also showed that nearly two-thirds of U.S. homes have detectable levels of cockroach allergens, with higher levels in high-rise apartments, urban settings, older homes, and low-income households. About 10 percent had cockroach allergen levels above the threshold for triggering asthma symptoms. Most homes in Northeastern cities had high levels of cockroach allergens.

 Essential

You can take steps to reduce your child's exposure to cockroach allergens by eating only in the kitchen and dining room, frequently vacuuming and dusting, putting nonrefrigerated items in sealed containers, keeping the garbage closed off and taking out the garbage on a daily basis, and blocking holes or gaps where cockroaches move in and out of walls.

Researchers have found that these cleaning practices, combined with proven extermination techniques and consistent maintenance methods, can bring these allergen levels under control.

Molds

Indoor molds and mildew can make themselves at home anywhere in your home—from damp basements to under the kitchen sink to along the bathroom windows. With mold, the triggers are the small spores that are released.

However, once molds are detected, they usually can easily be removed. Sometimes it's with a little elbow grease and a cleaning solution made with 5 percent bleach and a little detergent. If molds are found in your household on items such as carpeting or wallpaper, those items should be thrown away.

To avoid mold buildup, repair any external leaks (such as roofs or basement walls) and internal leaks (such as pipes or condensation). Ensure that the crawl space is dry and has plastic covering over it. Avoid storing damp clothing, shoes, newspapers, or other household items in damp areas of your home. Do not place carpets on cement floors as mold can accumulate underneath. And consider use of dehumidifiers in damp areas (such as basements) in your home. But remember to clean them periodically—or you could end up with even more mold.

Endotoxins

Recent research has discovered the presence of bacteria in household dust that produces chemicals, called endotoxins, which can trigger asthma and asthma-related symptoms. The research on the impact of these endotoxins on children with asthma is still limited.

However, researchers with NIEHS found that kitchen and living room floors had the highest concentrations of endotoxins. They found, though, that the likelihood of having recent asthma symptoms was nearly three times greater among individuals with exposure to high levels of endotoxins in the bedroom.

Overall, the study indicates that it is not just the concentration of the endotoxins that matters, but other factors such as duration of exposure, timing of the exposure, and genetic factors that can trigger asthma symptoms.

Animals and Pets

Your furry or feathered pets may be a trigger for your child's asthma. But, it's not—as most people think—the hair or feathers that may cause the symptoms but rather dander or dead skin particles from the animal, proteins found in the saliva, or urine.

Sometimes, a child's symptoms can occur within minutes after exposure to the animal. Other times, the symptoms may build up and become most severe up to twelve hours following contact with the animal.

 **Fact**

One of the most surprising findings from the National Survey of Lead and Allergens in Housing was that 100 percent of homes reviewed had detectable levels of dog and cat allergens. This was despite the fact that while dogs were present in only 32 percent of the surveyed homes and cats were in 24 percent, their allergens were still in the homes—often tracked in on shoes and clothing.

All cats or dogs produce a certain amount of allergens per week—specifically through dander and saliva. While some breeds produce more than others, all are capable of triggering symptoms— even so-called "hypoallergenic" breeds of cats or dogs.

These dander levels are usually highest in the winter in areas where the temperatures are cold and dogs and cats spend more time indoors. In new homes, built with a higher level of energy efficiency, the amount of inside air exchanged with outside air drops, causing people to breathe in the same air with the dander and other allergens.

While dander and saliva are the source of cat and dog allergens, urine is the source of allergens from rabbits, hamsters, and guinea pigs, so be sure to ask a non-allergic family member to clean the animal's cage.

At home, the most effective way to address triggers related to furry or feathered animals is to avoid contact with them and remove the pet from home—maybe giving it to a friend or relative. This, of course, may be a difficult decision, but it will help your child in the long run. You could possibly suggest other animals for your child such as fish, hermit crabs, or turtles.

Moving a furry pet to the outside may only partially address the problem since homes with pets in the yard still have higher concentrations of animal allergens.

If the decision is made to keep the furry or feathered pets in the home, try to make sure that your child minimizes contact. This means keeping a pet out of the bedroom or other rooms where your child spends a great deal of time. Some studies have indicated that weekly bathing of dogs or cats could reduce some of the allergens they produce. If you have removed the pet from the home, replacing bedding and carpeting that contains animal dander may be advisable because it may take weeks or months to remove it from fabrics.

In school, the most effective method to controlling exposure to animal allergens is to keep it free of feathered or furry animals. For some children, isolation measures may be sufficiently effective. They include keeping animals in localized areas; locating animals away from ventilation system vents to avoid circulating allergens throughout a room or building; keeping animals away from upholstered furniture, carpets, and stuffed toys; and keeping sensitive individuals away from animals as much as possible.

Outdoor Allergens

The great outdoors may not be so great if your child also has allergies to pollens and molds. These outdoor allergies, which are sometimes overlooked in asthma management plans, have been found to be major factors in triggering asthma symptoms.

Pollens

Pollens may be the size of less than the width of a human hair, but they can let their presence be known during warmer seasons. Billions of tiny pollens from trees, grasses, and weeds fly through the air—triggering allergy and possibly asthma symptoms. Generally, pollens from flowers are heavier and are less likely to become airborne.

 **Alert!**

Pollen season usually coincides with temperatures that encourage you to open the windows and air out your home. But if pollens are a trigger for your child, consider keeping those windows closed and, if available, running your air conditioner or ventilating system specifically when pollen is at its peak. If you do need to open your windows, remember that pollen counts are at their peak in the early morning or the late afternoon.

On days when pollen hits high readings, your child could experience an asthmatic episode—even if her asthma was controlled the season before. During this time, your child may have to increase use of quick-relief medications and antihistamines.

Sometimes, though, these allergy medications may gradually lose effectiveness, and symptoms may become more severe. Your child then could experience year-round allergies—both outdoors and indoors. Then other strategies, such as immunotherapy, may be considered.

Outdoor Molds

Molds are found most of the year throughout most locales and in most habitats. Mold spores, which float in the air as pollen does, usually are influenced by weather conditions such as mild, humid weather that encourages mold growth and windy weather that distributes the spores.

Outdoor mold spores begin to appear in the spring—reaching a peak in July in warmer states and in October in the cooler states. Molds often can be found outdoors in the South and on the West Coast throughout the year. They can be found in many outdoor locations—from the soil to rotting wood and leaf piles.

If your child is allergic to molds—and it might be a trigger to asthma, he might want to avoid some of those outdoor chores that involve digging, raking, and mulching.

Pollen and Mold Counts

While it's impossible to avoid all outdoor molds and pollens, you can keep on top of their levels on any given day and determine if your child should be prepared to take actions to help herself breathe better. The mold and pollen levels generally are reported daily as grains per cubic meter of air. Certified aeroallergen counters at many universities, medical centers, and clinics provide these counts on a volunteer basis. These levels often are found online.

Frequently, the American Lung Association (*www.lungusa.org*) reports this information; you can register online to receive automatic updates. The National Allergy Bureau, a section of the American Academy of Allergy, Asthma and Immunology's (AAAAI) Aeroallergen Network, offers a free service that reports current pollen and mold spore levels to the public (*www.aaaai.org/nab*). The reports come from certified stations nationwide. Pollen counts for your specific area also are available at *www.pollen.com*.

Keep in mind that sampling techniques, which are influenced by the type of device used and its community location, can affect counts.

Weather and Location

Weather also can impact can influence asthma and allergy symptoms related to pollens and mold. The symptoms generally are minimal on days that are rainy, cloudy, or windless, since pollen is less likely to be moving through the air on those days. However, hot, dry, and windy weather encourages greater pollen and mold circulation—thus increased symptoms.

Sometimes symptoms might by triggered right before thunderstorms when winds whip up tiny mold spores and pollen particles (some 1,000 times smaller than pollen grains) along the ground. These particles then are blown up at face level, where they could be inhaled deeply into the lungs.

Secondhand Smoke

Secondhand smoke, an irritant, is actually a mixture of the smoke produced by the burning end of a cigarette, pipe, or cigar, and the smoke exhaled by smokers. Secondhand smoke, also known as environmental tobacco smoke, has more that 4,000 substances that can cause major health problems including cancer.

Secondhand smoke can not only trigger asthma attacks but make asthma symptoms more severe. Exposure to secondhand smoke also has been related to new cases of asthma in children who have not previously shown symptoms.

Nearly one in three children under the age of eighteen years lived in families with at least one smoker, according to the federal Agency for Healthcare Research and Quality (AHRQ). In the Environmental Protection Agency's National Survey on Environmental Management of Asthma, children with asthma appeared to have more exposure to secondhand smoke than children without asthma. Parents were

responsible for about 90 percent of those children's exposure to secondhand smoke.

Question?

Is it okay to smoke in an area when children are not present?
Remember to keep your child away from tobacco smoke:
Do not allow family and friends to smoke anywhere inside
your home or motor vehicles—even when your child is not
there. While smoke can be very irritating in an enclosed area,
its odor can be trapped, for instance, in a home or vehicle's
upholstery or carpeting for a long time. This secondhand
smoke could then continue to trigger asthma symptoms.

Even outdoors, an individual sitting a few feet from a lit cigarette
can be exposed for short periods of time to substantial levels of con-
taminated air—compared with normal background air pollution levels, some researchers have noted.

Recent studies also have found that asthmatic children of different races may show different susceptibility to the toxic ingredients in
tobacco smoke. In one study, African American children with asthma
who were exposed to secondhand tobacco smoke reportedly had
significantly higher amounts of cotinine, a byproduct of nicotine, in
their bodies.

Other Indoor Irritants

Many other irritants can be found indoors—specifically in your home
or your child's school—that can aggravate asthma symptoms. Many
of these products may be found in areas ranging from your kitchen
cabinet to your bathroom counter to your child's art supply closet at

school. In general, anything that has an odor or can put particles into the air can be an irritant to children with asthma.

Chemical Irritants

Chemical irritants that could be triggers of your child's asthma include fairly recognizable everyday products including:

- Strong odors from perfumes, scented candles, hairspray, cooking fumes (especially from frying), paints, or varnishes.
- Small airborne particles found in coal dust, chalk dust, or talcum powder.
- Cleaning products including air fresheners, toilet bowl cleaners, mothballs, powdered carpet cleaners, and related products with volatile organic compounds.
- Various spray pesticides.

Consider using these products less often—or not at all. Also, if you continue to use them, carefully follow the instructions on the label, and make sure the immediate area is ventilated. Periodically review this list of chemical irritants with your child's health care provider because his sensitivities to these irritants can very easily change.

Nitrogen Dioxide

Nitrogen dioxide, an odorless gas, is produced by appliances that burn fuels such as gas, wood, and kerosene. Make sure that these appliances are vented to the outside in order to avoid irritation of the eyes, nose, and throat or shortness of breath. If you use a gas stove for cooking, always use an exhaust fan when you cook. Also, never use the stove to heat your home.

For unvented kerosene or gas space heaters, remember to use the proper fuel and keep the heater adjusted as recommended by the manufacturer. Also, keep a window slightly ajar or use an exhaust fan to provide ventilation.

For wood-burning stoves, make sure the doors are fit closely, and follow the manufacturer's instructions for starting, burning, and extinguishing the fire. For wood-burning fireplaces, remember to keep the flue open so the smoke escapes through the chimney. Use these only if they are the sole source of heat in the home as they are significant irritants to a child's airways.

Outside Irritants

When your child goes outside for a "breath of fresh air," sometimes that air may contain higher levels than normal of unseen pollutants or irritants that may affect her asthma and her lung development. Inflamed airways are usually very sensitive to environmental irritants that aggravate asthma.

You can monitor the air quality of the neighborhood you live and where your child attends school via radio or television broadcasts, the Internet, or other services on a daily basis. The air quality can vary by season or by other environmental events (such as smoke from forest fires).

While much of this area on environmental factors and asthma is still under investigation, research is now available to help you and your child breathe better outdoors.

 Essential

When the EPA calculates the Air Quality Index (AQI), it looks at five major air pollutants regulated by the Clean Air Act: particle pollution, ground-level ozone, carbon monoxide, sulfur dioxide, and nitrogen dioxide. Two key air pollutants that affect asthma are particle pollution (found in haze, smoke, and dust) and ozone (found in smog).

Particle Pollution and Smog

When your child has asthma, you may have noticed that his symptoms may get worse when the air is polluted. Air pollution can make it harder to breathe—causing symptoms such as coughing, wheezing, and chest discomfort.

To protect your child's health from air pollution, you can first observe if his asthma symptoms occur more often when he is physically active outside—specifically when the air is polluted. This may indicate that he is sensitive to air pollution.

Also, if asthma symptoms arise the day after he has been outside in the polluted air, this may indicate that his exposure to this air has increased his sensitivity to other triggers indoors, such as dust mites or mold.

To anticipate when the outside pollution might cause your child problems, keep in mind that:

- Ozone is often worst on hot summer days, particularly in the afternoons and early evenings. Urge your child to limit physical activities to early in the morning or later evening hours on smoggy days.
- Particle pollution can be bad any time of year, even in the fall and winter—especially when the weather is calm and the air pollution builds up.
- Particle levels have been found to be high within a third of a mile near major highways and near busy roads during rush hour.
- Particle levels can be high around factories, and when smoke is in the neighborhood air from wood-burning stoves, fire-places, or burning vegetation.
- Changing weather conditions, such as changes in temperature and humidity, barometric pressure, or strong winds, can trigger asthma. Cold weather—when the air becomes dry and chilly—could cause respiratory problems.

Newly Identified Environmental Triggers

Recent research also has been uncovering new asthma triggers. One of those triggers is related to "red tide toxins"—blooms of ocean algae that are concentrated along shorelines and produce highly potent aerosolized toxins.

The red tides, which occur worldwide, increase respiratory symptoms in patients with asthma. In studies along the Florida Gulf Coast, the red tide toxins were found to affect asthma patients in just one hour at the beach when exposed to the toxins. Researchers recommend that those with asthma choose another beach when red tides appear because they tend to be localized along the coastal waters.

Sometimes, the origin of various asthma triggers may begin far away. The U.S. Geological Survey has been monitoring the transport of dust through tradewinds from northwest Africa to the western Atlantic Ocean and Caribbean regions, noting that it may be responsible for a number of environmental problems, including the increased occurrence of asthma in humans. The dust comes from the expanding Sahara/Sahel desert region of Africa and carries a wide variety of bacteria and fungi.

Other Medical Conditions

Children with asthma also may have other medical conditions that could be aggravated. These conditions, if left unchecked, could worsen a child's asthma—or prevent them from getting better.

Viral Infections

Viral infections, including colds, flu, or viral pneumonia, can trigger or aggravate asthma, particularly in young children. The infections can irritate the airways (nose, throat, lungs, and sinuses), which in turn can trigger asthma flare-ups.

Another condition, sinusitis—an inflammation of the sinuses that are found behind the nose—is a common childhood condition that may be overlooked in its role as a trigger for asthma symptoms. Sinusitis may follow a cold or upper respiratory condition in a child, or accompany untreated nasal allergies. With sinusitis, mucus may linger in the nose—along with large groups of bacteria that encourage infections.

To avoid these infections, your child should think prevention: he should remember to wash his hands to prevent transmission of viruses. Also, you should think flu shot in the fall for your child.

Food Allergies

Asthma symptoms such as coughing, wheezing, or difficulty breathing—especially in infants and children—may be triggered by food allergies. For some children, eating certain foods (such as milk, eggs, peanuts, tree nuts, soy, wheat, fish, and shellfish) or various food additives (such as sulfites or MSG) can trigger symptoms.

Determining if an allergy to various foods exists requires using a medically supervised test where food is eliminated from the diet and a child's symptoms are monitored. Sometimes, though, the results may reveal false positives—indicating that the food is causing problems for the child when it is not.

If diagnosed with food allergies, avoid the identified foods that cause symptoms. Make sure you or your child inquire about ingredients when eating out and read food labels carefully. The best way to treat food allergy is to avoid the specific foods that trigger the allergy. This means becoming familiar with corresponding names for foods: For instance, "gluten" may mean "wheat."

Emotions

Anxiety or stress by themselves do not trigger asthma symptoms but can intensify them. However, these emotions may lead to greater fatigue and cause greater difficulty in coping with the asthma episode. Also, laughing, crying, and yelling can sometimes lead to airways tightening up—triggering an asthma episode.

Making sure your child has adequate rest, proper nutrition, and exercise—in addition to learning relaxation techniques—can help promote better well-being and better asthma management.

Medications

About 5 to 10 percent of adults with moderate to severe asthma may be aspirin-sensitive. Aspirin-induced asthma occurs less frequently among children, but it is still a condition for which you should be alert. Other painkillers, including nonsteroidal anti-inflammatory agents such as ibuprofen, also could trigger asthma symptoms. Acetaminophen, though, has been suggested as an alternative to these medications.

The signs of aspirin sensitivity may not always be immediately evident. Usually, the airways may begin to constrict anywhere from thirty minutes to two hours after using the medications. Sometimes it might not be clear if the medication is triggering asthma or if the trigger is what the medication is being used for—such as a cold. Before your child takes any over-the-counter medications, make sure you check with her health care provider.

Exercise

A majority of children with asthma have symptoms related to a variety of triggers, including when they exercise or play sports, known as exercise-induced asthma. On the other hand, some children will show asthma symptoms only when they exercise. However, this doesn't mean your child should avoid exercise or sports. In fact, it is important that they be active—to keep their hearts and lungs healthy and live the normal life of a child.

Working with your child's health care provider, an action plan should be developed that includes use of quick-relief medication and proper warm-up exercises. (See Chapter 19.) It also means anticipating —and avoiding, if possible—outside conditions such as cold, dry air, air laden with pollen or molds, or smog that could cause breathing problems.

More than likely, if your child's asthma is well-controlled, he can participate in almost any activity he desires.

Chapter 5

Complementary and Alternative Medicine

Perhaps you recently heard from friends or read a magazine article about a new diet or a relaxation technique that can help reduce asthma symptoms. Could it help your child? After all, many people with chronic conditions have turned to complementary and alternative types of treatments for years. But before taking this route, ask questions. Even today, many research findings behind these treatments have been mixed or poorly documented. That doesn't mean you have to rule them out. But, keep in mind: Is this something that can safely supplement—but not replace—your child's current medical treatment?

Complementary and Alternative Medicine Today

A variety of therapies and techniques have existed throughout history with the express purpose of healing or relieving various medical conditions or illnesses and/or emphasizing mind, body, and spirit connections. Asthma has been one of those conditions. Many of these therapies and practices may be familiar to you including acupuncture, yoga, hypnosis, chiropractic, herbal therapy, massage therapy, and music therapy. In almost all cases, they do not use medications prescribed by health care providers.

Essential

While it is difficult to specify a particular phrase or word that encompasses these many therapies and procedures, the term "complementary and alternative medicine" has been gaining acceptance in recent years.

The term complementary and alternative medicine refers to treatments used along with conventional treatments prescribed by your health care provider (complementary), or separate treatments used for an illness (alternative). Other terms you may be familiar with are integrative medicine, holistic medicine, or non-allopathic medicine.

Safe and Effective?

Determining if complementary and alternative therapies and practices are safe and appropriate for your child may take a little research on your part. Up until a few years ago, this could be difficult: Only a small number of scientifically valid studies were available that examined the safety and effectiveness of complementary and alternative therapies in treating asthma.

Often the reports were somewhat mixed. Sometimes, they were anecdotal. Perhaps a small group of people who received an alternative treatment may have reported their asthma symptoms improved. Sometimes the data was questionable—especially if no randomized clinical trials were used to get more objective findings on what treatments did or did not work.

No large, nationally representative study has been done on how many children use complementary and alternative treatments, according to the National Center for Complementary and Alternative Medicine (NCCAM). However, limited surveys suggest that many children and teens are using them, with some groups having a high rate of usage—

particularly those with chronic conditions (at least 50 percent by one estimate). Asthma was included in this group.

 **Fact**

> With expanding interest in complementary and alternative medicine among asthma patients, more in-depth research is beginning to appear in reputable medical journals and among research institutions. Also, many health care providers are now becoming more knowledgeable about complementary and alternative methods because their patients are asking for more information.

Children were likely to use complementary and alternative treatment if the condition was perceived as painful or uncomfortable; having an unpredictable course; disabling; or not having an established cure.

They also were more likely to use these treatments for the following reasons: one or both parents used it, word-of-mouth, cultural or ethnic traditions, improvement of quality of life, dissatisfaction with conventional medical treatment, for a greater sense of control, to participate more actively in health care, the influence of advertising, or a desire for a more "holistic" or "natural" approach to health care.

Heed Caution

But before taking any step, consult with your health care provider about the use of various complementary and alternative therapies. Find out what the advantages and what the dangers are—especially if the therapy involves ingesting or inhaling a product or stopping any prescribed medication.

Also, it's helpful to realize that children differ in how their bodies absorb, use, and eliminate medications and other materials. Children—especially infants and toddlers—may respond differently to a treatment than adults because their immune and central nervous systems are not yet fully developed. Even among children who are the same age, they may react differently to the same treatments because of variables such as body weight.

Alert!

Find out if complementary or alternative treatments or procedures could interact with current asthma medications—making them less effective in the long run. On the flip side, some treatments could end up creating risks with prescribed asthma medications because they act in a similar fashion as those medications.

Just typing the word "asthma" on an Internet search engine can bring up many "testimonials" touting the benefits of various "natural" solutions to asthma symptoms. But, be cautious of claims of what certain products or treatments can do for asthma—outside of conventional treatment. If it seems too good to be true, it most likely is.

Also check credentials of individuals offering various complementary and alternative therapies. Many states do have licensing requirements for practitioners such as chiropractors, naturopathic doctors, massage therapists, and acupuncturists.

If you consider this route, take it upon yourself to look, listen, and learn what could work with your child before you make the decision about complementary and alternative therapies.

Learning to Relax

While stress itself cannot trigger asthma, it can make asthma worse when it is present. Shortness of breath and decreased peak flow rates, for instance, have been found to occur when someone with asthma becomes emotionally upset.

Relaxation techniques have been suggested by various medical professionals as a complement to asthma treatment. While the research into how different relaxation techniques impact children with asthma is thin, the drawbacks of using these therapies is small. After all, many children, especially younger ones, generally enjoy being touched, held, and soothed. Your child might be comfortable with several methods that combine emotional processes, muscles, and breathing.

Massage Therapy

A small number of studies have shown some positive benefits of parents giving daily massages to their children with asthma. While the scientific evidence is sparse, massage does have some pluses on its side in that other than some parental time, it's free.

 Essential

Broader studies on massage have shown that it can be beneficial for both children and parents in terms of producing relaxation of chest and back muscles—especially when an asthma attack occurs—and helping children feel secure.

There are several types of massages you could consider that take a few minutes each to perform:

- Back massage—moving hands from neck and shoulders, down along each side of the spine and back again.

- Shoulder massage—using fanning motions along the collar bone, shoulders, back of the neck, and the bottom of the skull.
- Chest massage—gently rubbing from middle of chest to side of one half of body, then repeating on other side.

Health care experts familiar with massage therapy recommend that children sit up when massage therapy is used to relieve asthma symptoms so it is easier for them to breathe. It would be helpful to practice massage techniques—before an asthma flare-up occurs.

Meditation

Meditation has been found to be useful in promoting a sense of relaxation among patients of all ages with a variety of chronic conditions. While little scientific evidence is available to examine results of meditation and its impact on asthma among children, interest does appear to be growing in this area.

With many meditation techniques, an individual focuses on his breathing. This could be useful in detecting possible trouble signs related to asthma. Also, some health care providers have observed that the proper breathing techniques suggested for using an inhaler are oftentimes similar to methods used with some forms of meditation.

Yoga

Yoga is an ancient Hindu-based set of movements that are said to relate to mind, body, and emotions. Yoga, which emphasizes many physical and mental exercises or poses, also focuses on various breathing techniques designed to increase fitness, relax the body, and improve the way an individual breathes. No prescribed medications, however, should be replaced with the practice of yoga.

Essential

Yoga has been found in some studies to improve asthma symptoms when used with conventional medicine. Specifically, it also has been shown to improve peak flow rates, improve exercise tolerance, and create less overall anxiety and panic among those who tried it. Transcendental Meditation and other related forms of meditation have been found to create similar results.

Hypnosis

Hypnosis has been described as a daydream-like state where you shut out the area immediately around you, leaving you open to suggestions. Hypnosis has gained some interest for children with asthma because of its potential use for helping them to relax and to react to positive suggestions to encourage them to breathe easier.

Some studies have shown that hypnotherapy and self-hypnosis could reduce the seriousness and frequency of an asthma episode, but most showed equivocal evidence of effect. While self-hypnosis can be understood by just about anyone, it generally may be more helpful to be taught specific skills by a hypnotherapist. This person can provide techniques to reinforce suggestions used in regard to your child's asthma.

And, as for the idea that hypnosis could cause someone to lose control or start showing bizarre behavior, you could remind your child that it's a myth—something seen in cartoons, not in real life.

Biofeedback

Biofeedback is described as a way for individuals to alter certain bodily functions—from heart rate to muscle tension—by using techniques such as meditation or relaxation. Biofeedback has gained interest as a complement to asthma treatment. It has been linked in some studies to decreased medication use, decreased asthma symptoms, improvement of peak flow rates, and fewer emergency room visits among children.

At the University of Pittsburgh, ongoing studies have found that when an asthmatic child relaxes, his breathing slows down and becomes regular—the opposite of what happens during the early stages of an asthma flare-up. The treatment, called biofeedback assisted relaxation, uses a computer display to show children what their readings look like when they are stressed and when they are relaxed. The children practice to make the readings show a calm response, which can better help them control their bodies during an asthma attack.

The Arts Link

In searching for ways to make medicine a little more human, interest has increased in how the arts—music, art, and writing—could complement the treatment of chronic illnesses such as asthma among children.

Music Therapy

Music therapy has been gaining interest through school and clinical programs as a way to help children and teens address living with asthma. In New York City Public Schools, the Asthma Initiative Program uses music-assisted relaxation and breathing exercises that are combined with playing a wind instrument (usually a recorder) to complement medical treatment.

Researchers have found that by controlling her breath using a wind instrument, for instance, a child with asthma can help feel she has gained more control in her life—especially with a disease that can sometimes make her feel out of control.

In addition, children may learn how to play drums to learn about rhythmic and relaxed breathing, which can help them stay calm and focused if an asthma attack occurs. The musical approach used in New York City—and developed through Beth Israel Medical Center's

Louis Armstrong Center for Music and Medicine—is aimed at helping children understand how to breathe optimally and better maintain control over their symptoms.

Art Therapy

While self-discovery through art is not new, art therapy conducted in a health care setting is giving children and teenagers with asthma a different way to express how they feel about their chronic illness. An art therapist will look at an artwork's theme, sequencing, size, and details to understand a child's concerns and interest.

A child's concerns and worries about asthma can be translated into figures and shapes. At one California hospital, for instance, pictures that some children drew about their asthma depicted it as a weight on their chests or akin to being held underwater.

Writing Therapy

While people have kept journals to record thoughts and memories since early times, the art of journal writing has received a new twist in the health care community. The idea is that writing about an emotional event promotes better understanding of it.

In a health care setting, journal therapy would be conducted by a licensed health professional, such as a certified art therapy practitioner or trained psychologist or psychiatrist. The research in this area is continually evolving. One study noted that about half of patients with asthma who wrote about stressful experiences related to their condition experienced "clinically relevant" improvements after four months of writing therapy.

Chiropractic and Osteopathy

Chiropractic spinal manipulation is described as a way to stop stress or tension by realigning or balancing the spine—improving nerve function. In turn, this is designed to loosen the muscles and improve lung function. Some reports have shown that individuals with allergies or asthma may find it easier to breathe after treatment. However, in results from a few small randomized studies, no effective treatments were noted.

Osteopathy is similar to chiropractic in a number of ways, but osteopathy places more emphasis on soft tissue techniques designed to relax muscles. It usually is used to treat musculoskeletal problems, but has been used on asthma patients to help open up the chest. However, no documented improvements were found in two small studies.

Acupuncture

The ancient Chinese technique of acupuncture involves inserting fine needles into key points of the body as a way, according to acupuncture practitioners, to restore the body's energy flow.

Acupuncture is thought to signal the brain to release endorphins. These endorphins, in turn, can assist patients by reducing pain and promoting relaxed or calmer breathing. While acupuncture has been widely used in China to treat asthma, research in Western countries has not found a strong connection between acupuncture and improvement of asthma among children.

Infants as young as three weeks old can undergo acupuncture therapy. Instead of adult-sized acupuncture needles, an acupuncturist treating children may use thin needles to stimulate certain body points or may also use heat, massage, magnets, or lasers.

Homeopathy

The term "homeopathy" comes from the Greek words *homious*, which means "like" and pathos, which means "suffering." The concept behind homeopathy is that "like is cured by like," which means that the cause of any disease should be treated with a small portion of the substance that causes it.

What are described as homeopathic remedies are extracts that come from animals, plants, insects, or minerals. The remedies—which may be prescribed in forms such as tablets, powders, or granules—

are prescribed by doctors who have been trained in homeopathic techniques or homeopaths who are not medically qualified. While some research has found homeopathy can improve lung function, its value to improving asthma in children has not been proven by any current study. However, NIH clinical trials have been suggested to clarify the roles of herbal products in addressing asthma symptoms.

Food Nutrients

Many parents are showing interest in supplementing vitamins and minerals as a way to improve their child's asthma. Whether these nutrients are effective has been an ongoing debate among researchers.

This means while providing additional daily nutrients through foods or a multivitamin supplement probably won't hurt your child, more scientific evidence is needed that supports the use of specific nutrients in an asthma treatment program.

But, remember to discuss the addition of any supplements with your health care provider. Ingesting amounts over and above the usual daily requirements could be unhealthy for your child in the long run.

Magnesium

Much interest has been focused on magnesium because of its role (working with calcium) in contracting and relaxing smooth muscles, which have an important role in the process of breathing. Also, individuals with asthma have been found to have low levels of magnesium. Studies have looked at the intravenous use of magnesium sulfate when asthma patients have been hospitalized or encountering a medical emergency. However, no study information is available on how daily use of magnesium can improve asthma among children and adults.

Vitamins A, C, and E

The benefits of vitamins A (beta-carotene), C (ascorbic acid), and E (alpha tocopherol)—in their roles as antioxidant nutrients—have received much discussion as a way to improve and treat asthma symptoms among children. But so far, the evidence has been mixed and far from conclusive. Antioxidants help regulate your child's immune system so it doesn't overreact, which could trigger asthma symptoms, or underreact, which could increase the chance of infections.

Part of the interest in the medical community lies with the fact that asthmatic children were found to have lower blood concentration of two of these vitamins (C and E) when they had no symptoms. These levels were found to be lowest particularly among those with severe asthma.

Vitamin A has garnered interest in its role to protect your child's immune system and maintain epithelial cells and mucous membranes in your child's respiratory system. These are important in blocking substances that trigger asthma symptoms.

 **Fact**

Some studies have found that eating fresh fruit high in vitamin C (such as citrus fruits and kiwi fruit) could be beneficial for asthmatic children: wheezing, nocturnal cough, and chronic cough have been found to drop among children who consumed fresh fruit at least weekly.

Researchers also have been looking at the role that large doses of vitamin C—received as supplements—have in curbing airway inflammation related to exercise-induced asthma. One study found that supplements, combined with ongoing treatments, produced fewer drops in lung function following exercise when used by college athletes. Research is continuing in this area.

While the evidence is still being weighed, adding antioxidants naturally to your child's diet through fruits and vegetables is unlikely to draw much opposition from his health care provider. Although vitamin C appears (along with vitamin E) to have some healthful benefits in terms of managing some asthma symptoms, it should not be depended on solely for treatment of asthma. But, avoid overdoing doses of these vitamins (through supplements) because excessive doses could be seriously harmful to your child.

B Vitamins

The B-complex vitamins—such as B-1 (thiamine) and B-2 (riboflavin)—have important roles in supporting your child's immune system. The one vitamin that has gained particular interest is B-6 (pyridoxine) that has been found in some studies to be beneficial to asthmatic children—resulting in fewer asthma symptoms and flare-ups.

Zinc

Like magnesium, individuals with asthma have been found to have lower levels of zinc than those without asthma. No direct connection, though, has been made between a lack of zinc and asthma symptoms. However, it has garnered some interest as an antioxidant.

Omega-3 Fatty Acids

Much discussion also has come up over the use of oils from cold-water fatty fish—especially those that contain essential fatty acids, better known as omega-3s. These oils, and their anti-inflammatory properties, have caught the attention of researchers who are trying to find if they could hold promise for treating asthma. These oils can be found in a capsule form, but no positive effect has been found in relation to asthma.

Diet Changes

Debate continues on whether asthma can be improved by avoiding foods that are thought to be harmful, or by eating more of foods that are considered to be healthier. Into this discussion has been thrown new evidence related to the weight debate: children who are overweight or obese are more likely to have asthma than those children who have normal weight. (Also see Chapter 10.)

In coming years, the impact of a child's diet on his asthma symptoms is likely to become the subject of more study.

Food Sensitivities

A small percentage of children with asthma do have food allergies. When a child has an actual food allergy, he may react to foods such as milk, eggs, wheat, shellfish, soy, or peanuts. To detect these allergies, a child can undergo a medically supervised test in which a particular food is removed from his diet and symptoms are studied.

However, one idea that has been the cause of discussion among many parents is the so-called "hidden food allergies"—that a child has sensitivity to certain foods that can't be detected by health care providers.

This hidden trigger, though, has not been detected by any studies. If anything, health care providers have warned that a diet that eliminates foods suspected of causing allergies—without medically confirming this relationship—could cause more problems for the child. Without certain foods, these children could encounter nutritional deficiencies that could harm their health.

Healthful Diets

For years, advocates of healthy eating have pointed out how many processed or convenience foods—those foods made of refined wheats and sugars and unhealthy fats—were leading to weight gains among children. Those with an interest in asthma and nutrition cited how sugar could impair the immune system for hours, and how poor eating in general could trigger an asthma attack.

This emerging information on asthma and obesity, along with growing research into the impact of nutrients on asthma, has increased interest on the impact of foods—particularly those high in vitamins and minerals, moderate in protein, balanced with healthy fats, and high in fiber.

More research is needed in this area, but some studies of children who had diets that excluded most processed foods have shown interesting results. For instance, 690 Greek children ages 7 to 18 years who adhered to a "traditional Mediterranean diet" demonstrated few asthma symptoms such as wheezing and runny nose.

The children, who lived in rural Crete, had a diet high in fruits, vegetables, and nuts—including grapes, oranges, apples, and fresh tomatoes (the main local produce in Crete)—which contain many nutrients that may help with asthma symptoms.

Herbal Remedies

The history of herbal remedies goes back to the days of the ancient Greek, Roman, Chinese, Japanese, and Arabic societies. Today, herbal remedies can be purchased in a variety of retail establishments. But, unlike conventional asthma medications, you don't need a prescription to purchase them.

 **Fact**

The federal Food and Drug Administration (FDA) does not regulate herbal products the same way as prescription drugs. This means that herbal products do not have to meet standards for potency or purity required for prescription or over-the-counter medications in the United States. However, other countries, particularly those in Europe, do classify herbals as drugs.

This creates a double-edged sword. On one hand, herbal remedies are available to just about anyone who wants them. On the other hand, safety of the products can come into question due to improper labeling or possibly adulterated ingredients.

If considering the herbal route—and many people with asthma do—consider getting the assistance of a qualified naturopath or herbalist to help avoid the side effects of "going herbal."

Herbs and Asthma

Herbal remedies are botanical products that come from any part of a plant. This can include the root, stem, bark, leaf, flower, or fruit of the plant. When they are sold, they may be packaged as teas, tablets, powders, liquids, or capsules. Quite a few have been touted for their abilities to help with asthma symptoms.

In the adult market, herbal products have become very popular. These herbal products include: ginkgo biloba, green tea, licorice root, and black tea. However, these herbs do not have the scientific evidence behind them to recommend them for children under age eighteen.

Reviewing the Facts

The FDA classifies herbs (along with vitamins) as dietary supplements rather than drugs. Therefore, herbs are not subject to the same regulations as prescription drugs. The FDA, though, can remove an herbal product from the market if it finds it unsafe or makes false claims.

While the federal government also requires that herbal products carry labels to state how they affect the body, they are not required to carry health warnings. The labels, though, are not permitted to list any medical or health benefits.

Sometimes, various products may contain "hidden ingredients" —unnamed medicines such as steroids, anti-inflammatories, or sedatives—that act to reduce your symptoms. Although not common, individuals could experience toxic—and sometimes lethal—effects from improperly labeled herbs.

If you decide to use herbal supplements for your child's asthma, keep several points in mind:

- Make sure you have received an accurate diagnosis from a licensed health care provider.
- Speak to your child's health care provider about advice on using any specific herbal remedies—keeping in consideration your child's age, weight, and other pertinent factors.
- Find out if the products have been tested for safety and effectiveness.
- Avoid preparations made with more than one herb.
- Contact a health care provider if your child experiences an effect that concerns you.
- If you use supplements, do not increase the dose or treatment time beyond the recommended period.
- Ask what is known from scientific studies (published in peer-reviewed journals) about the remedies in which you are interested.

Medline, an online database that is part of the NIH's National Library of Medicine, provides information on both herbal and dietary supplements. The Web site (*www.nlm.nih.gov/medlineplus/drug information.html*) includes recent research and recommendations on whether children should use the specific supplements. A summary report on research regarding asthma and many types of complementary therapies is available at *www.nationalasthma.org.au/html/ management/infopapers/consumer/5004.asp.*

CHAPTER 6
Asthma Medications

The world of asthma medications is a constantly evolving—with new medications and new ways to control asthma symptoms frequently reported. Several years ago, asthma was thought of as an episodic disease that only needed treatment when symptoms flared up. Now research has revealed that it is a chronic inflammatory disease that needs treatment on a daily basis to control symptoms and prevent future problems, in all but the mildest levels of the disease. But while medical science has made leaps forward, children still appear caught in an old dilemma: remembering to take their medications as prescribed, even if they feel fine—and not just when their symptoms flare up.

The Medication Challenge

No doubt about it, asthma can seem like a complex condition to treat. When your child is first diagnosed with asthma, the discussions, for instance, of inhalers and multiple medications to reduce both constriction and inflammation of her lungs can seem overwhelming.

Once you receive a prescription or two, questions can still linger in your mind about whether the medication is being administered appropriately, if side effects are common, and if your child may be taking too much—or not enough—medication.

Today, more medications than ever are available to help children treat and manage their asthma safely and effectively. However, a void seems to have opened up between what is available and the appropriate use of available medications by children to manage their asthma.

A Larger Problem

Ongoing research has found that inadequate asthma control is common among children—even those who are prescribed recommended medications.

In one study, only 20 percent of children with persistent asthma were found to have their asthma under optimal control using their medications, according to a review of survey data from the Centers for Disease Control and Prevention. Another 43 percent had poorly controlled asthma—even when they were using their anti-inflammatory medications as recommended, and 37 percent had inadequate therapy with no preventive medication prescribed.

The poorly controlled asthma was linked with factors such as inadequate management at the health care provider level; failure to receive a written asthma management plan; no knowledge of how to use a peak flow meter; and no knowledge of how to recognize symptoms.

A solution, the researchers suggested, included using an approach that encourages, in part, more education by providers and community-based entities to promote better medication adherence.

Going Short and Long

Having a prescription is a start to better managing asthma. But, it is important that both you and your child educate yourselves on what the medications do, how they are similar or different, and how they fit into your child's treatment plan.

The main step is understanding that asthma medications are split into two groups to address two conditions (airway constriction and airway inflammation):

- Short-term quick-relief medications are designed to relax the muscle layers around your child's airways. They act fast—but their effect only lasts a few hours. They basically treat asthma symptoms (such as coughing or wheezing), but they will not reduce or prevent inflammation, which is the main underlying cause of asthma.

- Many long-term control medications are designed to prevent the longer term swelling and inflammation of airways and to prevent the occurrence and severity of asthma flare-ups. They are taken daily.

Except for mild cases of asthma, your child likely will be prescribed both types of medications to treat and control his asthma. There are a variety of combinations that your health care provider could prescribe that are examined here in more detail.

Quick-Relief Medications

The most popular "rescue medications" are known as bronchodilators or short-term beta-agonists. Initially, your child may need these medications several times a week, but usage should gradually decrease as she gains better control of her asthma symptoms. Side effects are minimal but can include nervousness, nausea, headaches, sleeplessness, or shaking.

Albuterol

You might be familiar with short-acting beta2-agonists through one of its most popular products with the generic name of albuterol, the seventh most commonly prescribed drug in the United States.

These medications, which are available in forms such as drypowder inhaler, metered-dose inhaler, nebulizer solution, injectables, or tablets, are designed to relax the smooth muscle surrounding the airways or bronchial tubes. They can be used for relief of symptoms related to exercise-induced asthma. These medicines usually take effect within minutes and can last for up to four to six hours.

New albuterol metered-dose inhalers with hydrofluoroalkane (HFA) are now replacing albuterol inhalers, which contain chlorofluorocarbons (CFCs) as a propellant. The Food and Drug Administration has ruled that American sales of CFC albuterol inhalers are prohibited by the end of 2008 due to rising global concerns about CFC's ozone-depleting properties. The medicine is the same, but the inhaler sends out a slower plume of medicine compared with the older inhalers.

 **Fact**

Albuterol also can be taken orally, but it might take a few hours for its peak to be reached. While oral albuterol can help mild symptoms, it may not provide enough medicine for those with moderate or severe asthma. Albuterol syrup may be used by young children, but it also may take longer to work and have greater side effects.

Side effects with albuterol are minimal but can include nervousness, nausea, headaches, sleeplessness, or shaking. Some examples are Ventolin HFA, Proventil HFA, ProAir HFA, and Accuneb.

Levalbuterol Inhalation Aerosol

Levalbuterol is a form of albuterol that may have fewer side effects compared to generic albuterol but is similarly designed for recurring episodes of bronchospasms. It comes in two forms—a nebulized form and in a metered-dose inhaler. An example of the metered-dose inhaler form is Xopenex HFA.

Pirbuterol

Pirbuterol has similar characteristics to albuterol. It has an autohaler dispenser that automatically releases a medicine dose when someone inhales. It does not use a space device and is not recommended for young children. Some side effects include difficulty sleeping, dry mouth, headache, or throat irritation. Examples are Maxair and Maxair Autohaler.

Anticholinergics

This medication group may be prescribed along with albuterol in cases of moderate to severe asthma—or when albuterol cannot be tolerated by a child. It can help relieve bronchospasms and/or reduce mucus secretions. Side effects include dry mouth. An example is Atrovent.

Oral Corticosteroids

These corticosteroids, taken by mouth, are usually used for short-term treatment as a rescue medication. They can be used in an emergency, and are designed to reduce inflammation of the airways that causes an asthma flare-up.

A short course (usually three to five days) might be recommended for a child who is having serious asthma symptoms that don't appear to be controlled by quick-relief medication. This short course would be used to decrease problematic or serious symptoms. Generally, these oral corticosteroids take about six to eight hours before they begin their work. Occasionally, children with significant asthma will require oral steroids routinely.

For the short course, some of the side effects seen would be mood changes or increased appetite. When oral corticosteroids are used for longer periods of time, more serious side effects are possible such as weight gain, increased blood pressure, a suppressed immune system, weakened bones, greater susceptibility to bruising, or decreased growth.

If a child is on oral corticosteroids for more than several weeks, medical experts recommend being tapered off the drug and moved to safer inhaled corticosteroids.

Prednisone

Prednisone is an older and well-known oral corticosteriod on the market. Generic versions are usually available. It can be taken in tablet form or as a syrup, but might meet resistance from children who do not like the taste.

Prednisolone

Prednisolone is similar to prednisone except this liquid form might be more agreeable in terms of taste with children. Brand names include Orapred, Pediapred, Prelone, Hydrocortone, and Medrol.

Decadron

Decadron is an oral corticosteroid that comes in pill form and can be used for emergency rescue treatment for asthma. It has a slightly longer effective time in the body so is usually used for a shorter period of time (two days) compared with prednisone.

Long-Term Control Medications

Rather than taking the route of using higher-dose inhaled corticosteroids, your child's health care provider is likely to take the safer route and prescribe the longer-term symptom control medications on the market. These medications can assist in opening airways and lowering inflammation. Not all, though, are recommended for children under the age of twelve years.

Mast-Cell Stabilizers

Cromolyn sodium and nedocromil sodium, which are available as metered-dose inhalers, are long-term asthma controllers used to decrease inflammation and improve lung function. They are not corticosteroids.

They may be used to prevent asthma symptoms related to triggers such as allergens or exercise if the medication is used prior to an exposure. They do not, though, provide quick relief of asthma symptoms. These medicines block the action of mast cells in the body that release various chemicals that cause inflammation in your airways.

Both drugs, which have been on the market for years (cromolyn since the 1970s and nedocromil since the early 1990s), have less potency than many of their longer acting counterparts and usually must be used about three to four times a day if inhaled. (For cromolyn, it's three to four times a day from a metered-dose inhaler and with a nebulizer.) Generally, they might be only prescribed to patients with very mild asthma. Side effects are very minimal and possibly include coughing, skin rash, and headaches. These drugs have a long history of safety—even with children. Examples are Intal (cromolyn) and Tilade (nedocromil).

Inhaled Corticosteroids

Inhaled corticosteroids, given in low doses, are recommended for children (even those under age five) requiring long-term asthma treatment.

 **Fact**

In its updated 2007 asthma guidelines, the National Asthma Education and Prevention Program (NAEPP) said that patients across all age groups with mild or moderate persistent asthma showed great improvement in obtaining long-term control for their asthma symptoms and in reducing flare-ups.

Like the older mast-cell stabilizers, inhaled corticosteroids work to control inflammation—making your child's airways less sensitive when asthma triggers appear. Unlike quick-relief medications, they may take two weeks to a month to see the full benefits from the medication and must be given twice daily to maintain their protective effect. Examples include Aerobid, Azmacort, Flovent HFA, Pulmicort, and QVAR.

Combination Medications

Combination medications are made from two types of asthma medicines that are joined together: Inhaled corticosteroids are usually paired with long-acting beta2-agonists. Generally, these medications are recommended for older children (ages four or up). Together they work in an inhalant form to open the airways and reduce inflammation. Brand names include Symbicort, Advair Diskus, or Advair HFA.

Combivent is a medication that combines two short-acting bronchodilators—albuterol and atrovent. It is used in adults more often than children and comes as a metered-dose inhaler.

Long-Acting Beta2-Agonists

These medicines are inhaled or oral bronchodilators (or muscle relaxers). They are not designed to treat the inflammation. These medications are strongly recommended to be used with inhaled corticosteroids to avoid asthma flare-ups.

 **Essential**

Long-acting beta2-agonists have been found to be helpful for treating children who have nocturnal asthma symptoms. They also are used to address symptoms related to exercise-induced asthma. Long-acting beta2-agonists are similar in action to the short-acting beta2-agonists used as quick-relief medications.

However, long-acting types have been found to be better for prevention since they last twelve hours. Examples are Serevent Diskus and Foradil Aerolizer.

Leukotrine Modifiers

Leukotriene modifiers are oral, anti-inflammatory medicines that can be used alone in cases of mild asthma or combined with inhaled steroids for patients with moderate asthma or asthma with allergic rhinitis. One of the products has been approved for use when symptoms arise when exercising. This medicine works to block leukotrienes, a chemical in the body that contributes to the airway inflammation. It also helps prevent swelling inside the airways, stops mucus from forming, and decreases muscle tightening around the airways. Side effects include headaches, nausea, or diarrhea. Examples of leukotriene modifiers are Zyflo, Singulair, and Accolate.

Oral Bronchodilators

A member of this group is theophylline, the generic name of one of the oldest asthma drugs on the market. It can be taken as a tablet, liquid, capsule, or time-released tablet, and works to relax and open up airways.

Theophylline is often combined with a moderate dose of inhaled corticosteroids to provide better control. The medication, though, may have numerous side effects in children—even at low doses. These include nervousness, nausea, restlessness, and headache. Among children who are already diagnosed as hyperactive, it could cause additional stimulation.

Theophylline also can interact with other medications, such as antibiotics or antacids, and can stimulate gastroesophageal reflux, which in turn could trigger asthma.

With so many brands of theophylline on the market, check with your child's health care provider if a change is made as the amount of medicine that gets into the bloodstream can vary with each product. Examples are Aerolate III, Slo-bid, Theo-dur, Theolair, T-Phyl, and Uni-Dur.

Subcutaneous Injection of Anti-IgE

This medication, known as omalizumab, is injected under the skin every two to four weeks in a health care provider's office. It can be used in combination with other agents to treat allergic asthma or allergy symptoms. It is designed to bind to immunoglobulin E (IgE), an antibody that is an underlying cause of asthma and allergies. The drug is designed only for children ages twelve and over. Side effects may include trouble breathing, chest tightness, dizziness, fainting, itching and hives, and swelling of the mouth and throat. It is utilized predominantly in children with severe asthma.

Getting What You Need from Medications

Correct administration of asthma medications is crucial in order to achieve the desired asthma control. For example, all metered-dose inhaler medications (also known as puffers) should be taken with a spacer device, most commonly a cylinder with a mouthpiece or mask for young children at one end and a rubber fitting at the other end that tightly surrounds the top of the metered-dose inhaler. The spacer acts as a holding chamber that gives your child time to slowly inhale her medicine when the inhaler is used—while preventing that medication from escaping into the air. In turn, the spacer will lower the amount of medicine that is deposited onto the back of her throat while increasing the amount that goes to her lungs.

It is important to receive instructions on the use of a spacer before using it with a medication, but it is easy enough that even infants can take the medication in this manner. Children will be able to inhale more medication with the use of the spacer than if they use the metered-dose inhaler on its own.

Once your health care provider has prescribed medication for your child, be sure you are clear on the following items:

- When do you give the medication? Should your child take it before a meal, before bedtime, when she feels symptoms coming on, before exercise?
- How should the medication be timed with other medications? If using both a rescue and a controller medication, for

instance, can they be used at the same time or should she wait until a specified time?

- What side effects should be reported immediately? Some conditions, possibly a drop in blood pressure or nausea, may require that you call your health care provider immediately.
- How will you know when and if the medication is working? While the results are more obvious with a quick-relief medication, it sometimes may take days or weeks to spot changes with the longer-term control medications.
- What side effects should you report with a follow-up visit? These conditions, such as headache, skin rashes, or nervousness, might indicate to your health care provider that a change in medications or strengths is needed.
- What side effects could your child expect from taking the medication? Some medications, when inhaled, may leave an aftertaste or could cause conditions such as a sore throat, hoarseness, coughing, or even thrush, a yeast infection of the mouth. Check with your health care provider about tips to prevent some of these side effects.
- How should a medication be prepared? What special directions (such as priming an inhaler or preparing an oral syrup) should you keep in mind before using the medication?
- What should you do if your child misses a dose? Should your child take the medication as soon as she can, or wait until the usual time before she takes it?
- Could this medication interact with others? If your child is taking a supplement or over-the-counter medication, check to see if it conflicts with the medication.

To make medication use a little easier, and to help your health care provider assess its effectiveness, consider using an asthma diary to record when medication is given and when side effects occur. It can be as simple as recording data in a notebook or on a calendar.

For more information on medications your child might be prescribed, you can view the online database that is part of the National

Library of Medicine of the National Institutes of Health at *www.nlm .nih.gov/medlineplus/druginformation.html*.

Side Effects and Safety Issues

Many of the medications your child could be prescribed have been around for years, while some may be fairly new. However, understandably, you have questions about whether they are safe for your child.

Inhaled Steroid Safety

Many parents are concerned about the long-term use of steroids in asthma medications. In fact, a phrase—"steroid phobia"—has emerged in the medical community over individuals who express fear over taking daily recommended doses of inhaled corticosteroid medications because of worries about how steroids could affect their health.

First, it's important to clarify the term "steroid." The controversial use of steroids by athletes to boost muscle mass and strength refer to an "anabolic steroid," which is a completely different compound from corticosteroids used in inhaled medications.

Also, a number of side effects have been noted with the use of oral corticosteroids over long periods of time such as weight gain, increased blood pressure, mood disorder, and decreased growth. However, oral corticosteroids are now usually prescribed for very short periods of time to decrease serious symptoms of an asthma flare-up.

Research from the Childhood Asthma Management Program found that growth may be slowed by inhaled corticosteroid use— but not by much. The study over a six-year period reviewed use of budesonide (an inhaled corticosteroid) by one group of children and nedocromil (a nonsteroidal medicine) by another.

At the end of the study period, the group taking the inhaled corticosteroid had a small decrease in growth velocity that was not sustained over time. They also had required fewer emergency room and hospital visits, and fewer emergencies that required use of oral steroids. Follow-up over four to seven years later of the children in that study revealed no adverse effect on growth or bone density.

 **Fact**

An NAEPP update obtained from large clinical trials found that the potential risk of a delay in growth linked to inhaled corticosteroids is temporary—and possibly reversible.

The NAEPP also concluded that other potential concerns, including reduced bone mineral density, suppressed adrenal function, and increased incidence of cataracts, are not considered significant risks for children.

Step Up, Step Down

You often may wonder if your child is getting too much medicine, not enough, or just the right amount for his asthma. Initially, it may be difficult to determine if the dose is right—since every patient has different symptoms at different times.

 Essential

Providers are being encouraged to step up treatment or step down, depending on how the patient is responding to the medication and the patient's symptoms. The goal is to place a patient on the lowest dose possible to maintain good asthma control.

When asthma symptoms become a problem, that dose can be increased; the dose can then be lowered when symptoms subside. In a study of the step-down therapy among 374 adult and children patients with asthma, two-thirds had at least one change in medication during a two-year period. Most of the changes were step-up doses that were in response to an asthma flare-up. Step-down changes were found to be less common. Part of the reason was that asthma care appeared to be episodic—with most health care provider visits occurring at a flare-up.

When visiting your child's health care provider next time to address his asthma, you may want to inquire if he could safely reduce his medication without anticipating any adverse effects. In the long run, this could help establish a better course of long-term treatment for your child. Asthma guidelines suggest reviewing the need to step down treatment if the child's asthma has been in good control and stable for at least three months.

What's in Your Medicine?

If your child is using inhalation drugs, particularly for use with a nebulizer, consumer groups are warning that you might not be getting what you want with medicines that are compounded at your local pharmacy. Compounding means that medications that are not commercially available for a single patient are mixed together for that patient.

Alert!

Some of these compounded drugs, which are not regulated by the FDA, may not contain the therapeutic ingredients to treat your child's symptoms, or they may contain ingredients that could hurt your child's airways, such as bacteria or preservatives.

Oftentimes, health care providers may not know that their patients are inhaling unapproved medications. The consumer groups recommend that parents purchase only FDA-approved brand-name and generic unit-dose medications.

Initial Daily Therapy

With so many controller medications to choose from, which should health care providers initially recommend for school-aged children?

 **Fact**

After studying 285 children ages six to fourteen years for forty-eight weeks, researchers at the Childhood Asthma Research and Education Network of the National Heart, Lung, and Blood Institute found that inhaled corticosteroids were the most effective initial daily therapy for children with mild to moderate persistent asthma.

Although a variety of medications are available to help children maintain asthma control, clinical trials directly comparing them had not been conducted. When the study was published in 2007, current recommendations in national and international asthma guidelines were based either on studies of single treatments compared to a placebo in children or on comparison studies in adults.

The researchers compared the effectiveness and safety of three asthma medicines for initial daily therapy for school-aged children: a low-dose inhaled corticosteroid such as fluticasone (Flovent) once a day; a combination of a lower-dose inhaled corticosteroid and an inhaled long-acting beta2-agonist (fluticasone each morning plus salmeterol twice daily); and a leukotriene receptor antagonist (montelukast once a day).

These results support the asthma clinical guidelines, issued by the NAEPP in 2007, which recommend inhaled corticosteroids as the preferred initial therapy for children with mild to moderate asthma.

Take the Medications

Sometimes your child's medications may work too well: She may want to drop daily medications because she has sharply reduced asthma symptoms or she knows she can count on her quick-relief medications at any time.

The Fire Beneath

Your answer to dropping medications should focus on the point that she is feeling better now because of her use of daily medications, along with other changes she may have made in her life (such as avoiding certain asthma triggers). While she may be breathing better now, let her know that a fire of sorts has been smoldering underneath in her airways.

Alert!

The quick-relief medication may make her feel fine now—it relaxes the muscles around her airways. However, what she doesn't realize is that inflammation in her airways could get worse if she just uses her quick-relief solution.

An asthma flare-up may be on the way, and she may have to take short-course action—such as an oral corticosteroid—to avoid problems.

Keeping on Track

During a calm time, look back on recent months with her to show how the medications have made changes such as fewer school absences, more time to play outside, or more restful nights in which she slept through the night.

A certain routine—such as taking medications after breakfast or before brushing her teeth in the morning—can help make using daily medications seem more routine with less hassle. (And by brushing her teeth, she can then get rid of the taste of the medicine that some children hate.)

As she becomes more mature, she can begin to take on more responsibility for herself—possibly even keeping her own asthma diary where she notes changes in her peak flow meter and symptoms. The eventual goal is that she will become responsible for her own health by controlling her asthma.

Circadian Rhythms

If you want to optimize how your child's controller asthma medications work, maybe you should consider his circadian rhythms.

The human body behaves differently throughout the day—following its own circadian rhythms, according to researchers. The rhythms also affect how the body responds to asthma and also allergy symptoms.

However, most inhaled corticosteroids—which are widely used by those with mild to moderate asthma—are taken two to three times a day, and research is ongoing to determine the best times to take those multiple doses. Overall, your strategy first should be consistency—that your child is taking his asthma medications daily as prescribed by his health care provider.

For those with allergies, taking those medications at night will help address symptoms first thing in the morning. This schedule will maximize allergy and asthma drug results—again only if individuals remember to take their medications each day, the researchers note.

 *Question?*

What is the optimum time of day to take an asthma medication to control symptoms?

Since asthma symptoms peak at about 4 A.M., researchers have suggested that patients with severe asthma, who require oral corticosteroid drugs, should take their medication at 3 P.M. Those with less severe asthma, who use steroid inhalers, may find drugs have their greatest effect when taken between 3 P.M. and 5 P.M.

Refill'er Up

Many inhaled medications can work wonders on your child's asthma—as long as they don't run out. Sometimes parents find out their children have been using a spent inhaler only after their children's symptoms cannot be effectively controlled as before. This is not an uncommon occurrence.

But, you can take steps to avoid using an empty inhaler by double-checking with your health care provider or pharmacist or carefully reading the directions yourself about the period of use established for the inhaler.

Possibly make a note to yourself: If an inhaler has 120 puffs, and your child uses two puffs per day on average, mark a date 60 days from the first day of use for replacement.

Some brands of HFA inhalers come with a counter to track how much medicine is left. For those devices without a counter, keeping a backup inhaler handy might be advisable—just in case.

Also consider designing a timetable for older children who are carrying quick-relief inhalers in school in case of emergency. Or, you might want to create a medications diary that lists when medications were used, or develop a set time each month when you and your child examine if and when a refill is needed.

CHAPTER 7

Devices

W hile having asthma is no fun for a kid, many medications have made it more manageable to avoid symptoms. And, helping deliver those medications quickly and safely are various devices—from inhalers to nebulizers. Using the right devices—and making sure the medications are delivered correctly with these devices at the right time—can sometimes be tough. But mastering this task can mean your child can better manage her asthma.

Metered-Dose Inhalers

Metered-dose inhalers, sometimes referred to by their acronym MDIs, made their first appearances in 1956 to safely house and dispense asthma medication. Their appearance made a difference in how asthma could be treated: Individuals with asthma could carry their medication anywhere and use it anytime.

The Changed MDI

The MDIs, which are small plastic devices that hold medicine in an aerosol container, are probably a familiar sight to those with asthma. The MDI pressurized container contains a chemical propellant, which is now being replaced. For years, the container used chlorofluorocarbons (CFCs), which are now being banned because of global concerns about their impact on the ozone layer. These inhalers will no longer be available by the end of 2008.

These are being replaced by inhalers with the same medicine but a different propellant called hydrofluoroalkanes (HFAs). The Food and Drug Administration has noted that HFA inhalers are safe and effective, and patients should not find any significant differences from their CFC inhalers.

 **Essential**

Changes are ahead for MDIs. The albuterol HFA sprays, for instance, have been found to have a somewhat different taste and spray strength. And, shelf life for some of the albuterol devices will be far shorter (at two months) for some of the new HFA inhalers. More frequent replacement is expected when compared with the older containers.

You will need to carefully read the directions on each inhaler to see what changes may have been made to dosage capacity and shelf life. Some of the inhalers with HFA will now use counters to track how much medicine is left. For those without counters, users can determine the life of the inhaler by dividing the number of puffs listed on the medicine with the number of days the medicine is expected to be used. But, medical advisors have suggested that these users keep a backup inhaler handy—just in case they run out.

Using an MDI

On the surface, using an MDI to deliver medicine looks simple enough, but the reality is that many patients usually do not use it the right way. When your child uses his MDI incorrectly, less medicine will get into his lungs to do its work.

To assist your child with using his inhaler without a spacer (see discussion in next section), you or your child should:

1. Remove cap from the inhaler and hold the container upright.
2. Mix the contents in the inhaler by shaking it several times, and turn canister bottom toward ceiling (so mouthpiece is on the bottom).
3. Have your child breathe out.
4. Use one of two methods to prepare to inhale medicine: close mouth around inhaler mouthpiece or hold mouthpiece an inch away from the mouth.
5. Press down canister and begin to breathe slowly and deeply.
6. Hold his breath as he counts to ten slowly (to let the medication into the breathing tubes).
7. Wait about a minute if another puff is to follow.
8. Have him rinse his mouth afterward to help decrease any aftertaste or unwanted side effects.

Remember to clean the inhaler as needed. If you see powder or residue in or around the hole where the medicine sprays out, you can clean the inhaler by taking out the metal canister from the L-shaped plastic mouthpiece. Rinse the mouthpiece and cap in water, and let them air-dry overnight.

Spacers

In the early years of inhalers, children often used an MDI by itself. However, today most children are likely to be prescribed a spacer (also called a holding chamber) with the MDI to make it easier for them to use.

The spacer, which comes in a variety of styles, acts as a medicine conduit between the inhaler and the mouthpiece held by the child. The spacer works to hold and slow down the spray ejected by the inhaler so a child can take more time to inhale the medicine deep into her airways.

 **Fact**

The idea behind the spacer is that larger particles from the aerosol spray will attach to the walls of the device. These are particles that (without the spacer) would end up in your child's mouth and throat. The finer particles in the inhaler medicine then will make their way to your child's airways—and help her asthma symptoms.

The one-way design of a spacer prevents a child from breathing back into the device. The spacer also requires less coordination than using the inhaler alone: A child can breathe in the medicine after the inhaler is puffed—not at the same time it is puffed.

Types of Spacers

The most common—and frequently prescribed inhaler—is a plastic tube with a space for the inhaler at one end and a mouthpiece at the other. Children as young as five years should be able to use this type of spacer comfortably.

Spacers also are available with a mask at one end that can be used by infants and toddlers. The mask should be fit securely around the child's face so he gets the medicine that he needs from the inhaler.

Bag-type spacers have an inflated bag in which the inhaler is sprayed. As the child breathes in the medicine through the mouthpiece, the bag shrinks in size. This type of space may work better with preschoolers and kindergartners who might like breathing in and watching the bag shrink as they take their medicine.

The bag device's life is short, though: The bags may last from one month to a year, while a plastic cylinder tube-type could last years.

An air entrapment device is slightly different than a spacer. With the device, the child sprays the inhaler as he breathes in deeply. He then holds his breath, and then breathes out. Using a series of internal baffles, the device filters out the medicine's larger particles, and permits the medicine to get through the child's lungs, while removing the amount that goes into the mouth. The device's smaller size has made it more popular among teenagers.

Using the Spacer

Keep a few extra tips in mind when using the MDI with a tube-type spacer:

1. After removing the cap from the MDI and shaking it, insert the end of the MDI into the larger opening of the tube. (The canister bottom should be facing the ceiling.)
2. Holding the tube securely, have your child place the mouthpiece between her teeth and then close her lips around it.
3. Press the inhaler and have your child breathe in slowly for about 5 seconds.
4. Have the child remove the inhaler while holding her breath for 10 seconds.
5. Repeat if another dose is required from the inhaler.

Keep in mind that each dose requires one puff of the inhaler: in other words, your child should not press the inhaler twice to get two doses—and then breathe in. Instead, press the inhaler once and breathe in, and then press again for a second dose if needed.

Dry-Powder Inhaler

Dry-powder inhalers or DPIs do not use propellants like MDIs. Instead, DPIs, which are also called breath-activated devices, deliver medicine to your child's airways using a dry powder. Children generally over the age of five can use DPIs, but they will require some new skills. Most of these devices have counters.

With a DPI, your child will need to take a quick, deep breath to inhale the medicine—rather than a slow breath as with the MDI and spacer. Because of the lack of propellant, this deeper breath will help the medicine move into your his airways better.

Types of DPIs

Four types of DPIs are on the market for treating asthma symptoms. One is the Diskus that is marketed under the brand names Serevent or Advair. The others are the Turbuhaler used by Pulmicort; the Twisthaler for Asmanex; and the Aerolizer inhaler for Foradil.

Using a DPI

Each of the DPIs varies in how it is used. With the Diskus, the device is twisted and a lever is pulled in order to use it. With the Turbuhaler, it is twisted in two different directions. The Aerolizer uses capsules so it's easy to see how much medicine has been used. Spacers are not used for DPIs.

The devices require that your child exhale first, and then bring the mouthpiece to her lips. She should use a fast, quick breath when the medicine is released, and then hold her breath for ten seconds. It's probably a good idea for your child to rinse her mouth when she is finished, and to clean off the device for the next use.

Nebulizers

A nebulizer is actually a device that includes an air compressor and tubing with a medicine cup that helps mix liquid medicine in the air. This creates a mist that can be breathed through a mouthpiece or a mask.

Nebulizers often are used for young children—particularly with quick-relief medications or inhaled corticosteroids. For infants and toddlers, a mask should be used; for children over age five, a mouthpiece should be used.

Alert!

The nebulizer should never be used by applying the "blow-out" method, which is circling the mist around the child's face rather than using a mouthpiece or mask. This is ineffective, especially when the child is crying, because he cannot properly breathe in the medicine.

A child should be reminded to breathe deeply and slowly—then hold that breath for five to ten seconds—when using the nebulizer. If the child breathes normally during the treatment, much of the medicine will not enter his airways.

If nebulizers are used correctly, they can do their job. But, the size and bulkiness of a unit hinders its portability. Smaller battery-powered nebulizers are available for traveling.

In terms of benefits of nebulizers over portable inhalers, researchers have not found any great differences between the two.

Using a Nebulizer

Using a nebulizer usually takes more time than the other devices. Once the device is set up, you will need to:

1. Place the medicine into the nebulizer cup, and attach the mouthpiece or the mask to the nebulizer.
2. Have the child wrap her lips around the mouthpiece. (A mask will require additional discussion with a health care provider.)
3. Once the nebulizer is on, the child should breathe in deeply and hold her breath for five to ten seconds.
4. The process should be continued until the cup is empty (about ten minutes).

Home Nebulizer Dangers

While home nebulizers may seem helpful in controlling asthma symptoms, researchers are concerned that if they are used improperly, they could lead to serious asthma complications and even death. This could occur, Michigan State University researchers reported, if the home nebulizers are not used according to the National Asthma Education and Prevention Program (NAEPP) guidelines.

Essential

The widespread prescription and use of home nebulizers in asthma may have the unintended consequence of contributing to an over-reliance on quick-relief medications and inadequate use of longer-acting preventive medicines. The result could be a delay in seeking medical care during an asthma flare-up and poor management of chronic asthma.

In the study, the researchers looked at all asthma deaths that occurred between 2002 and 2004 in people between the ages of two and thirty-four years old. During that time period, eighty-six people in the specified age group died as a result of their asthma, with thirty-eight of them children. Fifty-two people who died had a home nebulizer. They found that thirty of those people used their machines regularly—usually between once a week to six times a day. While about two-thirds of those who used their nebulizers regularly were prescribed either inhaled or oral steroids, only a third used them as directed.

Although thirty-eight of the people who died had peak flow meters, only eight used them daily, the researchers found. And, only nine out of the fifty-two people with nebulizers had written asthma action plans. Having the nebulizers for use at home may lead to a sense of complacency that they can handle any emergency, but sometimes an asthma flare-up may be more serious than anticipated —leading to serious or fatal results.

Storing Concerns

Once the medications are purchased for your child's use, you need to find the right place to store them. Usually, it makes sense to store them together—perhaps in a container placed in a cool, dry place. This should be out of the reach of younger children.

Alert!

Special attention needs to be paid to certain medications that are stored in dry-powder inhalers. They must be kept in an environment that is mostly moisture-free to prevent the powder inside from becoming damp. This means avoiding the bathroom medicine chest or sink, and near stoves or windowsills. If moisture causes powder to clump together, your child may not get all the medicine that he needs.

Also, metered-dose inhalers and spacers should always be stored with their caps on. Without the caps, small objects could become embedded in the openings and could be accidentally swallowed by your child when he uses the medication.

Peak Flow Meters

Portable and ready to go in a minute, peak flow meters can be an important tool in your child's arsenal of devices to manage her asthma symptoms. This small hand-held device, which measures how efficiently your child can move air out of her lungs, can move you away from just visually looking for asthma symptoms.

By having your child blow into the plastic or metal tube, a little pointer can indicate how much her airways are constricted. It will let you know if she needs some additional medications to help her breathing. It also will let you know if she's showing signs of exercise-induced asthma. And, it will let you know if she needs her quick-relief medication right now.

Basically, the peak flow meter focuses on getting a quick, objective measurement to comprehend how she is breathing at any given point in time.

Peak flow meters are available over-the-counter from a variety of vendors, and they're fairly easy for children at least five years or older to use.

Why Use Peak Flow Monitoring?

A peak flow meter lets your child measure variations in his breathing every day—no matter where he is. When his asthma is under control, his airways are open and he can forcefully exhale more air into the peak flow meter.

On those good days when he has few asthma symptoms, he can designate a "personal best" score—obtained from peak flow readings taken twice a day over a two-week period—that he can designate as a benchmark on his asthma action plan.

When his breathing is at or near this personal best, he is having a good day as indicated on the "green zone" (or in-control zone) on his asthma action plan. (See Chapter 2 for more information on this management plan.) His peak flow rates will be 80 to 100 percent of his personal best—an indication that his asthma is under control, and he has no asthma signs or symptoms.

However, if his airways are constricted and inflamed, his reading will be lower. He will find himself in the yellow zone (caution) if his peak flow rates are 50 to 80 percent of his personal best. If he no longer is able to blow as hard into the meter, this is a sign that his asthma is getting worse. If his peak flow rates are less than 50 percent of his personal best rate, he will be in the red zone (warning) on his action plan. This indicates an impending emergency where prompt action must be taken. This will make his peak flow rate lower.

When to Use It

Your child's physician may recommend using a peak flow meter at least once a day—usually before taking her asthma medication in the morning—if she has moderate or severe asthma. Current guidelines usually do not recommended daily peak flow monitoring for patients with milder cases of asthma—unless that patient, her family, and her health care provider find it useful in guiding treatment decisions.

To help better monitor her peak flow meter use, consider using it at the same time each day and recording her readings in an asthma diary. This actually can be any sheet of paper or a computer program where she can mark the reading and the data.

This information will help you, your child, and her physician to monitor: the severity of her asthma; the effectiveness of her current treatment and asthma management plan; if certain medications should be added or stopped; if signs or symptoms appear to point to an asthma flare-up; if emergency care might be necessary; and if exercise-induced asthma is being triggered.

Peak flow readings that show little change when your child is feeling well and when she is having what appear to be asthma symptoms indicate that it might not be asthma at all. But, if the peak flow values drop by more than 20 percent between that period of feeling well and feeling symptomatic, it may be signs of asthma.

Putting the Peak Flow Meter to Use

Using the peak flow meter to determine your child's peak flow rate requires just a few easy steps. Remember to have him hold the meter without holding the numbers and to remove any food or gum from his mouth:

1. Move the marker to the bottom of the numbered scale.
2. Connect the mouthpiece to the meter.
3. Stand up and then take a strong, deep breath (to expand his lungs).
4. Place lips around the mouthpiece, and blow hard and quickly in a single breath.

5. Review the final position of the marker. This will indicate his peak flow rate.

After repeating this procedure twice, have him record the highest reading of the three in his asthma diary for the next two to three weeks. And remember, to keep the peak flow meter operating correctly, continue to clean it—following manufacturers' directions. Finally, bear in mind that as your child grows, his "personal best" peak flow will increase as his height increases, requiring that a new "personal best" be documented in his asthma action plan.

Spirometry—and Beyond

In current asthma guidelines, the peak flow meter is a tool that is considered to be useful for providing ongoing monitoring of asthma symptoms. However, guidelines say it should not be used for providing diagnoses in a physician's office because reference values can vary between brands of peak flow meters.

In the office setting, a pulmonary function test—using a spirometer —is used for children about age five years or above. This test measures how much air can be emptied from your child's lungs (called force vital capacity or FVC) and how fast it exits her lungs (called forced expiratory volume or FEV).

For the test, which takes a few minutes, your child would be seated and asked to breathe into a tube that leads to the computerized spirometer. With her nose gently pinched shut, she would be asked to inhale as much as she could—then slowly and forcefully breathe out the air. She would be asked to do it twice again.

Determining If It's Asthma

The spirometer will record the information from her exhalations. It is programmed to take into consideration your child's age, gender, and height, plus the values obtained from the test. These results will be compared with the normal ranges of similar healthy individuals.

If the results fall outside the normal range, your child would be asked to take a quick-relief medication to help determine if she has asthma. This would help relax your child's airways. If she has asthma, the exhaled air should be expelled more rapidly—rising by around 15 percent.

The test, therefore, is used not only to indicate that asthma exists, but how severely her airways are blocked during the time of the test. This will help her physician in deciding what courses of treatment to follow and evaluate if treatment has been effective over time.

Other Diagnostic Tests

Although it is not widely available yet in the United States, a newer technology, called an impulse oscillometry system, is being tested on a limited basis at medical sites around the country. This test, which needs less effort than the spirometer and is easier for young children to use, can detect airway resistance and the airways' response to a quick-relief medication. The test can help detect how severe a young child's asthma is, and can assist physicians by alerting them sooner when appropriate treatments should begin.

Another method uses exhaled nitric oxide (eNO) testing to measure lung inflammation in children with asthma. The eNO machine is similar to a computer, with a small tower and monitor. A child using the system keeps a balloon icon steady on the monitor and controls its movement by breathing normally into the machine. The test gives a numeric reading of eNO levels that will correspond to the level of inflammation. If inflammation levels have increased, a decision can be made to better control the patient's asthma, including changing levels of medications or the actual medications.

Interest also has increased in analyzing sputum of asthma patients. The sputum is induced by inhalation of hypertonic saline aerosol. Ongoing research has noted that the test may be helpful when adjusting inhaled corticosteroid use among asthmatic patients.

CHAPTER 8

Infants, Toddlers, and Preschoolers

W hile dealing with asthma can seem challenging at any age, the younger age groups—infants, toddlers, and preschoolers—can seem more demanding because of their limited ability to speak and difficulties monitoring their breathing. Studies have shown this group is more at risk for respiratory failure. Even if you have cared for a child with asthma before—or if you've had asthma yourself—you may be apprehensive. This is not uncommon. Just remember it's good that you detected your child's asthma now so you can begin treatment as soon as possible.

Is It Asthma?

Several studies have shown that 50 to 80 percent of children who have asthma developed symptoms before their fifth birthday. In addition, children four years old or younger have the highest rates of hospitalization (59 per 10,000) and emergency room use (162 per 10,000) due to asthma—the highest of any age group.

If your young child is coughing or wheezing, you may wonder if he may be a part of that group. Oftentimes, though, it will be somewhat difficult for you—and even your health care provider—to initially make that diagnosis.

For years, medical professionals were taught that a child should not be diagnosed with asthma before the age of two. But, times have changed.

 **Fact**

Guidelines from the National Asthma Education and Prevention Program (NAEPP) of the National Institutes of Health no longer list exclusions for any age group. Instead, diagnoses are now based on a child's physical examination, symptoms, assessment of quality of life, medical history, and response to treatments.

For years, asthma during early childhood was often underdiagnosed. For instance, a child might be diagnosed instead with chronic bronchitis, wheezy bronchitis, gastroesophageal reflux disease, recurrent upper respiratory tract infections, or recurrent pneumonia. This meant those children did not get the correct therapy for asthma that they needed at the time.

On the other hand, symptoms such as coughing and wheezing do not necessarily mean that the diagnosis should be asthma. Nearly half of all infants actually may have a wheezing illness once in a while that is related to the small size of their airways or a particular type of virus. This usually disappears as they get older, and their airways get larger. Health care providers, therefore, should be wary of leaping ahead in this case and diagnosing asthma.

Sometimes, it could be other serious conditions such as cystic fibrosis, congenital heart disease, or maybe a parasitic disease. Health care providers should take time to rule out other conditions before starting asthma treatment.

So, you may ask, where is the best place to start? It helps to look for signs and indications that you can present to your health care provider. Even though you may feel you're on the sidelines when your young child has asthma, you still have a big job ahead in finding the right path for her to take in managing her symptoms. With a little guidance, you can make it.

The Warning Signs

Sometimes it may not be initially clear if your child has asthma, but several warning signs may point to asthma such as:

- A continuing cough, especially at night, with activity, or coughing longer than anyone else in the family after colds.
- Labored, rapid breathing—even when resting.
- Difficulty breathing in cold weather, especially when active.
- Greenish or yellow mucus found in his nose may indicate allergies or sinus infections, both of which can flare underlying asthma.
- Dark circles under his eyes may indicate allergies.
- Pale skin may indicate allergies.
- Changes in his sleep patterns due to coughing or waking at night with shortness of breath or chest pain.
- Changes in daytime behavior, such as misbehavior or irritability.
- More drooling than usual.

Also, if you or your family members have asthma, the likelihood that your child has it is higher. And, if your child is exposed to environmental factors such a secondhand tobacco smoke or various forms of air pollution, the likelihood of asthma could be increased as well.

A checklist could be a valuable tool in sharing information with your health care provider. The American College of Allergy, Asthma, and Immunology, for instance, has developed a specific asthma checklist test for children ages newborn through seven years (*www .acaai.org/public/lifeQuality/nasp/tests/0-7test.htm*) that you could use if you suspect your child has asthma. The checklist also poses questions for you and your child if asthma already has been diagnosed. This includes if your child gets scared because of asthma, and if you worry about how asthma may affect your child's health.

Guidelines for Young Children

The asthma guidelines released by the NAEPP in 2007 include an asthma severity scale specifically created for children from birth to age four who currently are not taking long-term control medication but have asthma symptoms. The different levels can give a health care provider a base by which to begin treatment. These levels are:

- Intermittent—Symptoms occur less than two days a week, no nighttime awakenings related to asthma are reported, quick-relief medications are used less than two days a week, and no interference is reported with normal, daily activities.
- Mild Persistent—Symptoms occur two or more days a week, one to two nighttime awakenings related to asthma occur monthly, quick-relief medications are used more than two days a week, and minor limitations are reported with normal, daily activities.
- Moderate Persistent—Symptoms occur daily, three to four nighttime awakenings related to asthma occur monthly, quick-relief medications are used daily, and some limitations are reported with normal, daily activities.
- Severe Persistent—Symptoms occur several times per day, nighttime awakenings related to asthma occur once a week, quick-relief medications are used several times per day, and normal, daily activities are reported extremely limited.

At the current time, data is inadequate to link flare-ups with levels of severity. However, for treatment purposes, the guidelines recommend that patients who have had two asthma episodes in the past six months or four wheezing episodes in the past year—and have risk factors for persistent asthma—may be considered the same as patients with persistent asthma (even if they fail to show signs of impairment associated with the other levels). Once treatment has started, your health care provider can determine if symptoms are well controlled, not well controlled, or poorly controlled for a child using current guidelines. (See Appendix C.)

Is Asthma Forever?

Every case is different. Sometimes very young children will grow out of the condition or show milder symptoms by preschool age or adolescence, but others will continue to have the condition throughout childhood.

 Essential

For many years, it was thought that an educated guess regarding a child's asthma could be made based on a family's history with asthma and allergies. However, researchers also are looking closely now at the how viral infections during the early years could be connected to asthma later in life as well.

The main point is don't automatically assume that your child will grow out of it: Only time will tell. The condition does need to be treated and managed immediately to prevent possible long-term problems. Just remember that half of all children with asthma symptoms generally develop them before their first few birthdays. The sooner the asthma symptoms are under control, the better she—and your entire family will feel.

When It's a Wheeze

Among infants, researchers have found that about 20 percent have wheezing only with upper respiratory tract infections. However, 60 percent of these infants no longer had wheezing by the time they reached preschool.

To understand wheezing better, researchers have put babies under one year of age who have asthma symptoms and wheeze into two basic categories: Those without allergies or a family history without allergies and those infants with allergic reactions or whose families had a history of allergies. The nonallergic infants were found to wheeze most frequently when they had an upper respiratory viral infection. But when they grew older, the airways of these "transient wheezers" grew larger and the wheezing stopped.

 **Fact**

For those infants with allergies who also wheezed with respiratory viral infections, the outcomes appear different: They were found more likely to be wheezing when they were ages six to eleven years. Sometimes, the asthma continued beyond childhood.

Australian researchers, studying the link between asthma and respiratory illness, have suggested that protecting infants with allergies from viral infections could prevent later development of persistent asthma. In a study of 198 children assessed from ages six months through five years, viral respiratory infections—usually rhinovirus or respiratory syncytial virus (RSV)—were found to interact with allergies during early infancy. This was associated with a "maximal risk" for subsequent asthma, the researchers said.

Food Allergies and Eczema

Other research has shown that infants with food allergies or eczema that appear before the age of three years may have a higher risk of developing asthma. Children may show wheezing or chest congestion during a respiratory illness.

While avoiding foods, such as milk or eggs, that can cause the food allergy, those actions usually did not prevent children from developing asthma or allergies later in life. However, it is very important to accurately determine if your child has an allergy to a food before restricting an important source of nutrition, such as milk.

Consulting with your health care provider or a pediatric dietitian may be needed.

Asthma or Another Condition?

If your child has one episode of wheezing, does that mean it's asthma for sure? In many cases—no. Younger children also can wheeze because of a variety of other conditions.

Respiratory Infections

Babies and toddlers frequently may develop "wheezy" bronchitis or bronchiolitis from an array of viral infections. These infections generally occur before their immune systems have matured.

 Essential

When your child wheezes for the first time—and has a runny nose, cough, and fever at the same time—it may be bronchiolitis and not asthma. This will probably be the case when "RSV season" arrives in the late fall and winter months. Other respiratory viruses can also trigger wheezing symptoms as well.

Since viral infections can be triggers to more serious asthma symptoms, it may be difficult to determine with a child's first wheezing episode whether it is an infection or asthma. Sometimes, a baby could have conditions such bronchitis and asthma at the same time.

However, if the wheezing symptoms continue to come back with every cold your child gets, asthma could be considered to be the culprit in this case.

Also, if your child gets pneumonia, bronchitis, or bronchiolitis several times or he has a persistent cough, especially at night and with activity, it might be asthma in this case.

GERD

Gastroesophageal reflux disease—better known as GERD or acid reflux—can lead to coughing and wheezing, especially at night, among children of all ages—including infants. GERD occurs when stomach acid travels up the esophagus and irritates its nerve endings, causing coughing and wheezing. Sometimes, it may reach the throat and be sucked or breathed into the lungs—irritating the airways. (See Chapter 3.)

Among small infants, GERD is usually easy to detect by observing the baby's wet burps and spit-up. However, for older infants and toddlers, some additional testing may be needed to determine if acid reflux is present and if it is triggering asthma.

Croup

With symptoms such as a barking cough and rough, troubled breathing, croup may sometimes be mistaken for asthma among children usually age four or younger. Croup is inflammation of a child's voice box and windpipe that is usually caused by an upper respiratory infection.

Cystic Fibrosis

Cystic fibrosis is another chronic condition that has symptoms similar to asthma. It is an inherited disease. Your child's health care provider may request testing for this disease in order to determine if it is—or is not—asthma.

Aspiration

Sometimes babies may have trouble swallowing, and they may cough and sputter when they drink fluids that appear to "go down the wrong tube." When fluids are drawn into the lungs while they breathe (also known as aspiration), this may produce symptoms similar to asthma such as coughing, congestion, and wheezing. Your health care provider can order special X-ray swallowing tests to rule this out.

Asthma Action Plan

Infants or young children should have written asthma action plans prepared by their health care providers that can be used to monitor and manage their asthma—just like older children with asthma (see Chapter 2). However, infants will need some special considerations—particularly because they can't use peak flow meters to gauge how much air is moving in and out of their lungs. Instead, you will need to review other signs—such as their asthma symptoms and breathing rate—to determine if they are in one of three zones:

- The green zone means the child is doing well in terms of breathing and her asthma symptoms appear well-controlled. There is no coughing or wheezing. Only routine controller asthma medicines are used, or in many babies, no medicine is needed here.
- The yellow zone means some symptoms are present, such as wheezing or mild coughing, and caution is needed. An inhaled quick-relief medication might be prescribed by your health care provider, in addition to any controller asthma medications if they have been prescribed in the past, to help with your child's breathing. The plan should state when to contact your health care provider and what to do if your child's symptoms fail to improve.
- The red zone can potentially mean an emergency is occurring. Even just one of these symptoms—such as persistent coughing, breathing difficulties that interfere with eating or sleeping, sucking in of the chest, or flared nostrils—means the child is in the red zone. In addition to the quick-relief medication, your health care provider might add an oral corticosteroid. An emergency contact for your health care pro-

vider should be listed, along with information on how and when to call 911 or emergency help.

Remember to keep this asthma action plan with you at all times, and to distribute it to relatives, daycare workers, babysitters, or other individuals who take care of your child. Also, remember to continually update the document as your child gets older—noting changes in symptoms and medications.

As your infant and young child grows and develops, her asthma action plan and peak flow meter readings (if she is old enough to perform them) should include her updated "personal best" rate. (See Appendix A for sources of asthma action plans.)

Lung Function

An asthma action plan for a young child can give you an idea of what your child's breathing capacity should be. This is helpful as you determine what zone your child is in.

Finding the breathing capacity for young children is different when compared with older children. Lung function or spirometry tests are breathing tests conducted in a health care provider's office or health care facility that measures a child's lung capacity when he blows into a tube connected to a computer that measures many aspects of his breathing capacities. This type of test, though, is difficult for young children to use.

New technology, called an impulse oscillometry system, is now being used at some major medical centers. In some studies, it has demonstrated airway abnormalities in children as young as two years old. (Also see Chapter 7.) The test can show how severe a young child's asthma is, and can assist health care providers in initiating appropriate treatments.

Breathing Rate Measurement

For most young children, their breathing rate or respiratory rate is commonly evaluated as an indication of their work of breathing. To get your infant's or young child's breathing rate, it would be helpful to use two adults. One individual watches the one-minute hand or the second hand on the clock, while the other watches the child's chest rise and fall, or in children under three years, watch the child's belly rise and fall. One breath in and then exhaling that breath counts as one breath. To quicken the process, watch the child's chest or belly for thirty seconds and multiply the number of breaths by two to get the respiratory rate. (See Chapter 2 for normal respiratory rates.)

**Fact**

The breathing rate at rest for an infant should be in the range of thirty to forty breaths per minute; for a toddler or pre-schooler, it's twenty to thirty breaths per minute. For comparison, the breathing rate of a child seven years or older should average around eighteen to twenty-two breaths per minute. Note that the younger the child, the faster her normal breathing rate is.

If the breathing rate at rest falls above fifty breaths per minute for an infant), forty or more breaths per minute for a toddler, or thirty or more breaths per minute for an older child, she is having trouble breathing and this should be correlated with any asthma symptoms such as coughing, wheezing, skin denting around ribs or collarbone, or using abdominal muscles to push air out. This requires immediate action (as noted on the asthma action plan).

Other Testing

Sometimes your health care provider may order a chest X-ray if your infant is having a wheezing bout to check if any other problem exists in the lungs. Allergy testing probably will not be requested for very young children who are wheezing—unless they appear to be reacting to an obvious trigger such as animal danders or foods or they have a significant family history of allergies with increasing therapy requirements.

Medications for Younger Children

Finding the right medication for your child starts with assessment of his asthma. If the condition is mild, usually a quick-relief medication would be appropriate. If the condition is severe or persistent, daily medicine, called controller medicine, also may be considered to reduce inflammation that causes asthma.

Working with your health care provider, the course of treatment would begin one of two ways. With a less-intensive method, the lowest dose of medication that may keep his asthma well-controlled at this stage of his life will be prescribed; if his symptoms are not controlled, more medication will be used (or stepped up) until control is achieved and maintained.

With the more intensive method, a higher level of therapy will be used to immediately control symptoms. It will then be stepped down to minimum therapy to maintain control.

It is important that an infant with asthma receive treatment quickly to alleviate symptoms. Rapid breathing for a prolonged period of time and poor fluid intake frequently occur when an infant does not feel well. It can lead to dehydration in an infant more rapidly than in an older child.

Alert!

If you find that the prescribed medication is not working for your child, let your health care provider know so changes in medication or dosages might be made. Also, additional assessments might be needed from a health care provider specializing in pulmonary problems related to children to determine if it is asthma or a different pulmonary problem.

Quick-Relief Medications

The quick-relief medication most often prescribed by health care providers for young children, including infants, has been albuterol. This medication can be taken by young children in one of three ways: orally (as a syrup), inhaled using a pediatric mask and metered-dose inhaler, or inhaled using a nebulizer.

Oral Medication

For infants that nurse or are bottle-fed, a pacifier can be used with a medication cup attached to it. An infant will suck the liquid past the taste buds and swallow the medication. Everyday teaspoons should not be used because the infant could get an incorrect dose.

Less medicine, though, goes to the lungs with this route. Also, more side effects will be experienced, and it may take up to thirty minutes before any effect is seen.

Inhaler and Spacer

This includes a holding chamber with pediatric mask, a device attached to the inhaler. While these devices are portable and inexpensive, they can be difficult if the child does not want to put them on. Keep in mind that inhaled medications will not work unless they reach the airways so make sure that the mask is snug. Talk to your provider for suggestions on doing this properly. The advantage to this method is that it delivers medicine directly to the lungs. It is much faster to administer to a young child and does not require a child to sit still for ten minutes, as when given by nebulizer.

When using the spacer, release only one dose at a time for the child to breathe in. If two doses are put into the spacer at once, the child will not get the full dose. It is important to check with your pharmacist to determine how often your child's brand of albuterol must be primed (firing of the unit to load the valve in the puffer) before using, especially if it has not been used recently. This will vary from product to product.

Nebulizer

This electronic air compressor delivers asthma medication as a mist and quickly gets the needed medicine to the lungs. However, it is an expensive machine. Children also must sit still for ten to fifteen minutes for the mist to work. With very young children, a face mask is required. This face mask, though, must be placed against the child's face so the right dose of medicine is being inhaled. If the mask is held even about a half an inch away, much of the dose will not be inhaled.

Preventive or Controller Medications

Longer-acting or preventive medications, often referred to as controller medications, for younger children are usually limited to inhaled corticosteroids, Singulair, or cromolyn. No oral medications are currently available for prevention of asthma symptoms.

Cromolyn, which is often used with milder cases of asthma, can be given one of two ways: through an inhaler or with a nebulizer. The nebulized product, though, contains more medicine than the inhaled version. It must be used several times per day to be effective.

Inhaled corticosteroids are usually used with children who have persistent asthma symptoms. They can be used through a metered-dose inhaler or a nebulizer.

Singulair is an oral non-steroidal anti-inflammatory medication that has been FDA approved for children six months and older. It is usually used as an adjunct controller medication with inhaled steroids for children with asthma and allergies.

Controlling Symptoms

An effective way to keep symptoms down is to avoid triggers that cause asthma symptoms to appear. These triggers can be found everywhere—in your home, in daycare facilities, and even outside. (See Chapter 4.) But you can take a few steps to make sure these triggers don't have the upper hand in aggravating your child's asthma.

Flu Shots

Viral infections are among the most common asthma triggers among young children. Unfortunately, they are difficult to avoid.

 *Fact*

You can take at least one step to avoid a viral infection by getting a flu shot each year. Prior to each year's flu season, the NIH guidelines call for the use of an inactivated flu vaccine for children six months of age or older.

The Centers for Disease Control and Prevention (CDC) has called for individuals with asthma to be vaccinated because they may be at an increased risk of getting complications from the flu. These risks include increased hospitalizations and increased use of antibiotics.

The CDC noted that among asthmatic children in 2005, one-third of children who were ages two to four years had a flu shot. This was the highest among all children. However, the CDC noted that this figure is still low.

The NIH guideline panel has cautioned, though, that the flu vaccine should not be given to a patient with the expectation that it will reduce either the frequency or severity of an asthma episode during the flu season.

Triggers at Home

Research has shown that removal of allergic triggers in the home—ranging from dust mites to cockroaches to mold—can sometimes be as effective as medication in controlling asthma symptoms. (See Chapters 4 and 16.)

For the young child, special attention should be paid to blankets, mattresses, and pillows where triggers, particularly dust mites, can hide. Washing bedding materials in hot water (over 130° Fahrenheit) at least weekly can help, along with using allergy-preventing mattress and pillow covers. Cleaning hard-surfaced toys and laundering stuffed animals weekly can also help reduce triggers.

Clean Hands

It's never too early to emphasize to young children the importance of washing their hands. Whether crawling on the floor or playing with toys, they can pick up germs and viruses that could lead to upper respiratory infections.

Exposure to Danders

Sometimes, exposure to a trigger may lead to the opposite effect and maybe reduce asthma symptoms. Take dogs, for example. Recent research has found that exposure to dogs in infancy and early childhood decreased symptoms later in life.

The research, part of the Childhood Origins of ASThma (COAST) project, evaluated the relationship of pet ownership on asthma diagnosis and wheezing in children. Dog exposure was found to significantly reduce the number of children who had tested positive for allergens.

Of the children studied, 18 percent of the children who had dogs at both birth and age three were diagnosed with asthma symptoms by age six; meanwhile, 34 percent of children who didn't have dogs at either age were diagnosed. Those with dogs at age three but not at birth had a 31 percent asthma rate, while those with dogs at birth only had a 25 percent rate.

The COAST project also explored cat ownership, but did not find such a correlation between cat ownership and reduced asthma rates. However, ongoing research is needed to confirm or reject this information and is continuing in this study and others. No recommendation has been made to own—or not own—any animal in attempting to prevent or minimize asthma in children.

Secondhand Smoke

Exposure to secondhand smoke can often trigger asthma attacks, make asthma symptoms more severe, and lead to increased use of medications. Approximately 11 percent of children age six years or younger are exposed to secondhand smoke in their homes on a regular basis (about four or more days per week), according to recent studies.

While an infant or young child with asthma may or may not cough or wheeze when exposed to tobacco smoke, research has shown that it still is irritating her lungs. Even in children without asthma, tobacco smoke can cause problems with chronic cough, congestion, and ear infections. However, when exposure is eliminated, a child's asthma symptoms usually improve.

Explaining Asthma

Coughing, wheezing, or a tightening feeling in her chest can be scary for a child—especially if she is younger. In addition, using medicine or a device that she has to breathe into can be equally daunting. It can be reassuring to hear from you what asthma is and what she needs to do to help manage it.

With some pictures—possibly from your health care provider's office—and some simple explanations, your child might be able to get a better idea of what the terms *asthma, triggers, nebulizer,* and *inhaler* mean. You can explain what her symptoms are and how that fits in with her own asthma action plan.

For example, you might mention that her lungs are located in her chest, and that when they are normal, the air goes in and out easily. You can point to her mouth and nose, and explain how the air goes down into tubes into her lungs. Then, you can note that when an asthma attack occurs, her lungs could become twitchy (when she breathes in a certain trigger such as dust or pollen). Her lungs then could feel tight and make a sticky, gooey substance called mucus.

An expanded dialogue of how to talk to your young child that was developed from NIH's Practical Guide for the Diagnosis and Management of Asthma, with input from asthma educators in Michigan, is available at *www.getasthmahelp.org.*

CHAPTER 9

Finding the
Right Child Care

Obtaining safe and reliable child care—whether for a few hours or for an entire work week—can be a challenge for any parent. However, for the parent of a child with asthma, finding the right care could seem like a daunting task. But it doesn't have to be that way. You can take several important steps to obtain quality care for your child either inside or outside the home.

Communicate Honestly

When looking for the right toddler, preschool, in-home, or extended child care program or service, some parents may consider underplaying the seriousness of their child's asthmatic symptoms over concerns that a child care provider may turn the child away. However, ignoring those symptoms could turn into a risky situation for both the child and the provider if the correct and up-to-date medical information is not presented when child care services initially are discussed.

Asthma symptoms that are not properly addressed can hinder a child's participation and growth within a child care program. As a parent, you can work with child care staff and health care professionals to remove obstacles while promoting your child's health and development.

The child care provider or program that you finally choose should be considered a partner in the care of the child with asthma.

With planning and organization, the child care experience can be a healthy and secure one for your child.

Outside the Home

Children with asthma need support in child care settings to keep their asthma monitored and under control in order to be as active as possible in the program. You should strive for good communications from the start with the director of the child care program and those who provide the care—discussing what your child needs in terms of safe and appropriate care.

You should be sure to discuss current care—what medications or treatment the child is using. Also, you should be sure to talk with other parents using the same child care services about how the facility approaches care for children with chronic conditions or special needs. And, talk to parents whose children don't have health problems to find out if it provides good care for them as well.

Essential

When you are visiting and evaluating a child care program for the first time, take along the child's asthma action plan that provides step-by-step guidance. You can use the action plan to help evaluate a potential child care program's willingness, concern, and preparedness to work with them on caring for your child with asthma.

Child-staff ratios by themselves in a child care setting will not necessarily predict the quality of care that the child will receive. However, warmer and closer social interactions have been found in studies to appear more between adults and children in facilities with lower ratios. Some also believe that smaller child care centers or in-home operations may be more advantageous to a child with asthma because exposure to common respiratory viruses—that may aggravate asthma symptoms—may be reduced. However, ongoing studies have not necessarily found this to be true.

Other studies have found that babies and young children who receive daycare services may be more likely to experience respiratory illnesses than those cared for at home. However, research at the Tucson Children's Respiratory Study has found that while two-year-old children in large daycare centers (those caring for more than five unrelated children) had more colds than those cared for at home, these children at ages six to eleven had fewer colds and a decreased risk of getting asthma later in life.

But no matter what the size of the program, you should look closely at the staff itself to determine if a program is right for your child with asthma. In particular, examine the role of the child care program's health advocate who is responsible for day-to-day issues related to health, development, and safety of all children, staff, and parents.

 **Fact**

The health advocate in a child care program is one who is licensed, credentialed, or certified as a director, lead teacher, teacher, or associate teacher. The health advocate also can be a health professional, health educator, or social worker who works at the facility on a regular basis.

The health advocate will be the primary parent contact for any health concerns, and will influence the organization and implementation of a strategy to meet the emergency needs of children with asthma or other special concerns.

You should also gauge how a child care program is prepared to meet medical emergencies related to asthma with personnel skilled in providing pediatric first aid, including management of blocked airways and rescue breathing. Also note if staff are qualified to provide cardiopulmonary resuscitation in case of emergency.

Inside the Home

Good communication is essential as well for working with caregivers inside a home setting such as grandparents or other relatives, neighborhood babysitters, or nannies. As with child care provided outside the home, an asthma action plan should be available to provide a useful guideline for providing needed care.

When calling on family members—such as grandparents—to assist with child care duties, take time to converse with them about what the child needs. You and your family should agree to work together and promote a sense of sharing, thoughtfulness, and consistency of care in the home environment.

When arranging for care with older caregivers such as grandparents, note how care of children with asthma has changed over the years. Some may mistakenly view asthma as a way for a child to get extra attention. However, others could perceive asthma as a condition that precludes a child from engaging in most active endeavors—even though medically this may not be the case.

Likewise, when employing a babysitter, au pair, nanny, or other individual to provide in-home child care, allow time for questions— well in advance—before actual child care is provided. If possible, hold a "dry run"—perhaps when you are at home—to discuss and review the special needs of your child and what to do in case of an emergency. Note what medications are used for your child and how devices, such as a spacer, are used. Make sure they know where these items are located.

Consider keeping an extra inhaler—just in case of emergency. Tape it in an easy-to-reach spot—such as an inside cupboard door in the kitchen. However, remember to keep it away from heat sources such as the stove. Double-check periodically to ensure the inhaler is up-to-date.

Always remember to post your emergency contact information— along with your insurance numbers and instructions—in a highly visible place (such as on the refrigerator or next to a kitchen phone) in the house along with the asthma action plan. Also, consider leaving a signed letter that gives permission to authorize treatment just in the unlikely case that you cannot be reached during an emergency.

At no time should you consider leaving your child under the care of an outside child care provider when asthma symptoms are not under good control.

Coordinate with Confidence

Successful coordination starts with parents who do their homework and apprise a caregiver of the child's needs before that child sets foot in the care-giving environment. But you also need to observe if a child care program has proper support to help your child keep his asthma under control and to make the transition from home as seamless, safe, and healthy as possible for your child.

The Asthma-Friendly Checklist

A good place to start is by inquiring what a child care program already has in place. The National Heart, Lung, and Blood Institute of the National Institutes of Health has developed a checklist with targeted questions that you can use to determine how prepared a child care setting is to assist the asthmatic child. They include:

- Is a medical or nursing consultant available to help child care staff write policy and guidelines for managing medications in the child care setting, reducing allergens and irritants, promoting safe physical activities, and planning field trips or outside activities for children with asthma?

- Have child care staffers been instructed on how to give medications prescribed by each child's health care provider and authorized by each child's parent?
- Is someone available to supervise an older child while taking asthma medicines and to monitor correct inhaler use?
- Do you have written emergency plans prepared for each child in case of a severe asthma episode? And, does the plan make clear what action to take, whom should be called, and when to call?
- Does a nurse, respiratory therapist, or other knowledgeable person teach child care staff about asthma, asthma action plans, reducing allergens and irritants, and asthma medicines?
- Is someone available to teach the child's classmates about asthma and how to help a classmate who has asthma?
- Does the child care provider help children with asthma participate safely in physical activities?

If an answer to any of the checklist questions is "no," you need to realize that the child with asthma in the child care setting could face barriers that may impact a child's attendance and participation in the program.

 Essential

When children are encouraged to be physically active, you should be clear about whether your child can take or be given his medicine before exercise. Also, you also should ask what modified or alternative activities are available for the child if he cannot participate because of the type of exercise or weather conditions.

Provider Special Care Plan

You should ask the child care program if they use a written special care plan that the program—and the child's health care provider—will have on file for a child with asthma. This care plan can list the usual information such as your phone numbers, and your primary care provider's and asthma specialist's numbers. But it also should list day-to-day points that providers can evaluate when taking care of the child such as:

- Known triggers for your child's asthma, such as colds, mold, exercise, strong odors, animals, or weather changes.
- Outdoor activities for which your child may need special attention, such as running hard, going outside on cold or windy days, jumping in leaves, or playing near freshly cut grass.
- Indoor activities for which your child may need special attention such as sitting on rugs or carpets, being exposed to chalk dust or glues, or providing pet care.
- Typical signs and symptoms of your child's asthma episodes such as fatigue, wheezing, quicker breathing, panting, or difficulty with playing, eating, or drinking.
- Recording of peak flow meter results by your child (if old enough).
- Information on how often the child has needed urgent care from a health care provider for an asthma attack in the past three months and past twelve months.
- Medications for routine and emergency treatment of asthma.

A sample of a special care plan form that can be used by child care providers may be viewed at the National Resource Center for Health and Safety in Child Care Web site at *nrc.uchsc.edu.*

Fact

To best monitor breathing with a peak flow meter, the following measures should be included on the special care plan used by the child care provider: the child's personal best reading, a reading that indicates when to give an extra dose of medicine, and a reading that indicates when it is necessary to get medical help.

Eye on the Environment

You should survey the physical surroundings of the child care site that you are considering to detect troublesome environmental triggers that could cause problems. While some trigger areas, such as dust in carpets and drapes, may be more evident, other triggers, such as fumes from pesticides, may be hidden. You need to keep several key trigger trouble areas in mind when looking for the appropriate child care placement.

Detecting Potential Triggers

The environment both inside and outside the child care site should be free of or have reduced amounts of known allergens and irritants, including dust mites, molds, mildew, pollen, cockroaches, and animal danders. When visiting the site, you need to discuss the needs of your child—and whether those needs can be sufficiently met by the provider.

In particular, you should determine if attempts have been made to eliminate or reduce use of plush carpets, feather pillows, stuffed animals, upholstery, or drapes; pets with fur or feathers; chalk dust; and flowering plants.

Alert!

As a parent, you also should use your nose as well to detect possible triggers inside the child care facility that could cause an asthma attack. These include fumes from cleaning products, secondhand cigarette smoke, perfumes, glue and other art supplies, wall paint, strong cooking odors, and even pesticides. Use of scented air fresheners may indicate a ventilation problem.

You can check to see if the child care provider has taken proactive steps to keep down possible asthma attacks by:

- Encouraging the use of nap mats, mattress covers, or crib covers that can be easily cleaned or laundered.
- Prohibiting pets such as furred animals (that produce danders) or birds in the immediate area where child care is provided.
- Prohibiting smoking inside and immediately outside the facility and near the playground.
- Discouraging the use of perfumes, scented cleaning products and soaps, and other products that produce odors or fumes.
- Quickly repairing leaky plumbing, air conditioning, sinks, or other sources of excess water.
- Promoting frequent vacuuming of carpet and upholstered furniture at times when the children are not present.
- Storing all foods in airtight containers, cleaning up all spilled foods and liquids, and correctly disposing of garbage and trash.
- Using integrated pest management techniques—using the least hazardous treatments first and advancing to more toxic treatments only as necessary—to get rid of pests.

- Promoting use of barrier floor mats near the building entrances.
- Notifying parents when carpets are cleaned, any painting is performed, or strong cleaners are used when children are present.

Outside of the child care site, attention should be paid to trees, grasses, and roadways surrounding it. While obviously unhealthy ozone levels and high pollen counts can't be eliminated, special alternatives should be put in place when a child should stay indoors to avoid potential allergens.

Also look at the traffic patterns around the school. Sometimes school buses, vans, or cars waiting for children or commercial vehicles making pickups or deliveries may idle their engines close to areas where children play or congregate. This produces exhaust that could pose problems for the asthmatic child. Some states have laws that prohibit this. Ask the child care facility what rules and policies are in place about idling vehicles, and also see yourself if this is being observed.

Conditioned Air

Also look at how the heating, ventilation, and air condition systems are used, and check how they are maintained. Improperly maintained systems can pose a serious threat to the child with asthma. In particular, is the ventilation system able to remove—rather than recycle—allergens and irritants back into the air? Are vents free of dust and dirt? Are the vents clearly visible throughout the child care facility, or are they hidden behind shelves, furniture, or books?

You should ask when windows at the child care site are open, and if so, for how long. While open windows may mean fresh air, they also may mean pollens coming in from trees and grasses and fumes from nearby auto traffic that could trigger an asthma attack.

Also, some inadequate air condition systems may create condensation that leaks through walls and ceilings. Likewise, dripping pipes and drains in bathrooms may create standing water. The lingering presence of water usually is accompanied by molds and mildews, which also may cause breathing problems.

Early Warning Signs

Besides avoiding various allergic agents in the environment, the child care provider needs to monitor activities such as exercise or playing in cold, damp weather—especially if your child encounters breathing difficulties or starts to wheeze.

The child care provider should immediately stop the child's activity and, if known, remove what may be causing the allergic reaction or remove the child from the current area. The provider should then calm the child, and use medication prescribed for an attack.

In Case of Emergency

Child care providers can use reminders from special care plans as guides for determining when emergency medical help is necessary. First, you should be notified immediately when emergency "rescue" medication is required and symptoms persist. Also, you should be notified if two or more doses of rescue medication are needed during the day and a peak flow meter shows 50 to 80 percent of normal—even with the rescue medication.

 Essential

Once participating in a child care program, you should discuss with providers the most effective ways to keep apprised of any changes related to a child's asthma—for instance, fatigue or lethargy—while attending the child care program so any problems can be quickly addressed.

Under a care plan, emergency help will be summoned if the child does not improve fifteen minutes after treatment with a rescue medication and shows the following signs or symptoms: difficulty walking, talking, eating, or drinking because of shortness of breath; gray or blue lips and fingernails; hunched over or sucked-in chest or neck muscles when struggling to breathe; highly agitated or sleepy; complaints of chest pains and tightness; red face with grunting; or peak flow that is less than 50 percent of normal.

Away from the Child Care Site

While you try to make sure that your child with asthma is monitored at home and at the child care site, one area may slip out of consideration: handling those emergency situations away from those locations such as on a bus or on a field trip. All drivers, passenger monitors, chaperones, and assistants should receive instructions on how to handle emergency situations that involve a chronic condition such as asthma and have all medications, asthma management plans, and equipment with them for all trips.

In this instance, a driver and chaperone should have an emergency list that includes parent emergency contacts, child summary health information, special needs, and treatment plans.

Alert!

Employees of a child care provider—such as bus drivers —should be trained to recognize the signs of a medical emergency, such as an asthma attack. They should know emergency procedures to follow, and have on-hand necessary emergency supplies or medications. They also should be able to map an appropriate route to an emergency facility if necessary.

Organize the Right Medications

Medications for use in the child care setting should be packed and clearly labeled for routine or emergency use for the child care provider. You can demonstrate to the child care providers how to use medications given routinely to a child and those used only in emergency situations.

The child care providers should confirm that they are trained in the proper use of devices such as inhalers or nebulizers.

To cut down on confusion on when to use routine or emergency medication, document that medication use through the written special care plan—which should be reviewed and approved by you as a parent—that indicates:

- When to use the medications (such as by symptoms or by time of day).
- How to properly use equipment (such as an inhaler either with or without a spacer).
- What dose of medication is needed for treatment.
- How soon treatment should begin to work.
- What is the expected benefit from the medication.
- What are the possible side effects.
- What are the most recent instructions from your child's health care provider.

Make sure that any changes in medications or dosages are communicated immediately to the child care providers and documented on their special care plan.

Plan Ahead

Even with the best of care, emergencies can arise. But you and your child's caregivers—together with health care professionals—can work together as a team to handle those situations effectively and efficiently in the child care setting.

You have a role in obtaining the necessary medications and medical devices and ensuring they are in the hands of the child care provider when needed (not at home or in the car) and that they can be properly used during any emergency episodes. You also should immediately apprise the caregiver, for instance, of any changes in medication or symptoms.

Likewise, child care providers should remind you to refill medications when necessary. They also can serve as an early warning system if they notice various symptoms that point to a possibly more serious condition.

While asthma can be a serious condition, it can be controlled in a large, medium, or single-provider child care situation with good communication, coordination, confidence, and, of course, cooperation.

CHAPTER 10

School-Aged Children

W hen it comes to monitoring your school-aged child's asthma, do not think of it as something that you only do from one health care provider visit to the next. Instead, it should be something that you and your child think about each day. What medications are needed, and when should they be used? What does your child come into contact with that triggers his symptoms? Let your child know that while asthma is now a part of his life, it doesn't have to control his life. By managing his symptoms day to day, he can still enjoy the same activities and pleasures his friends do.

Is It Asthma?

Keep in mind that 75 percent of all individuals with asthma usually show symptoms before the age of seven. And sometimes children lose their asthma symptoms around age six. (See Chapter 8.) But asthma remains a widespread condition for children ages six through twelve.

Diagnosis

To find out if your child has asthma, your health care provider will ask you a series of questions about her symptoms: about when she coughs, how she sleeps at night, or signs of labored breathing. (See more in Chapter 3.) The provider also might ask about possible triggers—maybe dust mites or cockroaches in a new home or animals in a school classroom. A family history of asthma will be reviewed, and other conditions such as bronchitis, allergies, or even vocal cord dysfunction will be examined as well.

A pulmonary function test can be performed on older children (usually age six or older) to determine how fast they can force air from their lungs. This common and frequently used test, called spirometry, measures how much her airways may be blocked. This test usually can be done at your health care provider's office or in a health care facility. A child breathes into a closed tube attached to a machine that measures how much and how fast she could expel a breath.

Newer methods are available, but they are found more at larger health centers. They include the impulse oscillometry system (IOS), which measures airway resistance while a child breathes normally, and another method, called exhaled nitric oxide or eNO, which monitors the amount of nitric oxide exhaled by a child. With either test, a health care provider can get a better idea how your child is breathing and what course of treatment is needed.

Guidelines for School-Aged Children

The asthma guidelines released by the National Asthma Education and Prevention Program in 2007 include an asthma severity scale created for children ages five though eleven with asthma who are not currently taking long-term control medications. The different levels can give a health care provider a base by which to begin or adjust treatment. These levels are:

- **Intermittent**—Symptoms occur less than two days a week, two nighttime awakenings related to asthma are reported, quick-relief medications are used less than two days a week, and no interference is reported with normal, daily activities.

- **Mild Persistent**—Symptoms occur two or more days a week (but not daily), three to four nighttime awakenings related to asthma occur monthly, quick-relief medications are used more than two days a week (but not daily), and minor limitations are reported with normal, daily activities.
- **Moderate Persistent**—Symptoms occur daily, more than one nighttime awakening related to asthma occurs weekly, quick-relief medications are used daily, and some limitations are reported with normal, daily activities.
- **Severe Persistent**—Symptoms occur throughout the day, nighttime awakenings related to asthma occur seven days a week, quick-relief medications are used several times per day, and normal, daily activities are reported extremely limited.

At the current time, data is inadequate to link flare-ups with levels of severity. However, for treatment purposes, the guidelines recommend that patients ages five through eleven who have had two asthma episodes in the year requiring treatment with oral corticosteroids may be considered the same as patients with persistent asthma (even if they fail to show signs of impairment associated with the other levels). Once treatment has started, your health care provider can determine if your child's symptoms are well controlled, not well controlled, or poorly controlled using the current guidelines. (See Appendix C.)

Asthma into Adulthood?

One question parents usually ask is whether their child will outgrow his asthma or will he still have asthma when he reaches adulthood? The answer is: It depends. Long-term studies have suggested that most children will improve during their teen years, and up to half will be wheeze-free by the time they turn into adults.

However, up to 80 percent of those symptom-free adults could demonstrate some bronchial problems and could end up redeveloping asthma.

Various risk factors, though, may point to persistent adult asthma such as a family history of asthma, exposure to secondhand tobacco smoke, direct exposure to smoke if the teen starts smoking, obesity, atopic dermatitis or eczema, exposure to the respiratory syncytial virus (RSV), wheezing at ages ten or eleven, a lower socioeconomic status, or earlier exposure to mites, cockroaches, and molds.

But one point that many studies have focused on is that the earlier asthma is diagnosed and actively treated in children, the less likely those children will face lung deterioration in later years.

A Step Each Day

While asthma is a chronic disease, it's not a condition that has to slow your child down. It does not mean spending a lot of time in a school nurse's office or a hospital emergency department. Instead, most children can lead a relatively normal life—without constant coughing, wheezing, or chest pain.

But it will take a little effort: monitoring breathing, using prescribed medications regularly, and watching out for triggers that can aggravate symptoms. Working with your child, you can help make a big difference.

Asking the Right Questions

A study from the Medical College of Wisconsin found that thousands of children's hospitalizations could be avoided every year if their parents knew more about their children's illness. Topping the list of most common reasons for hospitalization of children was asthma.

Overall, parents should know as much as they can about their child's condition, the researchers said. This includes what triggers can cause flare-ups, issues regarding medications, the importance of follow-up care, and how parents can educate children so that they can ultimately help themselves.

The underlying message is that parents should learn all they can about their child's condition so that unnecessary hospitalizations could be avoided. Much of this education should come from the child's health care provider who should emphasize the importance in curbing these hospitalizations.

Getting Kids Up to Speed

Each year, many children with asthma report experiencing restrictions in many of their daily activities such as going to school, playing, or participating in sports. Most of the time, it doesn't have to be the status quo.

Essential

Rather than think that asthma is a way of life, children should have the opportunity to know that they can self-manage their condition to help them get the most out of their lives. This can be done by talking with their providers or through local programs—at the school or community level—that give children the knowledge and skills to manage their disease.

Studies have found out that children who take part in school-based asthma education programs usually have decreased asthma flare-ups and reduced hospitalizations. (Also see Chapter 11.) At a minimum, each school-aged child should know that managing her asthma means:

- **Taking medications as prescribed.** Generally, many individuals with asthma will need two types of medication. One is a quick-acting medication that relaxes airways and is taken when symptoms flare up. The second medication is referred to as a controller medication and is used daily to decrease inflammation in the airways.

- **Taking medication when prescribed.** Sometimes a child may skip taking her medication because she feels okay. She should understand that she feels better because of the medication. She should not take medication only when she feels an asthma flare-up coming on.

- **Monitoring breathing.** A peak flow meter can keep track of how well air is moving through the lungs. It can detect when asthma symptoms are becoming a problem—and airways are inflamed—by flagging a lowered breathing rate on the peak flow meter.

- **Detecting early warning signs of asthma.** Coughing, wheezing, or shortness of breath may point to some potential asthma problems ahead if not addressed now. Some additional early warning signs of an asthma episode can include: throat clearing; irritation, tickle, or itchiness in the throat; frequent sighing; resting frequently or less active than normal; not able to keep up with friends; listlessness; cold symptoms; allergy symptoms; and coughing at night. Everyone's early warning signs are unique, but knowing them can help you act early enough to prevent an asthma episode.

- **Detecting triggers.** From not exercising outside in cold weather to avoiding secondhand tobacco smoke, a child can stop most of her asthma symptoms in their tracks.

- **Knowing when to seek additional help.** When symptoms are flaring up, she should know when to ask for assistance from adults including you, a caretaker, a teacher, or a coach. The child should also know the names of her medicines, when she usually takes them, and when they were last taken.

- **Participating in sports and other activities.** While exercise-induced asthma is common among children with asthma, there are steps she can take—from warm-ups and hydration to medication—to play comfortably. This should be done with advice from her health care provider.

- **Partnering with her "team."** While asthma is a chronic condition experienced by one person, it takes a team—including parents, health care providers, teachers, coaches, and school nurses—to understand and manage asthma every day.

Still, children often will have a hard time understanding why they have to take medicine every day—even when they feel fine. This is where you can play an important role by helping them develop a regular regimen. This could be keeping a chart that your child marks off when she takes her asthma medication. Or perhaps, offering rewards as incentive—especially for younger children—to keep track of their medication schedules.

Through these processes, children with asthma are learning that information is power. Along with asthma action plans and asthma diaries, they can find out that asthma is not just a chronic disease that can hit randomly at any time, but a disease that follows a pattern and can be controlled.

Hopefully, your child can find that each day. She can feel more empowered about tackling asthma—rather than worrying about asthma tackling her.

Getting the Right Asthma Action Plan

The goal of an asthma action plan is to help you and your child—whether he is at home, school, or on the playing field—better manage his asthma symptoms. (Also see Chapters 11 and 19.)

National statistics, though, show that this is an underused tool. According to the federal Agency for Healthcare Research and Quality (AHRQ), only 28 percent of the population reported even receiving an asthma management plan in 2006.

This plan gives your child a guide of what symptoms to look for to indicate that he is having a problem with his asthma. It spells out what medications are needed using green (doing well), yellow (caution), and red (medical alert) zones on his plan, and when professional help is needed.

The plan is somewhat different from the asthma action plan used by infants, toddlers, and preschoolers. Here, peak flow meter readings to monitor his breathing rate can be used once or twice daily—depending on the type of asthma action plan selected. Daily readings, which can be taken once or twice, should be compared to his "personal best" readings. These readings can be taken when he is reporting no asthma symptoms.

 *Question?*

Does my child need to use a peak flow meter every day?
If your child's asthma is fairly well-controlled, and she shows some reluctance to use the peak flow meter daily, check with your health care provider to see if she can do it every one to two weeks. This will let both you and your child know if her asthma is staying in the green zone, or if some possible problems are showing up.

If his peak flow rates start to drop and he begins to show asthma symptoms—such as coughing or wheezing—he will need to resume the daily readings.

If your child is doing occasional peak flow readings, consider going back to daily readings before a health care provider visit. Charting these readings—along with using an asthma diary (see next section) can give your health care provider a better overview of how your child's asthma is being managed.

When some children, especially younger children, are unwilling or find it difficult to use the peak flow meter, symptoms—such as wheezing, chest tightness, sleep problems—can be noted on the asthma action plan. A variety of sources for asthma action plans can be viewed in Chapter 2.

But remember, the asthma action plan is designed to help guide you and your child in managing his symptoms: It does not replace your health care provider's care. When symptoms change or use of medication changes, let your provider know. After all, the goal is to prevent an asthma-related emergency—before it happens.

In the Green Zone

When your child's ratings are in the green zone her lung function readings are about normal. These readings should be more than 80 percent of your child's personal best readings. Check with your provider if you want to know what the average personal best readings are for your child (based on height). However, keep in mind that these readings can vary child by child.

If you are monitoring by symptoms, your child's breathing should be good. She should not be experiencing coughing or wheezing, is able to sleep comfortably, and is playing with no problems. The breaths per minute should average around 21 or fall in the range of 16 to 25 breaths.

Alert!

The goal is for your child to remain in the green zone. If your child constantly moves back and forth into the yellow or red zones and correlates with other asthma symptoms such as shortness of breath, chest tightness, or coughing and wheezing, your child's health care provider should be notified to come up with adjustments to medication and a more suitable plan.

However, if your child never leaves the green zone, consideration might be given to lowering the dose of preventive (or controller) medicine.

In the Yellow Zone

When your child is in the yellow zone, his symptoms are getting a little worse. Possibly, he might be heading for an asthma attack. In the yellow zone, your child's peak flow readings generally will be between 50 percent to 80 percent of his personal best readings. These readings can be adjusted by your health care provider depending on your child's past medical history.

Symptoms in the yellow zone can include difficulties breathing; some coughing or wheezing; difficulties when playing or exercising; and trouble sleeping at night. Sometimes, though, symptoms may be absent, but peak flow meter readings may indicate possible difficulties.

The goal in the yellow zone is to get your child's asthma under control and to move back to the green zone. Your asthma action plan should tell you what to do—in terms of increasing medication—if your child's symptoms quickly return to the green zone and if they do not.

The asthma action plan should list a quick-relief medication (often albuterol) that is inhaled every several hours. Your health care provider likely will prescribe for your child a metered-dose inhaler, along with a device call a spacer. The albuterol is placed on one side of the spacer and the child breaths in a puff of medicine with his mouth on the other end.

Alert!

A preventive medicine—usually an inhaled corticosteroid—also should be listed on the action plan if your child has been diagnosed with persistent asthma by his health care provider. This medicine should be taken every day, whether well or sick, no matter what zone your child's peak flow is indicating.

When increasing any medicine dosage, let your provider know. If your child does not appear to be getting better in a few days, make an appointment with your health care provider.

In the Red Zone

In the red zone, your child's peak flow meter readings generally will be less than 50 percent of her personal best readings. This is the danger zone. That means aggressive steps are needed to reverse this condition. She will have trouble breathing, she will not be able to play or go about her activities, and she does not appear to be getting better.

Quick-relief medications are usually recommended to at least improve symptoms temporarily. But you will need to call your health care provider immediately. If you fail to reach a provider and your child is in the red zone—meaning he has significant asthma symptoms for more than fifteen minutes and albuterol is not alleviating symptoms—call 911 or go to the hospital. If your child cannot walk or talk or has lips or fingernails turning blue, call 911 immediately.

When in the red zone, oral corticosteroids, such as prednisone or prednisolone, will likely be used to help her inflammation. Check with your health care provider about keeping an emergency supply. Other medication adjustments will likely be necessary, at least temporarily.

Also, your "team"—you, your health care provider, and your child—need to discuss why your child slipped into the red. Questions to ask are whether your child was exposed to any new triggers or were some medications missed?

Asthma Diary

One way you and your child can work together in managing his asthma is by keeping a daily asthma diary. It doesn't have to be greatly detailed—maybe some space in a notebook, a calendar, or a computer spreadsheet, for those who love technology.

But either you—or your child if he is old enough and responsible —can note what medicines were used for the day and what activities were undertaken that could impact his asthma. For instance, did he visit a friend's home where dogs or cats are present or did he get a ride home in a car driven by a friend's parent who smokes?

Essential

The asthma diary can be helpful for periodic health care provider visits where your child's asthma is assessed. The data can be reviewed to determine if changes are required in medication or if triggers of asthma symptoms appear to be changing.

Usually the diary should include the date, time, and readings of peak flow meter measures (and whether they are in the green, yellow, or red zones of his asthma action plan), possible exposure to asthma triggers, and changes in daily activities.

On the Go

Whether it's going to band practice, a scout meeting, dance lessons, or a friend's house, your child is likely to be busy with her activities. But, you may be concerned about how protected she is from symptoms that could occur with her asthma.

Make sure she has her asthma action plan, quick-relief medication, and peak flow meter with her or with an adult in charge of the activity. Answer any questions the adult in charge of the activity may have about your child's asthma management or treatment—before the activity occurs. These questions include how to recognize symptoms, how to use the medication, how the medication works, your phone numbers, emergency phone numbers, and when to seek emergency help. (Also see Chapter 17.)

Next, scope out the environment for possible triggers. If the scout meeting is being held in a building undergoing renovation (with lots of dust) or a friend has an affectionate Labrador retriever (and your child is allergic to animal dander), you may want to rethink the activity or reschedule to an alternative time or place.

When Should Your Child Stay Home?

The decision can be difficult: Should your child stay home from school or daycare today or will he be okay if you let him go?

In the back of your mind, you may be worried about missing a work day or appointments. But on the other hand, you want to make sure your child will be comfortable and safe throughout the day.

Monitor the Symptoms

The first place to start is by examining his symptoms. If those symptoms—maybe coughing or wheezing—were detected early and treatment steps in your child's management plan were promptly followed, he probably can head off to school. However, make sure that he will be getting any needed medication on schedule during the rest of the day.

Also, if he's showing slight sniffles or sneezes, for instance, from an incoming cold or from the beginning of allergy season, he still might be fine to attend classes.

If your child, though, needs his quick-relief medication more than every six hours to relieve his asthma symptoms, you should have him stay at home. Or, if he will be going on an outdoor field trip, for instance, on a high pollen count day—and one of his triggers is pollen—he might consider remaining behind at school or at home for the day.

Essential

Your child should remain home—and even possibly see his provider—if he is not responding to his quick-relief medication and continues to have difficulty breathing. Also, if he appears tired or restless from a sleepless night related to his asthma or is using his stomach or neck muscles to pull air into his lungs, he should remain at home as well for the day.

A peak flow meter can be used to see whether he is in the acceptable or green zone or is heading toward the danger or red zone on his daily management plan. This reading can be compared to his "personal best" reading on his asthma action plan. However, the peak flow reading may not always be accurate if the child with the asthma symptoms has other ideas on his mind—such as getting "a free day off" from school—when he is blowing into the peak flow meter. So, use your best judgment with the peak flow meter reading and always correlate it with asthma symptoms. Just because a number is in the yellow or red zone does not mean the child's health is impaired.

The child's technique when using the peak flow meter should be observed to see that it is done correctly—or the data it produces may not be correct. The maneuver to perform accurate peak flow readings is totally effort dependent, meaning your child must do a vigorous hard and fast blow to trust the result. If he is not trying hard or blowing out long and slow instead of fast, the reading may be inaccurate, which results in inappropriate medications being used.

Symptoms—Or Not?

Sometimes you may run into the opposite problem: Your child wants to do something—maybe play basketball outside on the neighborhood court or use her new skateboard—but she doesn't appear to be breathing just right, in your opinion. She insists she feels fine, but you're not sure.

Again, if your child is comfortable using a peak flow meter, try it and see if she is close to her "personal best" reading—an indication that she can go outside. For younger children, watch their breathing while engaged in play or other activities. If they appear to be breathing harder or look uncomfortable while resting, consider guiding them indoors, selecting some less strenuous activities, and implementing your asthma management plan medications.

 **Fact**

Researchers have indicated, though, that children as young as seven years could dependably report on their own asthma health status. The researchers assessed data reported by the children for reliability, for validity, and by symptom and lung function comparisons. In all but one age category, scores were in the acceptable range.

Often parents and children may have different views on the impact of the disease. Some aspects may be difficult for parents to assess. This suggests that children can take more of a role in monitoring their own asthma status.

Asthma and Other Medical Conditions

For years, researchers have focused on which children are likely to have asthma, how it occurs, what treatments work best, and the impact of various triggers. But a new area that is opening up is the relationship between asthma and other common childhood medical conditions.

Obesity Link

One of the top health concerns about children today is obesity. For years, studies have shown that children with asthma were more likely than non-asthmatic children to be overweight. But, what has been less clear was whether children with asthma may become obese because they participate in less physical activity or whether obese children were more likely to get asthma.

Essential

Emerging research has found that children with asthma are more likely to be obese and less likely to exercise than those without the disease. One British study, for example, said a reason was that asthma was identified as a barrier to exercise by both parents and children.

Nearly half the children with asthma, ages seven to fourteen in the study, were overweight, as defined by their body mass index, which relates height to weight; within that group, 20 percent were obese. In comparison, only about 30 percent of the kids in the study without asthma were overweight or obese, while 7 percent were in the obese category.

Nearly two-thirds of the children said asthma was a top reason why the children skimped on physical activity. A third of the asthmatic children stated that better management and control of their asthma would help them be more active.

For most children with asthma, current studies have shown that participating in sports and exercise is possible with care or pretreatment—using quick-relief and/or longer-acting medications and warm-up exercises—before the activity. (Also see Chapter 19.) These children also should monitor their environment and avoid potential triggers—such as cold air or pollens—that could create asthma symptoms.

Mental and Developmental Health Link

More studies are being called for on other conditions that often accompany asthma such as depression, attention deficit hyperactivity disorders (ADHD), anxiety, and various learning disabilities.

These additional conditions—also known as comorbidities—can negatively affect a child's ability to cope with asthma, according to research from the University of Virginia Children's Hospital. If these conditions can be addressed at the same time, health care providers might be better able to help children with asthma and their families gain an additional advantage in managing their asthma, the researchers said.

Alert!

The research found that depression, anxiety, behavioral problems, and learning disabilities were common comorbidities among children with asthma. They also noted that the more severe the child's asthma, the higher the incidence of these types of problems.

More than 10 percent of asthmatic children were reported to have problems that lasted longer than a year and required counseling or treatment. Also, these children often missed ten or more days of school, which led parents and caregivers to be anxious about their children's academic and emotional development.

CHAPTER 11
School Days

A s the parent of a child with asthma, you probably know that asthma is one of the most common chronic conditions reported today among children. Unfortunately, some school employees have been found to underestimate asthma in terms of its prevalence and impact on children. And, many schools still lack comprehensive policies to make sure their students with asthma are safeguarded from potential problems found within their own buildings. But you can keep a few points in mind to help ensure that your asthmatic child's school experience makes the grade.

Classroom Challenges

Asthma is one of the leading reasons for children to miss school because of illness. Sometimes the causes of why a child's asthma is making him sick may be related to the school itself. Maybe there are no complete individualized student asthma action plans on hand to provide guidance when students' symptoms flare up. Or maybe the school ventilation system is not as clean and dust-free as it should be. Or perhaps mold has established itself under the window where your child's desk is located.

Making sure your child's health is protected at school is more than just the role of the school nurse. It actually is the role of all staff at your child's school—from the principal to your child's teacher to the facilities manager.

And, it's your role, too, in keeping school officials apprised of your child's health and pointing out potential triggers found in the school that could cause asthma symptoms.

 **Fact**

More than 14 million school absences annually are related to asthma. According to findings from the American Academy of Pediatrics Committee on School Health, many parents have kept their children at home over concerns that school employees will not be able to manage or quickly react to their child with asthma.

School Asthma Action Plan

Before your child even enters the school classroom, you can assist him by doing a little homework yourself. First, make sure you send into your school an asthma action plan for your child that includes daily management guidelines and emergency provisions in case of an asthma attack. This asthma action plan should be developed and signed by your health care provider or physician.

The plan should include your child's medical information, along with what specific steps should be taken in case of a medical emergency. Information also should be included on:

- Medications your child needs during school hours, along with medications that are required off the school premises or after school hours.
- Correct dosages of the medications, along with when they are used, how they are used, and the anticipated results.
- A specific plan of action provided for the school staff in case of an acute asthma emergency.
- Your child's optimum peak flow reading.

- Guidance for monitoring peak flow in case of an emergency, explaining what is the normal flow rate (the green zone), along with rates in the caution (yellow) or danger (red) zones.
- Specific triggers identified that can make your child's asthma worse.
- Procedures that should be followed in case of emergency, including when to call your physician and when to call 911.
- Phone numbers (including your health care provider's and your numbers) that should be used in case of emergency.

The plan should be signed by you before sending it to school. The asthma action plan then should be sent to the individual designated at the school who maintains the records, such as the school nurse. This person is responsible for educating appropriate members of the school staff—including teachers—about the action plan. The action plan should be renewed at minimum once each year your child is a student at the school to include updated information related to treatment and symptoms.

Essential

A set of medications with instructions also should be left at school. Remember to follow school regulations regarding medications: Generally, you are required to deliver medications unopened with prescription information attached.

Give permission to share your asthma management plan with all the relevant adults (including all teachers) who regularly interact with your child at school. Giving this permission avoids possible violations of the Family Education Rights and Privacy Act that prohibits unauthorized disclosure of a student's records—including health records. Each of the team members needs to know about your child's asthma and how to work together to reduce or eliminate symptoms.

Policies and Backup Plans

You need to know if your child's school is prepared in case an asthma-related emergency arises. Over the years, serious incidents at schools involving children with asthma have occurred because school asthma management policies or backup plans were not in place. This issue has become critical in recent years since many schools now do not have a nurse serving full time.

In one 2006 study, researchers found that many urban and rural schools in one state—Pennsylvania—fell short in following recommended best practices in child asthma management.

While the researchers did not study whether the shortcomings they found in Pennsylvania are present in other states, they noted that poor adherence to national asthma guidelines at school is widespread.

The researchers found in interviews with nurses at the 757 Pennsylvania schools that more than half of the secondary schools and three-quarters of the elementary schools had nurses present less than forty hours per week.

Also, asthma action plans were on file for only a quarter of the children with asthma—and many of those were incomplete. In addition, asthma-related equipment—such as peak flow meters, nebulizers, or spacers—were available for student use in about half of the schools.

What these findings mean is that in addition to having your child's asthma action plan on file at school, you should know what your child's school backup plan is in case the designated person (such as the nurse) is not available in an asthma-related emergency.

Alert!

Designated staffers—such as a principal or an administrative assistant—should be spelled out in the backup emergency plan, and the location of a child's action plan, medication, or backup medication should be clear to the those individuals.

Just remember that when an emergency arises, there's very little time to ask questions or hunt for missing directions and medications—especially when it comes to your child.

Asthma-Friendly School?

How do you know if your child's school will offer the proper support to keep her healthy and active—with her asthma under control? As a start, the National Heart, Lung and Blood Institute (NHLBI) developed a checklist:

- Is your school free of tobacco smoke at all times—even during school-sponsored events?
- Does the school maintain good indoor-air quality, and does it reduce allergens or irritants that can make it worse? Have any of the following been found: cockroaches, dust mites, mold, pets with fur or feathers, or strong odor from items such as art supplies, paints, pesticides, perfumes, air fresheners, or cleaning chemicals?
- Is the school nurse available in the school every day? If not, is the nurse regularly available to help the school prepare guidance related to medicines, physical education, and field trips?
- Can your child take medicines at school as recommended by her health care provider? Can your child carry her own asthma medication with her in school?

- Does someone teach the staff about asthma, asthma action plans, and asthma medications?
- Does someone teach students about asthma and what they should do to help a classmate with asthma?
- Does your school have an individualized written emergency plan, and do the plans indicate what actions to take, whom to call, or when to call?
- Does your child have good options for safely participating in physical education classes or recess? Does she have access to her medicine before exercise? Can she choose alternatives when medically necessary?

If you can answer no to at least one of these questions, your child may be encountering a barrier to asthma control. But these barriers are not insurmountable, and they can be tackled with the cooperation of the school staff, health professionals, and you.

Partnership for Better Care

Working to get better care for your child should not be a solitary effort. A strong partnership that includes you, the school staff, other families, physicians and other health care providers, and even students is needed to help young people with asthma.

Consider working with other parents to develop a resource library for all school staff and students for obtaining additional information about asthma through pamphlets, brochures, and other publications. Many local and national organizations offer educational materials for this purpose.

A good partnership can improve communication among all parties. In turn, it will help to promote improved attendance, alertness, physical stamina, and educational outcomes for your child—and other children—with asthma.

School policies that are supportive of partnerships have a number of points in common. First, they encourage families to participate in managing their children's asthma at school. They also provide opportunities for families to participate in decision-making regarding school policies and procedures impacting their children.

Working with Teachers and School Staff

Most schools are likely to have several students with asthma, which means that many teachers—plus school nurses—will be very familiar with helping children with asthma. However, you still have a role to play in making sure that your child gets appropriate attention for his condition and that all the relevant school staffers are familiar with what is needed to help your child during the school day.

Teachers and Asthma

In a classroom of about twenty-five students, teachers can expect to have at least two to three children with asthma. While you should check to see if your child's teacher has his action and daily action plans on hand, you also should ask if that teacher has had additional training from the school to spot asthma symptoms and to immediately address any emergencies that could arise.

In-service or professional development courses can be taught by a school nurse, a local hospital, or community organizations that focus on children with asthma. These courses can discuss when to refer a child to a nurse because of symptoms (such as wheezing, a pale and sweaty face, repeated coughing, or low peak flow readings), or side effects that are interfering with breathing or performing school activities.

Training also can assist teachers in learning about how to stop an asthma attack by encouraging relaxation or deep breathing (possibly by modeling the technique), providing warm water to drink, and, if needed, using quick-relief or rescue medication.

The message should be emphasized to your child that he must speak up—and not be embarrassed—to tell his teacher if he is experiencing any difficulties, such as labored breathing or wheezing, so the teacher can act promptly.

Additional training also can help teachers address the child's feelings, for instance, of being somewhat different than her classmates, anxiety over the use of medications, or embarrassment of having an asthma attack.

You should receive acknowledgement from your child's classroom teacher or teachers that they have received his asthma action plan. If possible (particularly for the elementary grades), review it with the teacher to see if any modifications are needed in the classroom such as removals or repairs to avoid various asthma triggers.

Alert!

Ask the teacher to contact you if your child's asthma symptoms are affecting his learning or interactions with peers. Concerns about possible side effects with medications—such as nervousness, nausea, hyperactivity, or jitteriness—should be reported to you.

Also, ask the teacher to set up a procedure addressing how missed schoolwork should be handled if your child has an asthmatic episode or is absent from school.

And above all, support the teacher's efforts to get your child to participate in all classroom activities. While there may be circumstances that may aggravate asthma symptoms on school days—such as changes in weather (hot, cold, or breezy) or poor air quality—your child likely will want to feel like "one of the guys."

School Nurse as Advocate

Schools with a full-time nurse can provide a valuable service to your child by monitoring her condition, overseeing the use of medication, or working with your family to suggest effective management strategies at home. However, many schools, because of budget cutbacks, do not have the resources for providing the services of a full-time school nurse.

Essential

Nurses—even if working part time in your child's school— still can be an important ally on the school staff for you and your child in asthma management and treatment. Make a point of meeting with the nurse to discuss the needs of your child.

The school nurse or other designated staff member can help review or develop your child's individual asthma action plan with your family and distribute it to your child's teachers. The nurse should also communicate with you throughout the school year to report attacks or update information found in the plan.

The National Association of School Nurses (*www.nasn.org*) has created a form that can be sent home to parents that can indicate whether your child's action plan is working. The forms flag signs that a child's asthma is not under control or where medication is not being used or is being used inappropriately.

And, the nurse is a "teacher" in that she can answer your questions about asthma, provide information and in-service courses to staff members about asthma's impact on students, and assist students and helping them with their self-management skills.

Principals and Head Administrators

Principals and head administrators have clearly defined roles as well. They should help initiate and implement an asthma management program throughout the school, and select the individual (usually the nurse) who is in charge—along with a backup designee if the nurse is not available.

Working with you, the school nurse, and medical professionals, principals or administrators can also help develop the policies that ensure medication administration is safe, reliable, and effective, and—when appropriate under current school system policies—permit self-administered medication. They also can clarify policies about taking medications during field trips, after-school programs, and other school-related events outside the regular school day.

Principals or administrators also can provide appropriate guidance for outside play—to protect students from extreme temperatures, high pollen counts, and air pollution that can affect children with asthma.

Other Staff Roles

Building maintenance staff can play important roles in the life of an asthmatic child by identifying indoor air quality problems including mold growth, improperly maintained ventilation systems, and possible chemical pollutants from chemistry or art classes.

They also can play important roles in minimizing allergen and irritant levels through regular cleaning and maintenance schedules. And, they can stop problems before they start by scheduling renovation or major repair work when students are not in the school building.

Guidance counselors, social workers, or school psychologists can smooth the path out for your child at school by making sure he is treated the same as all other children, except when addressing his asthma needs.

They also can help your child deal with the stress of a chronic condition—helping them address anxieties or pressures they might feel from time to time. And they can assist students in resolving issues related to school policies or practices, along with his asthma management.

They also can help school staff better understand what asthma is—an inflammation of the lungs and not something going on in a child's head or an excuse not to do something.

Gym, Sports Teams, and Outdoor Play

The individuals that teach or coach your child in sports or other physical activities need to have access to your child's asthma action plan. In particular, they should have an understanding of your child's premedication procedures, and then know—and have readily available—the child's quick-relief medications.

They also make sure that an asthmatic child's medications are available for any sports or athletic activities occurring away from school or outside of school hours.

A good instructor will encourage your child to participate in sports, but also respect her limits when she says she is unable to participate in an activity. Sometimes the instructor needs to recognize the need to adjust for the pace or intensity of activities—or substitute some activities—due to weather or air quality issues.

Understanding Your Child's Rights

State and federal laws have outlined protections for children with asthma in regard to what services they are provided in school and what can be done in school to treat their asthma symptoms.

Regulations and Asthma

Asthma may be considered a disability for a student—depending on severity—under Section 504 of the federal Rehabilitation Act of 1973, the Individuals with Disabilities Education Act (IDEA), and Title II of the Americans with Disabilities Act. Title II and Section 504 assure access to federally funded services for a handicapped individual, while IDEA makes available funds to help schools serve these students when those schools follow specific requirements.

Not all students with asthma are covered by IDEA. If a child is classified as disabled under the IDEA, the child will require special education and related services because of the asthma or another disabling condition.

Section 504 and Title II are more broadly defined than IDEA, and students who experience breathing difficulties at school may be considered to have a disability that qualifies them to receive services under these laws.

 **Fact**

Children with asthma may need what is called a 504 Plan or an Individualized Education Plan (IEP) to ensure that they receive health services or physical activity modifications that they need to help them learn in the school.

In some instances, a child may need an Individualized Education Plan (IEP), which is developed by a team that can include the child's parents, regular and special education teachers, a school nurse, and other education officials. Asthma action plans can be incorporated into the IEPs.

A helpful part of the IEPs is information about when, where, and how medication should be taken while in school—including when self-administration of medication is appropriate.

Self-Administration

If an asthma attack occurs, schools need a plan to deliver medication quickly from a central site. But another way of addressing this is permitting children—who are understand how to use an inhaler and are old enough to tell time—to carry the inhaler with them in school. Physicians generally have recommended that students carry asthma medication to provide them with a quick way to stop or prevent an asthma attack.

In some areas, though, the carrying of inhalers had run up against zero-tolerance policies regarding the carrying and use of any drugs during school hours. In recent years, almost all states in the country (forty-seven by the end of 2006) have passed laws that permit students to carry their inhalers with them in school.

Alert!

If your child is allowed to carry his own medications, make sure all necessary school permission forms are completed, and backup medications are provided to the school. All medications and related devices should be labeled with your child's name.

When deciding if your child should carry and administer asthma medications in school, you need to evaluate several factors such as:

- Does your child have a history of asthma severity—such as recently going to the emergency room or hospitalizations—that would underscore the need for self-administered medication?
- What is your child's attitude and seriousness about using the inhaler? (Is he aware of the signs and symptoms of when he needs it? Will he report use of the inhaler when he uses it? Does he know when and how to use a peak flow meter? Does he know how to use the inhaler and spacers correctly?)
- Does his previous history with inhalers (such as at child care or at friends' homes) show he will be responsible for correctly using them?
- Will he know when to check to see that he has enough medicine to relieve symptoms and when to order or replace with a refill?

- Is the school size large enough to preclude getting to the health office in a timely fashion in an asthma emergency?
- Can he tell time so he understands when a medication is due or needs to be taken?

The question of whether to allow a child to self-administer medication is not an easy one, but it is one that you—working with school staff and your medical provider—can discuss in determining the right asthma medication treatment for your child.

School Environmental Triggers

As the parent of a child with asthma, it is important to take a look—and smell—inside and outside his classroom and determine if there are potential asthma triggers. From the classroom ceilings to the carpeted floor, down long hallways, in damp boys' and girls' bathrooms, and through miles of heating and ventilating pipes, potential asthma trouble spots probably are found everywhere:

- Carpets or furniture that are emitting noxious fumes.
- Extensive renovations that involve painting, cleaning, and repairs that are taking place when the kids are in school.
- Dust and dirt on desk, wall, and floor surfaces.
- Storage areas covered with dust and dirt.
- Strong odors from chemical and cleaning supplies.
- Moisture from leaking pipes or window condensation that can lead to mold.
- Bathroom sinks and fixtures leaking.
- Animals in the classroom or school building (whose dander can be picked up by the ventilating system).
- Dirt and dust around the ventilation system outlets.
- Signs that pesticides were used recently for extermination work.
- Smells such as cigarette smoke on the school premises.
- Chalkboards without dustless chalk.

Putting Precautions in Place

While so many triggers exist, you can observe whether schools are taking aim at some of the targets to stop or slow them down. To address these challenges, schools can take many actions to eliminate exposure to these triggers.

To oust cockroach allergens or other four-legged pests, schools can use integrated pest management practices to prevent pest problems. These practices are a safer alternative to spraying to get rid of pests, which in turn could trigger asthma symptoms. It means cleaning food-contaminated dishes, utensils, and surfaces by the end of each day; regularly cleaning garbage cans and dumpsters; storing foods in tight canisters; keeping vegetation and shrubs at least one foot away from school structures; and filling or eliminating cracks and crevices in walls, floors, and pavement.

 *Essential*

Any renovations, which can create dust and paint smells in the school, should be scheduled during long vacations when the school building is empty. If new carpet is installed in the school, the spaces where carpet has been installed should be aired out for a minimum of seventy-two hours. The carpet installation also should only happen when the school is not in use.

Inadequate maintenance of the carpet can allow large quantities of dust, dirt, pollen, pesticides, mold spores, and other debris to build up. Therefore, regular and effective vacuuming with a well-functioning vacuum cleaner—with a high-performance filtration bag or system—is required, especially if young children are playing on that carpet where they are more likely to come into contact with those contaminants.

When possible, furry or feathered classroom animals should be removed from the school. But if this cannot be done, the animals should be moved away from sensitive students and ventilation systems.

Entry door barrier mat systems are important in trapping soil, pollutants, and moisture that could spread throughout the school. According to the International Sanitary Supply Association, most of the dirt in a building is tracked in on people's shoes, and that 85 percent of this could be removed if the mats are properly designed and placed. A combination of mat materials, textures, and lengths should be used: For a snowy climate, a scraper mat would work well; for a rainy location, an absorption mat would work; and for a muddy location, both of the mats could be used.

To prevent molds from developing, the school should fix moisture problems promptly and thoroughly dry wet areas within twenty-four to forty-eight hours. Moldy, hard surfaces should be cleaned with water and detergent or bleach, and then dried thoroughly.

Strong policies should be in effect at the school—and on its grounds—to enforce no-smoking policies and eliminate secondhand smoke exposure.

Portable Classrooms

While additional classrooms placed outside the school building have many names—such as portable, relocatable, modular, or trailer—they are becoming popular features around many schools whose student populations keep increasing. While these classrooms can provide additional space for lower costs, they may pose some additional difficulties for your child with asthma.

The most common problems with portable classrooms include: poorly functioning heating and cooling systems that provide minimal ventilation with outside air; seeping or dripping water and mold growth; exhaust pollution from nearby school parking lots or loading areas; and chemical off-gassing from pressed wood and other materials.

The outdoor air intakes should not be located underneath the portable units because these areas usually are not well ventilated and are prone to moisture, biological contaminants, and other pollutants. Also, lack of an exhaust in the heating and cooling system with an outdoor air intake could result in insufficient removal of pollutants from the room.

 **Fact**

Outdoor air should be supplied continuously into a portable classroom when it is occupied, according to the EPA. However, many heating and cooling system packages often just operate when the temperature of a space is different from the thermostat's set point. To provide a continuous outdoor air supply, the thermostat fan switch should be set in the "on" or continuous mode when occupied.

Overall, the EPA suggests that the portable classroom should be moved away from locations where vehicles (such as school buses, delivery trucks, or parent pick-up vehicles) idle; where water accumulates after rains; or where there are other major sources of air pollution (such as a highway).

No carpet should be used at the entryways to the classrooms with direct outdoor access. Instead, use waterproof mats over carpeted entryways to slow down tracking of dirt and allergens, and to provide areas used for drying clothing and umbrellas.

School Buses

About 24 million children spend part of their school days traveling in school buses. While school buses have been found to be a safe way to get children back and forth on the road, questions have arisen over the years about the exhaust that children, as passengers, may be breathing from the diesel vehicles.

Essential

A move has been on to try to reduce children's exposure to diesel exhaust by replacing older buses with less polluting buses, but this may take time. Concerns are still raised about how diesel fumes currently impact children—particularly those with asthma.

Children can reduce their exposure to exhaust fumes by sitting near the front of a bus or riding on a bus that has windows open, which allow exhaust fumes to escape. But these options might not always be available to your child. If your child rides one of the older types of diesel buses back and forth to school, monitor whether her asthma symptoms seem to get worse on the bus. If your child's symptoms seem to flare up, check with your pediatrician and determine if you should look at other ways for your child to travel to school.

School-Based Asthma Education Programs

One of the strongest tools in addressing your child's asthma in school is education. Numerous studies have shown that children educated about asthma have improved school performance and fewer missed days.

One example of a school-based asthma education program is the American Lung Association's Open Airways For Schools, a free program for elementary school children and their parents. It is designed to teach children how to take control of asthma, how to reduce exposure to environmental triggers, and how to use their medications properly.

When children are educated about asthma, they learn that while asthma may be a fact of their life, it does not have to mean it will hold them back from life at school.

CHAPTER 12

Teenagers and the Asthma Challenge

While the teenage years can be a tough time, it can seem twice as hard for the teenager who has asthma. Whether your teen has had asthma for years or is newly diagnosed, this condition will bump up against the classical teen attitudes of wanting to blend in with peers, not appearing to be different, or wanting to try new things. But, there are ways that you can make asthma and adolescence easier—to assure your teen that she can fit in with the crowd while making sure she gets the appropriate treatment she needs.

Asthma and the Teenage Lifestyle

Current statistics show that the rate of asthma among young people has more than doubled in the past quarter century. Just like anyone else with asthma, teenagers may react differently to their condition. Some worry that they will have to miss participating in sports or fun activities, even if they had been given an okay by their physicians. Others may use asthma as an excuse to get out of physical education class or work around the house. Others may just deny they have asthma and will turn away from treating it effectively.

More than half of young people who have asthma will see a decrease in symptoms during their teen years. Others, when asthma becomes part of their teen lives, may become frustrated or irritated about how this condition seems to hover over them—just like so many other issues at this age.

You as a parent know that even though they say they feel fine now, they are headed for serious trouble if they fail to treat and monitor their asthma.

**Fact**

Statistics from the Centers for Disease Control and Prevention show that while adolescents (ages eleven through seventeen) are less likely to be hospitalized than their younger counterparts with asthma, they have a proportionately higher death rate from asthma when compared with the younger group. Early studies suggest that inadequate asthma management may play a major role.

Although asthma still poses dangers, you need to realize that your teen now wants to do many things—maybe play soccer, hang out at friends' houses, go to parties, ride horses, or learn to drive a car. But while he may be busy, you still have a role in your teen's life—albeit an evolving one—to make sure he is protected from his asthma symptoms.

Parental Support

The role that you take on as a parent should be a little less "intrusive" —at least from your teen's point of view—than when she was younger. Consider letting your teen take on more responsibility for her asthma care in a way that fits in appropriately with her often hectic life—but protects her from serious asthma complications.

In other words, don't let asthma become a battleground between you and your teen. Support the point that your teen needs to take her asthma medications so she remains healthy. But state this in a matter-of-fact way rather than as a threat or an ultimatum.

Chances are if you focus on this as a make-or-break deal, you're likely to meet strong resistance because she might feel you're challenging her independence.

 Essential

While asthma can pose potential dangers to teenagers—particularly those with severe asthma—avoid overreacting in most cases to what they can't do (with the exception of smoking). Instead, focus on—and encourage—what they can do as they grow older and get ready for life outside your home.

Daily Monitoring

Depending on the age of your teen, gradually shift over to him the responsibility of taking his medications on a timely basis. For instance, agree on the time when he'll take his medication each day, and when he needs to ask for refills (well in advance of running out).

This doesn't mean totally ignoring what your teen is doing. If you notice, for instance, that his asthma medication container has not moved for several days from a spot on his bedroom dresser, it's time to step in to find out what is happening. Sometimes your teen—despite what he says to you—may not be ready just yet for additional responsibilities involved with managing his asthma.

This is where an asthma diary can be useful.

It may take a step-by-step process to help a teen move ahead with taking his medication on schedule. But during this time, remember to treat this relationship with your teen as a partnership—with the goal of stopping asthma symptoms.

Solo Medical Visits

When your teen was much younger, you most likely sat in the examining room with the physician during the visit. But as your child becomes older, you might be encountering more resistance from her to your presence in the exam room: She probably would like time by herself to speak with her physician.

While you might be used to asking the physician questions— sometimes even dominating the visit, it might be helpful for the teen to begin talking one-on-one with the physician about various concerns on her mind, including asthma.

Letting a teen visit her physician alone might give her more of a feeling of power over dealing with asthma—and could make her more responsible for herself in the long run.

Get the Right Treatment Plan

Whether it is to start—or to continue—controlling asthma symptoms, a teen needs to talk to his physician about creating and using a personalized asthma action plan. Working with his physician, this means listing severity of symptoms, asthma triggers, exercise modifications, peak flow meter personal best readings, and control medications.

 *Fact*

A teenager's asthma action plan can provide good protection against potentially problematic situations by indicating, for instance, when she should use medication when participating in a competitive sport. It also can help avoid possibly scary or embarrassing episodes such as having an asthma attack at a friend's party where partygoers are smoking.

But like the best-laid plans, implementation of an asthma action plan sometimes may fall short. Perhaps your teen might forget to take his medication as prescribed at the right time or he might find it embarrassing to use his peak flow meter to get readings when eating out with his friends. Sometimes he might think—incorrectly—that he is feeling better without his daily medication and doesn't need it. But there are ways for your teen to get back on track and make sure he is taking care of himself.

 **Fact**

It's easy for a teen to underestimate the severity of his symptoms. A peak expiratory flow meter can help detect if his lungs are not functioning as well as they should. Generally, he might not notice that his lung function is not good until it is at 50 percent of his personal best peak expiratory flow—a level that could put him in danger if not treated promptly.

Medical Check-Up

Teens need to meet with a physician or health care provider on a regular basis. For teens already diagnosed with mild cases of asthma that have been under control for at least three months, a visit about every six to twelve months would be advised; for teens with moderate asthma, a visit every three to six months would be recommended; and for teens with uncontrolled or severe asthma, a visit every one or two months would be called for.

The discussion should focus on the goals of treatment: to avoid long-term lung damage related to underlying inflammation of the lungs; to decrease the severity and frequency of asthma episodes by avoiding triggers; to treat asthma symptoms as they occur; and to support a healthy quality of life that lets a teen participate in daily activities at home, school, and in the community.

During an office visit, the health care provider will ask the teen about symptoms and peak expiratory flow readings—whether they have been holding steady, improving, or getting worse. The provider also will ask about any asthma attacks, including those that occur during exercise or at night.

To better keep track of these events triggering asthma symptoms, your teen can keep a personal asthma diary either online or on paper. The diary can be used to record ongoing information for each day of the week on points such as:

- Her personal best peak expiratory flow meter reading.
- Daily morning and afternoon/evening peak expiratory flow meter readings.
- Scores from the peak expiratory flow readers that indicate either the green zone (80–100 percent of the personal best reading); the yellow zone (50–79 percent of personal best); or the red zone (below 50 percent of personal best).
- Symptom scores based on: no symptoms such as wheezing or coughing; mild symptoms that may occur during physical activity but not while resting; moderate symptoms that prevent sleeping or keeping active; and severe symptoms that occur even when resting and can cause difficulties with walking and talking.
- Notation if quick-relief medications are used to address symptoms.
- Triggers, location, weather, air quality, and type of environment where asthma symptoms occurred.
- Any visits to the physician, hospital, or hospital emergency room due to urgent medical treatment related to asthma.

Monitoring lung function with a peak expiratory flow meter lets her detect—and then treat—any problems quickly. Your teen can ask the physician or health care provider to explain what control medications should be used daily or what quick-relief medication should be used and when. She should also review how to correctly use the medications and make sure she's getting enough to control her symptoms.

These discussions can help the teen feel that she's more in control. It also will help underscore what will happen if your teen follows—or declines to follow—her action plan. The teen should be reminded to check in with her physician to review her action plan or daily personal asthma diary and to ask questions if problems arise.

Either you or your teen should check to see that an up-to-date action plan is on file with her school, physical education teacher, and sports coach. This lets them know what medications she is using, whether exercise modifications are needed, what symptoms should be monitored, and when emergency assistance might be required.

Guidelines for Teenagers

The current asthma guidelines released by the National Asthma Education and Prevention Program include an asthma severity scale created for children and teens from ages twelve though adult with asthma who are not currently taking long-term control medications. The scale can provide a health care provider a base by which to begin or adjust treatment. These levels are:

- Intermittent—Symptoms occur less than two days a week, two nighttime awakenings related to asthma are reported, quick-relief medications are used less than two days a week, and no interference is reported with normal, daily activities.
- Mild Persistent—Symptoms occur two or more days a week (but not daily), three to four nighttime awakenings related to asthma occur monthly, quick-relief medications are used more than two days a week (but not daily), and minor limitations are reported with normal, daily activities.
- Moderate Persistent—Symptoms occur daily, more than one nighttime awakening related to asthma occurs weekly (but not nightly), quick-relief medications are used daily, and some limitations are reported with normal, daily activities.

- Severe Persistent—Symptoms occur throughout the day, nighttime awakenings related to asthma occur seven days a week, quick-relief medications are used several times per day, and normal, daily activities are reported extremely limited.

At the current time, data is inadequate to link flare-ups with levels of severity. However, for treatment purposes, the guidelines recommend that patients ages twelve through adult who have had two asthma episodes in the year requiring treatment with oral corticosteroids may be considered the same as patients with persistent asthma (even if they fail to show signs of impairment associated with the other levels). Once treatment has started, your health care provider can determine if your child's symptoms—as in the younger age groups—are well controlled, not well controlled, or poorly controlled using the current guidelines. (See Appendix C.)

Medications

Many good medications on the market work well to address asthma symptoms. But for the usually busy teen with asthma, the issue generally will narrow down to simplicity and portability. Basically, the simpler the course of treatment, the more likely the teen is to follow his daily regimen.

Get Informed

Teens need to understand what medications are available, and when they are appropriate to use. Medications generally fall into two categories: quick-relief medicines and preventive medicines.

Quick-relief medicines, such as the anti-inflammatory bronchodilator sprays, rapidly open airways when inhaled. They are to be used when a teen is having an asthma attack.

If a teen has periodic symptoms including wheezing, coughing, or troubled breathing, she would use quick-relief medicine. However, overuse of a quick-relief medication could harm your teen.

These medications should be used quickly when asthma symptoms appear: The longer the teen waits to use the medicine, the longer it takes to end the symptoms. Following an asthma episode, a teen may need to take the quick-relief medicine for several days.

The quick-relief medicines can be inhaled fifteen minutes before intense and vigorous workouts—and also afterward, if needed—to reduce the occurrence of exercise-induced asthma.

Preventive or longer-acting medicines help stop asthma attacks by keeping lung airways from becoming inflamed. Teens with more severe asthma symptoms usually will need to use preventive medicines daily to allow them to participate in normal activities.

 *Question?*

What symptoms indicate a need for teens to use an asthma preventive medicine?
These symptoms include: two or more attacks of wheezing per week; two or more nighttime asthma attacks per month; asthma flare-ups that continue for several days; a need arising for urgent medical care despite proper inhaler use; and asthma triggered by pollens during the usual growing season.

Teens also have a high rate of using complementary and alternative treatments. In one national survey of about 1,300 young people fourteen to nineteen years old, 80 percent said they had used these treatments at least once in their lifetime, and 50 percent said within the past month.

Teens, though, need to first be aware that the complementary and alternative treatments should not replace their current medications. Also, they should check with their physician if they are using treatments such as herbal remedies. They may not be aware that some alternative treatments could end up creating risks with pre-scribed medications because they act in a similar fashion as those medications. (Also see Chapter 5.)

What to Choose

When looking for the right medication to use, convenience likely will mean better compliance when it comes to teenagers. Once-a-day medications may appeal to the teen rather than taking those medica-tions that need to be used several times a day.

For asthmatic children, spacers are a familiar tool. But by the time they reach their teenage years, the large bulky spacers may get the thumbs down in terms of portability. If those tubes don't easily fit in pockets or purses, they're bound to be left behind. So smaller—and even attractive—spacers will be preferred. Health care provid-ers have found that some teens may prefer dry powder inhalers to get their needed medication because their size is smaller, and no spacer is needed.

Cool Versus Safe

Teens need to realize that failure to comply with use of the right medication at the right time can have consequences. It's not uncom-mon that a teen may feel better after taking daily medication—and then stop using it. He might begin just relying on quick-acting bron-chodilator spray when an asthma event occurs, which could prove to be problematic—especially if he forgets to carry his inhaler with him the one time he has an asthma attack.

In a worst-case scenario, teens with severe cases of asthma can die. But uncontrolled asthma also can lead to other problems, too, including depression, fatigue, and low self-esteem. This, in turn, can lead to emotional outbursts and poor school performance.

Alert!

Some of the most common mistakes that a teen can make in treating her asthma is delaying the start of prescribed asthma medications, failing to replace those medications promptly, or not renewing them at all when they run out. Relying on nonprescription inhalers and medicines to take their place will not be helpful to the teen in the long run.

Therefore, it's important for the teen to realize that her asthma needs to be managed daily using medications appropriate for her and in a timely manner.

Is It Working?

Sometimes the medication prescribed by your teen's health care provider may not be working very well to control his asthma. In this case, your health care professional likely will see if he is using the inhaler correctly. If he is, then his health care provider may change the dosage, switch to another medication, or add a medication to the current treatment.

Also, the provider may suggest other medications, such as leukotriene pathway modifiers, or possibly mast cell stabilizers (cromolyn sodium or nedocromil), or theophylline.

If your teen's asthma still does not improve with the different treatments, he may need more intensive treatments involving larger doses of corticosteroids or other medications. This may require a visit to an asthma specialist.

Controlling Symptoms

Aside from using medications, your teen needs to look around and identify what could be possible triggers to her asthma symptoms.

Sometimes it might be as close as a pet cat or someone smoking in her best friend's car. Other times, asthma might be related to eating or exercising. But whatever it is, your teen may have to make some adjustments in her life when it comes to addressing her asthma.

Saying No to Smoking

Each year, more than a million teens become regular smokers—some of them are teens with asthma. This could not be a worse choice because cigarette smoke makes their asthma worse by irritating their airways—causing them to narrow and disrupting the normal flow in and out of the lungs.

 **Fact**

Cigarette smoking actually can increase the risk of an asthma attack for your teen. In fact, cigarette smoke is one of the more common causes of asthma aggravation. You need to let your teen know that smoking can permanently damage his airways. Those teens who smoke are not as likely to see long-term improvement in their asthma—basically reducing the odds of outgrowing it.

Teens may choose to smoke—even if they have asthma—for a variety of reasons: For instance, they think smoking makes them look cool or it helps them to control their weight. But the fact is that cigarettes have nicotine that is very addictive. If your teen smokes, he should talk with you or his physician about how to quit.

Secondhand cigarette smoke is a common trigger of asthma attacks, as well. If your teen's friends smoke, tell him not to sit or stand near them when they smoke and not to ride in their cars. Also, if members of your family smoke, talk with them about it, and encourage them to consider quitting.

Triggers at Home

On the home front, your teen should be encouraged to keep her bedroom as neat and dust-free as possible by cleaning regularly. In this area, she may need a little help—especially with dusting and vacuuming—since it could aggravate her condition. In her room, you might consider minimizing carpet use and instead use bare floors to cut down on dust and dust mites that can trigger asthma symptoms.

This also means laundering bed sheets in hot water at least once a week to get rid of dust mites. Special mattress and pillow covers, with their closures taped over, can be considered, too.

For the heating and air-conditioning system, change air filters regularly and consider using filters especially designed to capture many potential allergens. Keep air vents clear of dust and dirt. Also consider using a dehumidifier to keep the humidity in the house at less than 50 percent to keep down molds and carpet dust mites.

Giving away a beloved furry or feathered pet might not sit well with a teen. But if a teen is allergic to their dander, at least keep the pet out of her bedroom at all times.

Alert!

Since carpets and upholstered or cloth-covered furniture capture pet dander, minimize the use of the items—or keep pets away from them—in rooms of the house that your teen often uses. Also, consider giving the pets a weekly bath to keep down dander.

While teens are constantly bombarded with messages of smelling good, they may have to put some brakes on their habits. Various scents from perfumes, colognes, aftershave lotions, creams, and deodorants could trigger asthma symptoms. Also, scented products

—ranging from candles to incense and air fresheners—could cause problems as well.

Food and Asthma

When you think of teens, you might think of their "food groups" such as pizza, hamburgers, chili, sodas, or burritos. But many of these foods may end up aggravating your teen's asthma.

Sometimes a little food may come back up their esophagus with stomach acid—creating what many people think of as heartburn. The medical term is gastroesophageal reflux disease or GERD. Since the same nerves that control the esophagus's reflexes are also connected to their bronchial muscles, stomach acid irritates these nerves and can trigger asthma symptoms such as coughing.

 Essential

Advise your teen to refrain from eating large meals before bedtime and to avoid those foods that are spicy, high in fat, caffeinated, or acidic. This will cut down on the potential for heartburn and possible asthma symptoms. Your teen also may want to elevate the pillows at the head of her bed by several inches to avoid that heartburn.

Also, encourage your teen to consider including in his diet more fruits, vegetables, and omega-3 fatty acids, which are found in tuna, salmon, and nuts. These foods have been linked in recent studies to helping improve respiratory function.

Exercise

Exercise is a great way for teens to keep fit. But, since most teens with asthma also have exercise-induced asthma, they may back away from activities related to physical education or sports. However, working with a health care provider, teens can find ways to manage and treat exercise-induced asthma and become active—just like their friends.

Your teen can control symptoms by using medication (usually a bronchodilator) at least fifteen minutes before competition. She will need to take time to warm up before exercise, and then cool down. Also let coaches and physical education teachers know that your teen has exercise-induced asthma and make sure they have a copy of her asthma action plan.

While sports that involve shorter periods of exertion (such as baseball or gymnastics) may be better tolerated by your teen than sports that require longer periods of exertion (basketball or soccer), she can still participate in most sports with proper medical supervision and physical conditioning.

She will, though, need to keep her eye on weather conditions since colder, drier air can trigger an exercise-induced asthma episode. She also may need to double-check outdoor pollen counts or ozone alerts, which also could trigger symptoms.

College Bound

Older teenagers with asthma will need to take on new responsibilities as well when they move away from home and high school and into a new world such as a college campus. As a parent, there are several tips that you can tell your teen to keep in mind as he makes the transition:

- Have your teen tell his health care provider that he will be moving from home, and that he would like to coordinate the transfer of care to a new provider.
- Advise your teen to fill his prescriptions before he leaves, and have his physician call a local pharmacy with his prescription so he can continue to get refills while living away.
- Make copies of his personal asthma action plan that he can present to his campus health service, his resident director,

and his roommate. (The plan should list medications being used and health care provider contact numbers.

- Request a non-smoking room and/or roommate, and avoid secondhand smoke since smoke is a common asthma trigger.
- If possible, try to get a dorm room that has wood or vinyl flooring rather than carpeting.
- Advise him to carry his inhaler at all times because he might run into unexpected conditions (such as cigarette smoke at a party) that might trigger his asthma symptoms.
- Become familiar with his on-campus health center—just in case he has to visit there if his asthma symptoms bother him.
- Make sure mattresses, box springs, and pillows are covered in airtight plastic or allergen-proof fabric covers.

 Essential

College students returning home for Thanksgiving should prepare for the "Thanksgiving Effect"—a flare-up of asthma and allergy symptoms that occur after being away from home and possible asthma-symptom triggers such as the family pet. Since squeezing in an urgent visit for care can be difficult during the holiday, students should think ahead and develop an action plan with their physician.

Although it may seem counterintuitive to some students, cleanliness also will have to be a top priority when away from home. Your teen will need to completely clean the living area when moving in to guard against dust mites, mold, and cockroaches. And once in his new locale, he will need to take precautions—such as storing food in secure containers and cleaning the floor after meals—to make sure unwanted asthma triggers don't pay a visit.

Teen Support

In the age of the e-mails, blogging, and text-messaging, teens with asthma are realizing that they are not alone. Numerous resources are available to help teens with asthma communicate with one another—to commiserate, answer questions, and just kind of hang out in their local communities or in cyberspace.

Educational Programs

Local community programs are available specifically for teens such as the "Power Breathing" program from the Asthma and Allergy Foundation of American (*www.aafa.org*). This national program is designed to teach the basics of asthma and assist teens in learning skills to manage asthma in social situations, in school, and at work.

Also check with local chapters of AAFA and other national groups, such as the American Lung Association, about community educational support groups that can provide your teens and pre-teens with information from health care professionals, emotional support, and the opportunity to meet new friends.

Online Support

Support is also close at hand on a teen's computer or cell phone. Numerous online groups have been started up to let teens talk with each other either through instant messaging or e-mail about signs, symptoms, triggers, and treatments for the disease.

To find the group that your teen feels comfortable with, she can get suggestions from her friends who have asthma or use a search engine to find a group that focuses on teens.

Whatever method your teen uses, she should be reassured that asthma is not a condition meant to slow her down: As she takes charge of her asthma, she'll soon realize that she can confidently move ahead with other parts of her life as well.

CHAPTER 13

Finding the
Right Provider

The foundation for your asthmatic child's medical care starts with your "team"—you, your child, and health care providers. But who should those providers be? Your family physician or your pediatrician? An asthma specialist? And how about nurse practitioners or respiratory therapists? Are these all providers who will take time to answer your questions and are they familiar with the latest developments in asthma? Your selection should not depend solely on the credentials but on the role you see that provider playing in managing your child's asthma—and in communicating clearly with you.

Forming the Team

Asthma-related visits by children to physician offices have more than doubled since the early 1990s—from less than forty visits per 1,000 children under age 18 in 1990 to eighty-nine visits per 1,000 in 2004, according to figures from the Centers for Disease Control and Prevention.

While part of this increase is related to the rise in the number of children with asthma, it also represents a change in how asthma management is viewed. Rather than just visiting a medical office when symptoms flare up, more families are taking time to monitor their children's asthma symptoms and find ways to prevent those symptoms from occurring through medication and lifestyle changes.

This means working more closely with a health care provider year round.

There are several types of health care providers who treat asthma that you may consider for your child:

- Family physicians or general practitioners who have a broad knowledge of a host of medical conditions and are knowledgeable about asthma since it is a common condition.
- Pediatricians who specialize in the care of infants and children and are very knowledgeable about asthma.
- Allergists/immunologists who treat the allergy symptoms related to asthma.
- Pulmonologists who specialize in treating people with lung diseases, including those with severe or poorly controlled asthma.

Also, look at those individuals working alongside those physicians who play very important roles in providing and enhancing the asthma care that your child receives. These include pediatric and family practice nurse practitioners, respiratory therapists, physician assistants, and patient educators who can provide critical help and information to you and your child to promote successful asthma self-management.

Who's Right for You?

Sometimes it might be easier to select the provider you've been seeing all along—for instance, your family physician or pediatrician—who may know you and your child's history. But while this provider may be excellent at treating your family members, you need to determine if the skills and demeanor are there to provide continuing care for an asthma patient. Some of the areas you also may want consider when evaluating a health care provider include:

- Has she discussed developing a treatment plan or asthma action plan for your child—and reviewed the details?
- Does she discuss possible allergens, irritants, or other medical conditions (such as gastroesophageal reflux disease, food allergies, or vocal cord dysfunction) that could cause your child's symptoms?
- Does she explain what can happen to your child physically during an asthma attack, why the prescribed medications were selected, and when to seek emergency help?
- Does she encourage physical activity and participation in most sports activities? And, does she let you know what you can do to prevent or reduce symptoms related to exercise-induced asthma?
- Does she encourage you and your child to learn more about your asthma?
- Does she offer reading pamphlets, booklets, videos, or local support group contact information?
- Is the health care provider familiar with complementary and alternative therapies that you are interested in knowing more about? Could she recommend different providers?

The leading goal, though, should be does this health care provider emphasize prevention of asthma and what should be done every day to avoid an asthma attack? With careful treatment (and following a treatment plan that likely will evolve over time), many children with asthma—including yours—can achieve good asthma control.

The Therapeutic Relationship

Besides the right medications, an asthma health care provider should be able to keep your—and your child's—trust, and to promote what is called the therapeutic relationship. Both of you should feel comfortable when speaking to the health care provider, and he in turn must be sincere and honest with you—telling you the ups and downs of the medications being used and what the future holds for your child.

Establishing this type of relationship—where doubts or concerns can be expressed freely—helps set up a scenario where your child will strive for better understanding of his condition. This means avoiding situations that could trigger asthma attacks and being better able to deal with emergencies and severe asthma attacks without panic if they should occur.

 Essential

Take the time to choose the asthma health care provider that you believe is right for your child. Try to build a good relationship—where you and your child feel confident to ask for advice or even to complain if something seems to be ineffective or uncomfortable. Asthma is a very individual condition, and what works for one child may not always work for another.

If you see that you are not achieving results with this health care provider, do let him know. Hopefully, you will be able to work it out. But, if this falls short, then consider another health care provider. Remember, all team players need to work together.

Guidelines

Also, you should know if your child's health care provider is familiar with current guidelines that are designed to promote better asthma outcomes among patients of all ages.

Every five years, the National Institutes' of Health National Asthma Education and Prevention Program (NAEPP) releases new health care provider guidelines that are based on the latest research on monitoring and treating asthma. These guidelines are designed to help providers deliver care that promotes good asthma outcomes.

 **Fact**

> Shortly before the latest guidelines were released in 2007, a study showed that only 20 percent of children with persistent asthma had a level of control that was considered optimal. These findings were surprising because if the guidelines—which address medications, environmental triggers, and action plans—were followed, the children should have experienced few or no asthma symptoms, including asthma flare-ups, according to the study.

Researchers found several potential reasons for this low level of control, including children not using the daily medication consistently, exposure to environmental triggers such as secondhand tobacco smoke or allergens such as mold, or receiving little education about what to watch out for or what to do in the case of an asthma attack.

Using those guidelines, a health care provider can help your child work toward controlling his asthma by making sure he is taking his medications properly and flagging those trouble areas that could trigger asthma. The ultimate goal should be a better quality of life (with few asthma symptoms).

Role as Educator

Asthma can be a condition that continually varies for a number of reasons. While most days can be great for your child in terms of controlling her asthma, certain days may not. Stress, changing environmental conditions, or even forgetting medications can modify your child's asthma symptoms.

A health care provider, plus members of her team, should be able to act as educators—providing guidance to you ahead of time on what symptoms to look for and what to do. This can be listed on your child's asthma action plan that the health care provider should help develop. (Also see Chapter 2.) The health care provider (along with colleagues or support staff) should also be available to answer questions and provide guidance and treatment if an emergency arises.

It is also helpful if the health care provider can speak to the child in terms that she'll understand about her lungs and airways, medicines, and peak flows. Asthma symptoms can be scary, but it can be reassuring for the child's provider to explain what asthma is and how it can be prevented.

When Is a Specialist Needed?

In many instances, most primary care health care providers can treat mild or moderate asthma cases efficiently. However, sometimes a child's asthma may be harder to treat. Because of his asthma, a child may not be resting well at night, exercise or sports may be difficult, or numerous trips are being made to the health care provider's office or hospital emergency room.

It then may be time to bring in a specialist such as the allergist/immunologist who is trained to diagnose and treat asthma when an allergic component is suspected. Pulmonologists may be called in when an asthmatic has a co-existing condition such as bronchitis.

Coordinated Care

Choosing a specialist does not have to mean leaving a primary care health care provider. Oftentimes, care can be coordinated between the two health care providers. After the initial visit, a child usually will only have to be seen by the specialist about once or twice a year.

The partnership between the specialist and primary care provider can vary. Sometimes the primary care provider can be the point person who creates an asthma action plan, and works with the specialist to coordinate care. Other times, the specialist can take the lead and relay information on the patient's progress back to the primary care provider.

Guidelines for Specialty Referral

The NAEPP guidelines suggest that a referral to a specialist may be appropriate if a child:

- Has had a life-threatening asthma attack.
- Is not meeting the goals of asthma therapy after three to six months of treatment.
- Shows signs and symptoms that do not appear typical for asthma, or the diagnosis for asthma is not certain.
- Has other conditions that complicate asthma or its diagnosis such as sinusitis, nasal polyps, aspergillosis, severe hay fever, vocal cord dysfunction, or gastroesophageal reflux disease.
- Needs additional diagnostic testing such as allergy skin testing, rhinoscopy, complete pulmonary function studies, or bronchoscopy.
- Requires additional education and guidance on complications related to asthma and its symptoms.
- Has severe asthma requiring continuous oral corticosteroid (prednisone) therapy or high-dose inhaled corticosteroids.
- Has required more than two bursts of oral corticosteroids in one year.
- Is under the age of three and needs daily anti-inflammatory medications.

In addition, children with significant psychiatric, psychosocial, or family problems that interfere with their asthma therapy may need referral to an appropriate mental health professional for counseling or treatment, the guidelines suggest. These characteristics have been shown to interfere with a patient's ability to adhere to treatment.

Advance Visit Preparation

Since the health care provider visit usually may only last minutes in a busy practice, get the most out of your time with your child there. A little preparation can reduce the frustration you might feel if you forget to mention something.

Essential

Before the visit, write down a list of things you need to tell the health care provider—specifically noting any concerns or questions you may have about your child's treatment or medication. If this is an initial visit, write down the names of dosages of any prescription medications. Also, write down any over-the-counter medications, along with supplements, that your child may be taking.

If you are not clear about what the health care provider said, ask him to repeat it for clarification. If it helps, repeat back in turn what your health care provider has told you and ask if you've got it correct. You can also ask for reading materials, Web sites, or brochures on asthma or other topics that were addressed during the visit.

Keeping Up-to-Date

For a productive and helpful visit to your child's health care provider, remember to bring along a few items. This includes a copy of your child's asthma diary—if you or your child has been keeping one.

A diary, which can consist of notebook pages, jottings in a calendar book, or even a computer spreadsheet, can help you and your health care provider see trends in terms of asthma symptoms. (Also see Chapter 10.) These trends can help indicate, over a period of weeks or months, how your child has been controlling his asthma and what possible triggers he may have encountered.

It also may indicate a need for adjustment to his asthma action plan or a visit to his health care provider—and possibly a specialist —to get his asthma under control.

Some of the signs of trouble are:

- **Inhaler use.** If your child is using his quick-relief "rescue" inhaler more than twice a week, his asthma may not be under control. This may require a visit to the health care provider.
- **Sleep quality.** If your child awakens more than once a week due to asthma or can't go to sleep because of asthma symptoms, he is showing poor control under current asthma guidelines.
- **Daytime quality of life.** If your child is experiencing asthma symptoms in the daytime at least once every day, this also means your child's asthma is not in control.
- **Peak flow.** If your child's peak flow is less than 80 percent of his personal best score (the caution zone on his asthma action plan), or if it changes significantly from day to day, his asthma is not under control.

Don't wait for multiple trouble signs to appear. One by itself should be enough to alert your health care provider.

Communication 101

Health care providers often encounter the "doorknob syndrome" during patients' office visits. This occurs just when a patient is about to leave an exam room: She places her hand on a doorknob and mentions that she forgot to ask a question or was unclear about a detail. This could have happened to you. But, there are ways you can communicate more effectively with your provider about your child and her asthma during your visit—instead of just before you leave.

On a Different Wavelength

A survey conducted by the Asthma and Allergy Foundation of America (AAFA) found that asthma patients and mothers of children with asthma and their health care providers may not always "speak" the same language when it comes to discussing asthma control.

This means health care providers were interested in one set of goals, while patients or individuals with children were concerned about another. In the long run, this could lead to what AAFA called less than optimal disease management.

The survey found that health care providers and patients agreed that the most important factors describing asthma control included having few or no asthma symptoms, being able to continue with activities of daily life, not having to use inhalers frequently, and reducing the severity of asthma symptoms. The agreement, though, mostly stopped there.

Health care providers generally asked quantitative questions such as how many triggers a patient had or how often a patient used a fast-acting inhaler or rescue inhaler or experienced asthma symptoms.

Meanwhile, patients and parents were focused on how asthma symptoms could interfere with daily living. For instance, you might be concerned if your children could attend school on certain days or play a sport.

To bridge this gap, AAFA created a "conversational roadmap" that patients or parents of an asthmatic child could fill out when they visited a provider. Helping patients such as children volunteer more information about their asthma could help health care providers determine the best asthma management options for them, according to AAFA.

These questions could be used to expand the dialogue, for instance, by examining how a child's lifestyle has changed since the last visit (for instance, more or less stress, a new school, or a new pet) or if asthma is preventing a child from taking walks or cleaning house. (The questions are available at *www.aafa.org*.)

Problems with Medications

Another point that may be missing from a dialogue to achieve better asthma control is the use of medications. While health care providers say they are prescribing them, some children may not be using them for a variety of reasons.

For instance, in one study from Johns Hopkins University of children ages five to twelve, a third of caregivers or parents reported not getting an asthma controller medication for their children—even though most of the health care providers said they had been prescribed the medications during patient visits. Almost two-thirds of the children had persistent asthma.

The researchers attributed this underuse of controller medication to poor communication between health care providers and caregivers/parents about the severity of asthma symptoms, the prescribed regimen, or other medications that the patient is using.

In 2006, the Global Asthma Physician and Patient (GAPP) Survey reported results on the first-ever worldwide quantitative survey in regard to asthma attitudes and treatment practices among physicians and patients. The survey found a particular concern about medication side effects and how that could hinder their further use. One-third of those surveyed said they experienced short-term side effects such as hoarseness, fungal infections in their mouths, or sore throat.

 **Fact**

The Global Asthma Physician and Patient (GAPP) Survey found that key barriers to the best management of asthma—particularly the timely use of medications—were linked to communication.

About 19 percent of the patients said that they were not aware of the short-term effects, although only 5 percent of the physicians questioned thought that patients were unaware of those effects.

The patients' limited knowledge of side effects may be linked to a communication gap between themselves and physicians, the survey observed: 73 percent of patients who currently are on or have taken asthma medication in the past said they never discussed short-term effects with their physicians. However, 90 percent of physicians said they sometimes or always discussed short-term effects of medications.

If your child is reluctant to use a medication, find out why. If it's causing a side effect—such as a sore throat, a bad taste in his mouth, or an upset stomach—check with your health care provider to see if this is normal or if something else is needed.

Similarly, if the medication doesn't appear to be doing what you think it should for your child, find out why as well. A visit with your health care provider may reveal that the medication is not being used properly by your child or maybe another medication may be needed.

Get a Clear Understanding

While talking to your child's health care provider can be helpful, sometimes it can be intimidating and confusing—especially if the supporting written or verbal information is not clear to you or is written in a language with which you are not totally familiar.

Actually, this is a very common problem. According to the Partnership for Clear Health Communication, a coalition of patient, business, and medical groups, low health literacy—the ability to read, understand, and act on health care information—affects 90 million people in the United States.

This means that you might not be alone in trying to decipher what treatment and management techniques you will need to adopt to care for your child. Fortunately, a move is on in the medical community to improve these literacy levels, and make sure that all individuals understand what the medication is for and how it should be used.

**Fact**

> Reading ability was the strongest predictor of asthma knowledge: Nearly double the patients—89 percent versus 48 percent—who read below the third-grade level had poorer inhaler technique compared with patients reading at the high school level.

To improve understanding, the partnership recommended three questions (adapted here for parents with children) that individuals can ask at each medical appointment:

- What is my child's main problem?
- What do I need to do?
- Why is it important for me (and my child) to do this?

Keeping those three key points in mind may be able to promote better health care outcomes.

Follow-Up Visits

Along with patient self-monitoring, return visits to the health care provider for periodic asthma assessments should be made every one to six months. The frequency of the visit will depend on the asthma severity, with the first follow-up visit conducted within one month of the first visit.

Fact

> Return visits will help determine if any changes in severity or asthma symptoms have occurred, if a child's exposure to triggers has changed, and if use of devices such as peak flow meters or spacers need to be reviewed to see if they are being used correctly.

In addition to the physical exam, the other areas that should be reviewed are:

- The child's symptom history, which includes daytime and nighttime symptoms in the past two weeks and symptoms while exercising.
- Use of quick-relief medications in the past week and the past month.
- Need for oral steroids and understanding how often and how long they should be used.
- Any emergency or hospital care.
- Lung function readings, using either spirometry or a peak flow meter.
- Number of times your child's peak flow readings may have gone under 80 percent.
- Any problems related to using or taking medications.
- Assessment of how a child is using, for instance, a metered-dose inhaler or a peak flow meter.

And again, don't be afraid to ask questions if you're not sure about how your child's asthma is being treated. It's a lot of information to process, and your health care provider should make sure that you have a good understanding and that all your concerns are addressed.

CHAPTER 14

Insurance and Paying for Care

W hen you put them together, costs for physician visits, prescriptions, diagnostic tests, and sometimes hospital visits for an asthmatic child can add up. Today, both private and public health insurance can help to cushion those costs, but premiums, co-payments, and deductibles can still mean considerable expense. In addition, many children are falling through the cracks and not receiving coverage for their asthma—even though they might be eligible for public insurance. Health care coverage is an issue that will continue to drive the debate of how asthma can be best managed among all children.

The Costs of Asthma

Study after study has shown the importance of developing the asthma "team"—you, your child, your family, your primary care physician, a specialty nurse practitioner, a pulmonary specialist, or a respiratory therapist. The goals are to diagnose the severity of your child's asthma, monitor medication and device usage, draw up an asthma action plan, answer asthma-related questions, and provide assistance when emergencies arise.

It sounds simple enough. In reality, though, these goals are being met only part of the time. A large part of the reason is costs—being able to pay for care that promotes active asthma management and good long-term outcomes.

These shortcomings are illustrated by findings that indicate the types of medical settings in which individuals receive health care for asthma differ for those with private health insurance and those without health insurance, according to figures from the National Ambulatory Medical Care Survey of the Centers for Disease Control and Prevention (CDC).

 **Fact**

In 2003, approximately 30 percent of medical visits for asthma by those without health insurance occurred in emergency departments, compared with 6 percent of visits by those with private insurance. Asthma is a condition that can usually be managed well in collaboration with effective primary care and, if controlled, would result in fewer visits to the emergency department, the CDC noted.

In addition, the CDC said that in 2005, 3.8 million children—just over 5 percent of all children in the United States—had one asthma attack in the previous year. Broken down even further, two out of every three children with asthma had had an asthma attack in the previous twelve months.

According to many medical experts, most asthma attacks can be minimized with patient education, proper medication use, and avoidance of triggers. If your child was one of those who had an asthma attack, maybe it's time to see whether you're getting the most out of your health insurance plan or—if you don't have an insurer—how you could qualify for coverage for your child to help improve her outcomes with asthma.

If your child currently has no coverage, look closely at coverage by Medicaid and the State Children's Health Insurance Programs. In 2007, a study from the Urban Institute found that while more than 93 percent of low-income parents surveyed had heard of at least one of the programs, only 55 percent believed that their child was eligible for public coverage. In reality, these programs have the potential to cover almost all lower-income populations.

Comparing Commercial Health Plans

Health plans come in many forms such as health maintenance organizations, point-of-service plans, or even the newer consumer-driven health plans with high deductibles.

Perhaps you have obtained coverage from one of these plans through an employer or trade group. In selecting or joining a plan, you'll probably be interested in comparing with other plans how it provides services for children with asthma.

Regional Ratings for Asthma Care

The National Committee for Quality Assurance (NCQA), an independent organization that accredits health plans, began in 2005 to add comparative scores to its annual online "living with illness" reports to show how health plans help patients manage four select chronic conditions, including asthma.

The living with illness reports are viewed through a plan report card (available at *hprc.ncqa.org*). On the report card you design for your area, click on "more details" under a plan's "living with illness" category.

For asthma, plans are evaluated on the appropriate asthma medications given to enrolled members ages five to fifty-six with asthma. The health plans have bar graphs that indicate how they compare nationally and regionally with providing services in that asthma category.

The report cards themselves also have information on access to needed care, delivery of good customer service, review of qualified providers, and access to health plan activities that help people avoid illness.

State Ratings

Some states also have been doing their own ratings on how managed care plans do their jobs with chronic illnesses such as asthma. A Web site on health insurance plan quality ratings (*www.consumer healthratings.com*) provides access to various states' comparisons for providing asthma care.

For instance, California has an annual report card that ranks managed care organizations on making sure that "adults and children with asthma get the right medicine and know when and how to take their medicine" (*www.opa.ca.gov/report_card*).

If your state is not listed, you might be able to access its health insurance site by going through the National Association of Insurance Commissioners Web site (*www.naic.org*).

The Plan for You

While comparing plans is a start, you still need to evaluate if a commercial plan can provide quality asthma care for your child. If you are in a position in which you have several options from which to choose, keep in mind various points:

- What are the co-pays associated with office, medication, and hospital visits?
- Is there a substantial financial penalty for using out-of-network physicians?
- Are providers accessible off-hours or is e-mail access to providers promoted by the plan?
- Can you access your child's patient health records online?
- Do referrals to an asthma specialist need to come from a primary care physician?
- Are prescriptions included with the plan, and are the medications your child uses listed on the plan's formulary (the list of drugs for which a plan will pay)?
- Are devices used for asthma covered—either under prescriptions or under durable medical equipment?

- Is a structure in place to easily handle disagreements or complaints?

One key area to examine is if the plan has some type of disease management program that can offer education and information for your child and even your family. In particular, these programs monitor trends (such as multiple emergency room visits or constant refills of quick-relief medications) that could indicate poor control of asthma symptoms. Some programs offer interactive assistance—sometimes through telephone or computer—to monitor symptoms or medication use, for instance, to evaluate whether your child's asthma is being controlled.

Preexisting Condition Limit

A preexisting condition limit refers to a plan limiting payment for a specified time for a medical condition if it is present when you sign up with the plan. A few individual and small group plans have this regulation, which could be a problem for individuals with asthma. However, if you change plans that are sponsored by employers, the rule usually won't apply for those employers that have at least fifty workers.

Medical Emergencies

It is helpful to find out what your insurers' policies are when you are traveling. If you think your child's life might be endangered because of an emergency or if he might incur permanent damage because of his asthma, you'll be encouraged to seek the closest medical treatment. In most instances, your insurer should pay for this care.

If your child's condition is less serious—and he is enrolled in a managed care plan—you will need to call the plan's "pre-authorization" phone number listed on your insurance card for further directions regarding his asthma in order to receive coverage.

Medicaid

Medicaid is a state-administered program that receives federal funding and covers more than 55 million Americans. Each state sets its own guidelines regarding eligibility and services.

Medicaid does not pay money to those who are insured; instead, it sends payments directly to the health care providers. Depending on the state's rules, you could be asked to pay a small part of the cost (co-payment) for some medical services. Eligibility for a child is based on the child's status—and not the parent's.

 **Fact**

While Medicaid has been framed as a program for the poor, not all low-income individuals are eligible for the program under current laws. Other requirements must be met including age (children must be under the age of nineteen years); disability; income and resources; and legal status as a citizen or a lawfully admitted immigrant.

The one fact that is true for all the fifty-one Medicaid programs across the country is that they are different from one another in everything from scope of service to eligibility. This makes it difficult to determine if children with asthma are getting the continuing care they need in each state to manage their asthma.

Changes could be ahead for families with an asthmatic child as states begin to recast their Medicaid programs and change the way they provide care. Many appear to be looking at adopting more disease management strategies and promoting better compliance with current preventive practices and treatment guidelines. But, this could also create more state programs that are even more variable than before.

State Children's Health Insurance Program

Since 1997, the national program known as the State Children's Health Insurance Program (SCHIP) has provided health insurance to low-income children and teenagers who do not have private health insurance coverage and are not eligible for Medicaid. SCHIP is jointly financed by federal and state governments, and each state administers its own program.

As of September 30, 1999, each state and all territories had an approved SCHIP plan in place. SCHIP has been considered the single largest expansion of health insurance coverage for children since the initiation of Medicaid in the mid-1960s. Several states cover entire families.

Alert!

SCHIP is designed to provide coverage to "targeted low-income children"—or those who live in a family with income less than 200 percent of the federal poverty level (FPL) or whose family has an income 50 percent higher than a state's Medicaid eligibility threshold. Some states have expanded SCHIP eligibility over the years beyond the 200 percent FPL.

SCHIP gives states three options when designing their programs. The states can: use SCHIP funds to expand Medicaid eligibility to children who previously did not qualify for the program; design a children's health insurance program entirely separate from Medicaid; or combine both the Medicaid and separate program options.

Eligibility and Cost Sharing

Eligibility for SCHIP is targeted toward uninsured low-income children. However, certain groups of children cannot be covered under SCHIP. Those ineligible include: children who are covered under a group health plan or under health insurance coverage; children who are members of a family that is eligible for state employee insurance based on employment with a public agency; children who are residing in an institution for mental diseases; or children who are eligible for Medicaid coverage.

A child can remain in a state program as long as she qualifies. While no limit is placed on the amount of time a child can remain in the program, she will need to renew her coverage periodically—about every six to twelve months. As long as the child continues to meet the eligibility criteria established by her state, she can remain in the program.

States can require individuals who are enrolled in SCHIP to pay some costs. However, they may not charge cost sharing for preventive services or immunizations or impose cost sharing that exceeds 5 percent of a family's gross or net income.

For little or no cost, this insurance under SCHIP pays for: physician visits, immunizations, prescription medicines, hospitalizations, and emergency room visits. The states have different eligibility rules, but in most states, uninsured children 18 years old and younger whose families earn up to $41,399 a year (in 2007) for a family of four are eligible.

For contact information for each state or to learn about eligibility requirements, see the state section at the site *www.insurekids now.gov* or call 1-877-543-7669 and ask to be directed to your state's program.

Patient Assistance Programs

Patient assistance programs are programs set up by drug manufacturers that offer free or low-cost prescription drugs—both brand name and generic—to individuals who are unable to pay for their medication.

Alert!

Patient assistance programs have also been called indigent drug programs, charitable drug programs, or medication assistance programs. Many popular and often prescribed drugs—including many asthma medications with which you may be familiar—may be found in these programs.

All of the major drug companies have their own patient assistance programs, but they may have different eligibility and application requirements.

How They Work

Eligibility will vary by program. Generally, individuals must be in families that have incomes up to 200 percent of the federal poverty level. For a family of two in 2007, an income below $27,380 meets 100 percent federal poverty guidelines. When calculating 200 percent of federal poverty guidelines, this would indicate an income of $54,760 for a family of four. The individual cannot have prescription coverage from any public or private source and must be a resident or citizen of the United States. Some companies may require that a patient have no health insurance at all.

Information on medication available through the various patient assistance programs and applications for the programs are found at *www.rxassist.org*. RxAssist is a pharmaceutical access information center created by Volunteers in Health Care, a national resource center for safety net organizations that operates out of the Brown University Center for Primary Care and Prevention in Pawtucket, RI.

On the applications, the programs will ask about prescription coverage, eligibility for public insurance programs, and income and asset information. They also may ask for: proof of income, such as federal income tax statements or pay stubs; Medicaid or insurance denial letters; a prescription from a physician; and patient consent forms that are included with the application.

Most applications will require the signature of the physician, the patient, or both.

Special Assistance for Children

To help you wade through the vast information on public and private assistance programs available to help children in need, a Web site (*www.kids.pparx.org*) and phone number (1-888-477-2669) have been set up by the Partnership for Prescription Assistance. The partnership, which includes the YMCA, Easter Seals, and the Pharmaceutical Research and Manufacturers of America, established the site so parents and others could access more than 475 public and private patient assistance programs—many of which provide medicines for free or very little cost.

While children may be eligible for many of them, forty programs are available that specifically address children's needs. The children's Partnership for Prescription Assistance will work to connect qualified, low-income children and their families with discount prescription drugs—direct from the pharmaceutical manufacturer.

Buying at Discount

If you are considering purchasing asthma medications and even devices online for your child to save money, the federal Food and Drug Administration has compiled suggestions of what to look for—and what to be wary of—at *www.fda.gov/buyonlineguide*. Among the suggestions are:

- Use only medicine that has been prescribed by your doctor or another trusted professional who is licensed in the United States to write prescriptions for medicine.
- Make sure a Web site is a state-licensed pharmacy that is located in the United States. Find a list of state boards of

pharmacy on the National Association of Boards of Pharmacy Web site at *www.nabp.info*.

- Make sure the Web site has a licensed pharmacist to answer your questions.

And most important, don't buy from sites that offer to prescribe a prescription drug for the first time without a physical exam, sell prescription drugs without prescriptions, or sell drugs not approved by the Food and Drug Administration.

These drugs may be counterfeit or "copycat" medicines, may be too strong or too weak, have dangerous ingredients, have expired dates, have not been checked for safety and effectiveness, or are not safe to use with other medicine or products that your child uses.

CHAPTER 15

On the Home Front

H ome may be where the heart is, but it is also where your child's asthma attacks could be triggered. Dust mites, cockroaches, pollens, animal dander, and molds may sound like something from a horror movie, but the truth is they are found in all homes—even yours. This certainly doesn't mean you're a poor housekeeper. But, there are steps you can consider to get many of these microscopic organisms and other asthma-provoking allergens out of your house—and away from your child.

Keep Your Home Free of Allergens

Tiny organisms and particles that can trigger asthma symptoms are found everywhere. While you'll never be able to totally eradicate them, you can find ways to substantially decrease their numbers within each room of your home.

But before you take aim, check with your child's health care provider to see exactly what triggers might be causing his asthma symptoms. These should be included on your child's asthma action plan completed by his health care provider.

Eradicating these allergens, though, will involve some tough decisions—such as whether to ban a pet from a room or a house. It may mean replacing carpeting, draperies, and upholstered furniture with materials and fabrics that are easier to clean and maintain. Or, it may mean changing the way items such as toys, clothes, or shoes are stored and maintained, or looking at how the air is cleaned and humidified in your house.

These are issues that you and your child will need to discuss so you can come to an understanding of what the culprits are—and how they should be addressed. It also will take multiple efforts throughout your home—generally on a room-by-room basis—to get effective results. Not all results will be seen immediately; for example, it can take weeks to months for pet dander to be minimized in a house despite your best efforts.

A Multifaceted Approach

While taking one step—for instance, eradicating the presence of dust mites in your child's bedroom—can be helpful, research has shown that multiple steps throughout a home can have an even stronger impact.

Removing various allergens from the home was found to be effective in reducing symptoms among children (ages five to eleven years) with moderate to severe asthma—specifically if a multipronged approach was used, according to a 2004 study from the National Institutes of Health (NIH). The study examined the children's sensitivity to certain indoor allergens and evidence of exposures at home to known asthma triggers, including tobacco smoke, dust mites, cockroaches, pets, rodents, and mold.

The study focused on educating the families, who lived in seven inner-city areas, about how to reduce all allergens to which a child was found to be sensitive. The families were assisted with other measures such as using allergen-impermeable covers for their children's bedding and air purifiers with HEPA (high-efficiency particulate air) filters in key locations within their homes, including the children's bedrooms. Cockroach extermination home visits also were provided for those allergic to cockroach allergens.

The greater the drop in household cockroach or dust mite allergen levels, the greater the reduction in asthma symptoms—suggesting that the allergy-reducing measures can make a difference, the researchers said. Also, the benefits of the home intervention occurred quickly: The researchers found a significant drop in symptoms just two months after the study began.

The researchers also noted that earlier studies that focused on controlling a single allergen or tobacco smoke met with limited success. Since many children with asthma are usually sensitive to more than one allergen, taking a multifaceted, home-based approach showed promising results that families can achieve by using recommended practices of allergen reduction every day.

 **Fact**

Children in the group in which educational/preventive measures were used to reduce multiple household allergens were found to have far fewer asthma symptoms compared with a control group: an average of twenty-one fewer days of asthma symptoms in the first year and an average of sixteen fewer days during the follow-up year.

Taking Aim at Triggers

These allergens can be found just about everywhere in your home. And, while you can't see them with the naked eye, they are there—often hidden in the dust. The National Institute of Environmental Health Sciences (NIEHS), a part of NIH, describes house dust as a "component of who you are"—not just dirt but "a mixture of potentially allergenic materials," such as: fibers, food particles, mold spores, pollens, dust mites, plant and insect parts, hair, animal fur and feathers, dried saliva and urine from pets, and flakes of human and animal skin.

The allergens most likely to be considered asthma triggers within that dust come from:

- Cockroaches, which are considered to have the greatest impact on childhood asthma in many American cities. Cockroach allergens appear to come from several sources such as saliva, fecal material, secretions, shed skins, and dead bodies.
- Dust mites, or more specifically, the feces of dust mites, which are microscopic relatives of the spider and live on mattresses, bedding, upholstered furniture, carpets, and curtains. These tiny creatures feed on the flakes of skin that people and pets shed daily and they thrive in warm and humid environments.
- Pets and animals, which have allergens that are actually proteins secreted by oil glands and shed as dander, proteins in saliva that may stick to fur when animals lick themselves, and aerosolized urine from rodents and guinea pigs.
- Molds, which produce tiny spores and can be found almost anywhere.
- Endotoxins, which are chemicals produced by bacteria.

And beyond the dust are triggers in the air that also could make your child's asthma worse such as secondhand smoke from cigarettes, cigars, and pipes; wood smoke or particulate matter that gets in the air from fireplace or woodstove use; nitrogen dioxide, an odorless gas from improperly vented fuel-burning appliances that can irritate eyes, noses, and throats and may cause shortness of breath; and chemical irritants that are found in some products in your home such as cleaners, paints, adhesives, pesticides, cosmetics, or air fresheners.

Asthma Control in the Bedroom

Your child's bedroom may be her haven—her escape from everyday pressures related to school, peers, and just growing up. But it also is a retreat for tiny organisms, dust particles, or mold she cannot see.

But you and she should pay attention to them because they may be triggering her asthma—and they are all around her.

Allergens can hide just about anywhere in her room—in her comfortable pillow, on her favorite stuffed teddy bear, in her clothes drawers, and even in her rug. They also can be found in the shoes in the corner she wore to school this morning and or the damp sweatshirt thrown next to her bed that she wore when she rode her bike this afternoon.

Therefore, according to recent studies, attention to allergen control in the bedroom—in consideration of the large amount of uninterrupted time spent there—could significantly reduce important allergen concentrations and therefore improve asthma control.

 **Essential**

Making your child's bedroom hostile to asthma triggers but comfortable for her means starting out with the four cleaning C's: cleaning up clutter, cleaning out carpeting, cleaning out closets, and—most importantly—cleaning completely.

Clean It Up and Move It Out

Getting your child's room in shape may take some preparation. Guidelines created by the National Institute of Allergy and Infectious Diseases suggest that a starting point is cleaning the child's bedroom completely—"just as if you were moving."

This includes emptying and cleaning all closets and storing contents, if possible, in a location elsewhere while the room is cleaned. Also recommended is placing clothing in zippered plastic bags, plus moving shoes off the floor and into boxes—if they cannot be moved elsewhere.

 **Fact**

> If possible, remove carpeting and underlying padding in the room since they make dust control difficult by capturing and trapping dust and particles. If carpeting or upholstered furniture are to remain, vacuum and/or steam-clean them thoroughly. If not thoroughly dried, however, mold may develop.

If wooden, laminate, linoleum, or tile floors are used in the bedroom, clean weekly and scrub the surfaces thoroughly to remove all traces of dust. Wipe these hard surfaces with water, wax, or oil, and cement any linoleum or tiles to the floor.

Consider using flat shades that pull up and down—rather than blinds or interior shutters—to reduce spaces where dusts and allergens can accumulate. If curtains are used, make sure they are cotton or synthetic, and can be laundered easily and often. Keep doors and windows closed after cleaning the room until your child is ready to use it.

Maintaining the Clean

It may not be the easiest job in the world, but once your child's room is cleaned, it will need to remain that way. Depending on your child's reaction to the triggers, you will have to decide who will be responsible for follow-up cleaning and dusting—you or him.

Cleaning can be done wearing a dust mask that covers the nose and mouth and gloves. Also, remember to stay out of the freshly vacuumed area for at least twenty minutes to allow any dust and allergens to settle after vacuuming or cleaning the floor.

 **Fact**

No food should be eaten in the bedroom. Recent studies have found that if food leftovers were present in the bedroom, higher levels of cockroach allergen were present in the bedroom dust samples.

The floors, furniture, tops of doors, window frames, and sills should be wiped with a damp cloth, a special dust-catching cloth, or an oil mop that holds onto the dust. Avoid using a plain dry cloth since that will throw more dust back into the air.

Carefully vacuum any carpeting or upholstered furniture that remains in the room while cleaning the room thoroughly and completely at least once a week.

Also, consider washing the curtains (if they remain) often in hot water (at 130 degrees Fahrenheit), and air out the room completely. And, designate a new hamper site outside his room for damp and dirty clothes; these items—if carelessly tossed aside after play or stuffed back in drawers—can become a home for mold and mites in drawers and other dark places. The same goes for shoes: find separate storage or boxes to keep them in—rather than just under his bed or on the floor.

Beds and Bedding

Depending on the age of your child, she could spend anywhere from 30 to 40 percent of her life in her bed. Accompanying her in that bed could be unwanted critters such as dust mites, which could be one of her asthma triggers.

NIEHS researchers found that in a study of indoor dust in homes of seventy-five areas across the country, 45 percent of the U.S. housing stock (about 44 million homes) had bedding with dust mite allergen concentrations that exceeded 2 micrograms per gram of dust, a level associated with the allergy development. Of those homes, over

23 percent (about 22 million dwellings), were estimated to have bedding with dust mite allergen concentrations that exceed 10 micrograms per gram of dust, a level associated with the trigger of asthma symptoms in asthmatics who are allergic to dust mites.

But, there are ways you can keep these mites and other unwanted microscopic visitors away. First, consider shielding bedding by using special mite-proof mattress, box spring, and pillow covers. Also consider:

- Putting electrical or duct tape over the covers' zippers.
- Washing bed sheets at least once a week in water heated to 130 degrees Fahrenheit to kill dust mites and their eggs; for white fabrics, consider using bleach when washing. Also, avoid fuzzy wool blankets or feather- or wool-stuffed comforters and mattress pads; instead, use cotton or synthetic blankets and covers that can be easily laundered.
- Making sure that pillows are made of materials such as Dacron or other synthetic fiber; don't use foam, feather, or "down" pillows. Consider washing your child's pillows about once a month, and replacing mattresses every ten years and pillows every five years.
- Keeping only one bed in the bedroom: If two beds have to be in the same room, prepare each bed in the same manner as the bed for the child with asthma.

If your asthmatic child sleeps in a bunk bed, she should sleep in the top bunk. The beds themselves should have wooden or metal frames. And don't use furniture—such antique or old dressers or chairs—that had have been stored in attics or basements.

Asthma Control Throughout the House

Allergens that can trigger asthma symptoms can be found throughout your house—and not just your child's bedroom. To asthma-proof your home, keep in mind a number of actions you can take room by room.

In the Living or Family Room

The room where your family comes together—to play with toys, watch television, play video games, read, or just hang out—can mean lots of fun and relaxation. It can also mean danger and worry in terms of the allergens found there that can trigger asthma symptoms.

Dust mites can make their homes here—as well as in bedrooms—by laying their eggs in the upholstery, along with their droppings and sheddings that can cause asthma symptoms. In addition, mold can be found on the upholstered furniture, as well as on curtains, drapes, and carpeting.

And, since the living area is frequently the site of snacks, the crumbs and morsels left behind on floors and furniture may become meals as well for cockroaches.

 Essential

To keep insects and other organisms out of your living space—and out of your lives, consider taking steps such as using easy-to-clean flooring, including wood, laminates, or tiles, and avoiding carpeting where moisture can get trapped and assist mold in growing.

Once a week, vacuum furniture and curtains or drapes if you're not using blinds and other easy-to-clean window treatments. Also, consider using washable slip covers and cushions that can be laundered in 130°F hot water weekly.

Using tannic acid or benzyl benzoate on carpets can remove some dust mite residue, but these chemicals must be applied repeatedly to be effective.

If you have potted plants in your living or family rooms—or any other room of your house—you may want to find a new home for them to help contain mold. For those you keep, consider spreading aquarium gravel over the dirt to stop that mold.

Asthma Control in Kitchens

One of the big culprits in the kitchen are cockroaches whose droppings and sheddings can trigger an allergic asthma attack. Also, molds and odors can invade kitchens—causing problems for your asthmatic child.

In the war on cockroaches, remember to never let food or trash remained uncovered in the kitchen. This means storing food (including pet food) in airtight containers inside or outside of the refrigerator. Use a covered trashcan or sealed trash bags to keep the cockroaches out as well.

After cooking, wipe the stovetop to remove food particles, and immediately clean crumbs and spilled food from floors, tabletops, and countertops after food preparation and meals. Also, wash dishes immediately after eating, rather than letting them accumulate in the sink. Clean the faucets and sink to remove any mold and food debris.

Alert!

If necessary, use poison baits, boric acid, and insect traps to kill cockroaches in the kitchen area. This is because some liquid or spray pesticides possibly could aggravate the symptoms of the asthmatic child if they are used.

Periodically check under the kitchen sink, the dishwasher, and the refrigerator for plumbing leaks that could create mold. In the refrigerator, remove excess moisture inside as well to prevent mold growth, and occasionally check—and replace if necessary—moldy rubber seals around the door. Also, check through and discard any moldy food in the refrigerator.

For cooking odors, consider installing and using an exhaust fan over the stove and oven to remove cooking fumes and reduce moisture. Oftentimes, many stovetop hoods only filter cooking particulates without venting outside.

Asthma Control in Bathrooms

Warm, humid bathrooms and cold, dank basements are the perfect breeding ground for several asthma triggers. In the bathroom, molds can appear in many places—under the sink, on the shower curtain, on the rubber bath mat, on towels, on bath tiles, or around the faucets.

In the bathroom, make sure you remove the mold as soon as you detect it. This means fixing any leaky pipes found under the sink, in the shower or tub, or around the toilet, and cleaning sink, tub, and toilet surfaces regularly. It also calls for laundering, at least weekly, bath towels, washcloths, floor mats, and tub/shower mats used by your child, along with those "guest towels" that hang by themselves in the bathroom.

If available, use a fan or vent (or a slightly opened window if not available) to keep the air continually circulating in the bathroom, while decreasing the amount of mold.

Asthma Control in Basements

Whether your basement has a recreation room, a laundry room, or a storage room, it's a favorite space for allergens. In the basement, dripping water pipes, leaky washing machines, or dusty corners could trigger attacks, too.

As in other rooms in the house, cockroaches could find a home where they leave their sheddings and droppings. Rodents, such as rats or mice, could also creep in, and mold grows in moist areas of the home, especially around beams and pipes, where it releases spores that could trigger allergic asthma symptoms.

To eliminate allergens from the basement, identify and repair leaks, seams, and cracks in the foundation that may let moisture seep in. Find ways to keep humidity down below 50 percent in the lower level by waterproofing the foundation or using dehumidifiers. If mold does appear, clean it promptly. Also, fix leaks in pipes, around the water heater, around washing machines, and central heating and cooling systems.

"Air" Conditioning

In your effort to combat indoor allergens, keep two other factors in mind: air filtration and indoor air humidity. With a growing number of cases of asthma in recent years occurring among children who spend much of their time inside, attention has been given to indoor air in preventing asthma symptoms.

 Essential

Just finding better ways to condition the air will not serve as a sole solution to eradicating asthma triggers in your home. Probably many sources of asthma symptoms—such as dust mites—are found in heavier concentrations, for example, in and on furniture, floors, carpets, and other furnishings.

In your quest to find the best way to condition air in your home, though, you will find that there is no one-size-fits-all answer. Depending where you live, many variables need to be taken into consideration: presence of pets, pollen counts, outdoor climates, household renovations, or even wood or cigarette smoke.

Cleaning the Air

Many products on the market—such as central air furnace filters and portable filtration systems—are geared at cleaning your home's air. But keep in mind that no federal standards exist spelling out the relationship between air filtration products and improvement of health symptoms. However, standards from manufacturers and manufacturing groups are available to guide you in determining if various products could help in your quest to have cleaner indoor air (see Chapter 16).

To maintain good air quality inside your home—and help your child breathe better—many low-cost or no-cost solutions are available for you. They are:

- Prohibit of any kind of smoking inside your home.
- Use air conditioning—in your home and even your car—on days when the pollen or mold counts are high or when ozone or pollution warnings are issued.
- When pollen counts are high, consider going outside—only if necessary—later in the morning because the counts are usually highest between 5 A.M. and 10 A.M.
- When air quality is poor for the day, consider opening doors and windows—if it is necessary—in the early morning hours before pollution has had a chance to build up.
- Avoid the presence of nitrogen dioxide (NO_2)—an odorless gas byproduct of fuel-burning appliances such as gas stoves, gas or oil fireplaces, wood stoves, and space heaters—by making sure they are all properly vented to the outside.
- Avoid using spray pesticides around the house.
- Use unscented or nonaerosol household cleaning products, while avoiding scented candles, powdered carpet cleaners, or room fresheners.
- Remember to change your central air and portable air filters regularly, following the manufacturers' directions.

Humidifying the Air

Data from the National Survey of Lead and Allergens in Housing indicates that the strongest independent predictor of dust mite allergen levels is indoor humidity. It found that homes with relative humidity above 60 percent have three to four times higher mean bed dust mite allergens than homes with relative humidity below 60 percent. This increased relative humidity also was associated with higher levels of cockroach and mold allergens in the home.

 **Fact**

For personal comfort and a healthier environment, the ideal relative humidity in your home should fall between 35 percent and 50 percent. Consider using a digital hygrometer, a simple device that can be purchased in hardware or other retail stores that measures indoor relative humidity, to determine the level throughout your home.

Generally, only use a humidifier in your home only when conditions require it—such as when the relative humidity drops below 35 percent and the air is very dry—such as during cold weather or in certain parts of the country such as the Southwest. This dry air could irritate your child's throat and airway linings. Remember to use the correct moisture setting for existing conditions and to clean any unit thoroughly

Pets and Problems

Detectable levels of dog and cat allergens are present in every home—even in those with no pets, according to a study from the NIEHS and the U.S. Department of Housing and Urban Development. Although allergen levels predictably were higher in homes with an indoor dog or cat, levels previously associated with triggering an allergic reaction were also common in homes without the pets.

Since dog and cat allergens can be transported on clothing, the researchers theorized that communities, particularly those in which dog or cat ownership is high, may be an important source of these pet allergens.

But when you and your family—like many millions of others—own a furry or feathered pet or two and it appears to be a trigger to your child's asthma, what should you do? A preventive strategy would be to remove your pets from your home if possible. If this cannot be done, make it a policy to keep pets confined to a specific area of the home not used often by the child and to keep pets completely out of your child's bedroom—especially his bed.

 **Question?**

Why should pets stay off your child's bed?
While your child may like to snuggle with a pet at night, he may not know that it not only brings in dander, but mold and pollen from outdoors. When materials such as dander settle on bed linens, a food source is developed for dust mites. All of these could be triggers for his asthma.

Also keep in mind that your child can wheeze and cough with and without your pet being present. While an animal may be out of sight, their allergens may not be because pet allergens are carried on very small particles. As a result, pet allergens can continue to circulate in the air and remain on carpets and furniture for weeks and months long after a pet is gone.

If you keep your pet in your home, consider confining it to certain rooms or areas. And, if possible, bathe pets weekly to reduce the amount of allergens.

Also, remind your child after playing with a pet to wash his hands and clean his clothes to remove pet allergens. Around rodent cages, he should wear gloves to avoid contact with soiled litter cages. And, of course, dust and vacuum around pet areas often.

Other Kid-Healthy Tips

Aside from cleaning and maintaining rooms in your home to keep your asthmatic child healthy, keep in mind several other areas that may be problematic.

Toys

Dust mites, mold, and pet dander accumulate in and on children's toys, especially when pets play with them, and can trigger allergic asthma symptoms.

 **Essential**

Encourage your child to play with washable toys made of wood, rubber, metal, or plastic. Store all toys in a closed toy box or chest. Consider reducing the number of stuffed toys your child has—keeping the washable toys—and sharply limiting those that she might want to bring to bed.

To keep them as mite-free and dust-free as possible, launder the stuffed animals weekly and dry them in a hot dryer. For unwashable stuffed toys, place them in the freezer in a plastic bag once a week for twenty-four hours to kill mites, and then shake them out.

To take the guessing game out of the task of how to clean and maintain your child's toys, the Asthma and Allergy Foundation of America and Allergy Standards Limited (ASL), a testing organization, established a program (*www.asthmafriendly.com*) in 2006 that tests and labels toys. Those approved toys, which are available at major retailers, come with unique registration codes and instructions to help parents keep them in "asthma friendly" condition.

Holiday Decor

Children love holidays, but sometimes the decorations you use might harbor some unexpected—and not completely welcomed— surprises for those with asthma and allergies.

First, if you carry items from dusty basements or attics or take them from garages and storage areas, you may be stirring up dust and molds. If decorations are dusty, consider taking them outside and wiping them off—before putting them up.

Some experts even recommend cleaning off artificial trees if used during the Christmas season to get rid of molds and dust from the branches. For those looking for real trees, consider Scotch pines and Douglas firs—which are usually found on most tree lots. But still be cautious: the trees' pine oils, strong smells, and pollens and molds may trigger asthma symptoms.

As for household decorations, lean more toward plastic, metal, and glass items, which are easier to clean and trap less dust than fabric decorations. If you do have fabric decorations, consider washing them, if possible.

New Habits, New Look

To eliminate triggers, your child may have to make some changes on the home front as well, such as:

- **Cutting clutter.** If it can collect dust, it can also collect dust mites. So, suggest to your child that she remove knick-knacks, trophies, books, magazines, and newspapers from her bedroom.
- **Eliminating wall hangings.** Encourage her not to put up pennants, pictures, photos, or other dust catchers on the walls of her room.

- **Storing books.** Most of your child's books should be stored in another room rather than on shelves in her bedroom or playroom.
- **Catching a few winks on her bed.** Encourage your child to take naps only on her bed—and not the couch in the family room.
- **Keeping a clean entrance.** Encourage your child to wipe her feet on a door rug when she enters your home and to hang up her coat outside of her room.
- **Find a place for laundry.** Encourage your child not to toss dirty clothing on her bed and in her drawers—but in a hamper or laundry bag for laundering.
- **Specify eating locations.** To cut down on visits by cockroaches, keep snacking and eating (and dirty dishes) confined to kitchen or dining areas—and clean up immediately afterward.

While making changes may seem difficult at first, practice will make them easier over time. But assure your child that the pay-off—better breathing, fewer medicines, and reduced asthma attacks—will prove to be worth her effort in the long run.

CHAPTER 16

Products to Use (or Not) in the Home

W ith more children diagnosed with asthma, more products have been appearing on the market that focus on eliminating allergens in your home. What do you really require to meet the needs of your child, and is it worth the extra money? The answers at times could seem confusing. But, armed with background knowledge, you can get a better idea of what will—or will not—work for your child, and how you can get the most out of what you already have. You may also be surprised to know that some products you think of as being helpful sometimes may be a hindrance in preventing asthma-related symptoms.

Household and Portable Room Filters

Whether air filters—used with any type of household heating, ventilating, and air conditioning system or as part of a portable room unit—are necessary tools in the arsenal against allergens in the home has been part of an extended debate among asthma and allergy experts. While allergens are found mostly in surface dust, questions have arisen as to whether removing those materials from the air in a home make any appreciable difference. But others have argued that any reduction in allergens in the home environment is a positive step forward for the asthmatic child—especially those homes with pets.

Using filters in the home may also have its benefits when opening windows at any time during the year is not an option. When the "fresh air" outside contains, for instance, pollens and molds, filtered indoor air could provide your child with relief from his asthma and allergy symptoms.

But getting the full benefit of filtered air requires some diligence on your part—including cleaning and maintenance of filters and air cleaning units—to make sure your child gets the full benefit from the products you do use. And, as the asthma and allergy experts advise, air filtering should not replace a thorough cleaning to remove allergens found in dust in your home.

Household Heating and Cooling System Filters

Your child's respiratory defense system, which includes her nose, sinuses, and windpipes, are designed to filter out particles she breathes that are about three to five microns in size (or about 5 to 7 percent the size of a human hair). However, surrounding her are even tinier particles—less than 1 micron in size—that make up to 99 percent of the particles flowing in the air through your home.

Breathing in these particles could pose problems for your asthmatic child—such as allergic reactions or asthma attacks. As part of a strategy to lower your home's particle count, air filters that work within your home's heating and cooling system may be considered.

 Essential

When selecting a filter (what is often called a "furnace filter") for a centralized heating and cooling forced air system, look for the minimum efficiency reporting value (MERV) rating, which measures a filter's ability to trap small particles.

These filters generally have a rating from one to twelve: The higher the MERV rating, the more efficient the filter is and the more particles (such as various allergens and mold spores) it can filter.

High-efficiency furnace filters with at least a MERV rating of ten or higher will be more efficient in capturing indoor pollutants.

Filter performance is influenced by the size and density of the material used, along with the size and volume of the particles being filtered. Generally, the more efficient the filter is at capturing small particles and allergens, the more expensive it is.

The types of filters available for forced air heating and cooling systems include:

- Less expensive panel filters that have a layer of fibers, which are often fiberglass, that are covered by a honeycomb-shaped grille. The primary function of these filters is to capture larger particles from the air and to protect the forced air system's fan, while decreasing the amount of dust on heating and cooling coils.
- Reusable filters, which are designed to be washed and reused, are generally less ineffective at capturing small particles.
- Pleated filters that are not electrostatically charged are made of a variety of materials and are somewhat more expensive—but more efficient—than fiberglass filters because the pleats provide a greater surface area to trap air contaminants.
- Electrostatically charged pleated filters are designed to assist in attracting and holding microscopic particles such as dust, pollen, mold, pet dander, and smoke.
- High Efficiency Particulate Air (HEPA) filters are designed to remove submicron particles (99.97 percent of all particles 0.3 microns in diameter or larger) with high efficiency. The filter, made of fine submicron glass fibers within a matrix of larger fibers, generally will not fit within forced air heating and air conditioning systems found in most homes. Instead, it will need a separate setup with a fan and filter.
- A step beyond using the furnace filters is a whole-house electronic air filtration system that attaches to—and is distributed through—your home's heating and cooling system. It requires professional installation. While it generally has a

high MERV rating, it is far more expensive than purchasing individual filters and could require frequent (for example, weekly to monthly) cleaning to maintain its effectiveness.

Whatever air filters you use to help protect against allergens, be extra diligent about keeping those filters clean. They need to be changed at regular intervals—from about once a month for the inexpensive models to about every two or three months for pleated varieties. Labels on the products should indicate time frames.

Alert!

Also take a periodic look at the air filter if your heating and cooling system experiences heavy seasonal use, you have a remodeling or construction project going on in your home, you have a smoker in your home, or you have a pet on the premises. More frequent filter changes will be required to compensate for the extra dust and residue in the air.

To remind yourself to change the filter, schedule those changes to coincide with other household activities, such as paying a monthly bill, or post a sticky note near the thermostat or on the outside of the heating and/or cooling unit—so you'll be less likely to forget.

Also, filters are available that can be cut to size and placed over room vents—such as those in your child's bedroom—to provide another layer of filtration. However, carefully follow manufacturer's directions on installation on selected vents so you don't accidentally strain your home's heating and/or cooling system.

Portable Air Filtration Devices

For filtering air just within a room or small section of a home, portable devices are available on the market—either as tabletop models or floor units. Since your child is likely to spend at least a third of his day in the bedroom, that would be a good location to keep it if you purchase the air filter.

The filters fall into several categories:

- HEPA filters, which are designed to remove 99.97 percent of airborne pollutants (including tobacco smoke, household dust, and pollen) 0.3 microns or larger from air that go through the filter.
- ULPA filters, which are ultra-HEPA filters that are designed to capture 99.999 percent of all airborne particles 0.3 microns or smaller that pass through the filter—including tobacco smoke, household dust, and pollen.
- Electronic air filters, such as electrostatic filters, which use a static charge on the filter that gets airborne particles to stick to it.
- Ion generators, which use electrical charges to take allergen particles out of the air. The ions stick to particles, causing them to attach to nearby surfaces, such as walls or floors, or to a filter with a magnetic-type attraction.
- Gas-phase filters, which cannot eliminate allergenic particles but remove odors and non-particulate pollution such as cooking gas, gases emitted by paint or building materials, or perfumes or fragrances.
- Hybrid filters, which contain two or more components of the particle-removing devices.

Another filtration device—ozone generators—have been marketed to clear the air of various particles. However, many consumer groups have opposed use of these types of devices because of the high amount of ozone they emit in the air—which could end up irritating an asthmatic child's lungs.

The other devices, such as electronic air filters and ion generators, for the most part do produce what is called an "ozone byproduct." This byproduct should be similar to what other household devices in your home—such as ceiling fans and hair dryers—produce. The level of ozone byproduct produced by most of these air filtration devices should be well within the range of current federal standards—if the products are properly installed, and kept continually clean and well maintained.

 **Fact**

No federal guidelines or standards have been published to indicate how well low- to medium-efficiency air cleaners—the usual types of models found in homes—actually work. However, standards have been developed by private standard-setting trade associations that can be used in comparing what various air cleaners deliver.

The Association of Home Appliance Manufacturers has created one rating system for air cleaners called the Clean Air Delivery Rates (CADR) (*www.cadr.org*). Three CADR numbers are usually found on the back of an air cleaner's box: one for tobacco smoke, one for pollen, and one for dust. The CADR indicates volume of filtered air delivered by an air cleaner. The higher the tobacco smoke, pollen, and dust numbers, the faster the unit filters the air.

To make sense of the CADR numbers, follow the two-thirds rule—using your room's area size. For instance, if you had a room that was 10 feet by 12 feet (or 120 square feet), you would want one with at least a dust CADR of 80. If your room size is smaller, the unit will clean the air more often or faster; if the room is larger, it will be less effective. If you have ceilings higher than 8 feet, you'd need an air cleaner rated for a larger room.

Another measurement, called the Air Changes Per Hour (ACH) rating, can let you know how frequently the air purifier exchanges all the air in a given room.

Also the Environmental Protection Agency (EPA) recommends that you consider other factors as well when considering the use of air cleaners in your home:

- Gases and odors from particles collected by the devices could be redispersed into the air.
- Some devices scent the air to mask odors, which may lead you to believe that the odor-causing pollutants have been removed.
- Ion generators, especially those that do not contain a collector, may cause soiling of walls and other surfaces.
- Noises from some portable air cleaners may be bothersome, even at low speeds.
- Maintenance costs, such as costs for the replacement of filters, could be significant, and should be considered with the initial cost of purchase.

Also like the filters used with a forced-air heating, cooling, and ventilation system, proper installation, use, care, and maintenance is necessary to ensure that you get the most benefit from the air cleaners. They should be placed away from a corner of a room, and at least a few feet away from the walls to support maximum air flow. This means frequent cleaning and filter replacement to ensure proper functioning.

Tobacco Smoke and Filters

If you smoke, will using filters cut down on the amount of secondhand smoke generated by smoking? According to various researchers, the most effective way to eradicate environmental tobacco smoke—or "secondhand" smoke—is to eliminate the main source of smoke: Persuade any smokers in your home to quit smoking.

Some air cleaners can help to reduce secondhand smoke to a limited degree. However, no household or portable air filtration systems can completely absorb secondhand smoke particulates. These invisible particles are of concern since they can be inhaled deeply into the lungs and could trigger asthmatic symptoms.

Air Duct Cleaning

The cleaning of air ducts in a heating, cooling, and ventilation system has been heavily marketed as a way for families like yours to help control a child's asthma. While research in this area is limited, asthma and allergy experts have pointed to other targets that should be considered first in lowering allergens in the home—particularly cleaning surfaces such as floors and furniture, while keeping humidity low to discourage mold and dust mites growth.

Duct cleaning generally refers to the cleaning of various heating and cooling system components of forced air systems, including the supply and return air ducts and registers, grilles and diffusers, heat exchangers, heating and cooling coils, fan motor, and the air handling unit housing.

 Essential

According to the EPA, pollutants that enter the home through both outdoor and indoor activities—such as cooking, cleaning, smoking, or just moving around—can cause greater exposure to contaminants than dirty air ducts. Overall, no evidence has been shown that a light amount of household dust or other particulate matter in air ducts poses any risk to your health, the EPA has noted.

Duct cleaning has not been shown to actually prevent health problems, nor have studies conclusively demonstrated that particle (e.g., dust) levels in homes rise because of dirty air ducts or go down after cleaning, the EPA said. This is because most of the dirt that accumulates inside air ducts adheres to duct surfaces and usually does not enter your home's living space.

Therefore, unless the ducts are infested with vermin, (e.g., rodents or insects) or clogged with excessive amounts of dust and debris (such as from pets or from a remodeling project) that are being released into your home from the registers, the EPA does not recommend that air ducts be cleaned, except on an as-needed basis, because of the continuing uncertainty about the benefits of duct cleaning.

The Right Humidity

Relative humidity is defined as the amount of water in the air relative to the amount of water in the air when it is saturated at a specific temperature. When that relative humidity moves past 50 percent in your home, dust mites and mold will thrive—possibly triggering asthma symptoms.

There are many sources of indoor humidity including water vapor coming in from the outside, which is usually the top source of humidity during hot weather. Then there is the air drawn through a home's crawl spaces or passed through soil and cracks in your home's substructure. Or, it might be caused by activities in your home—such as bathing, laundering, or cooking—or through evaporation of water that originates from leaks or condensation.

Dehumidifiers

Activities such as using vents in bathrooms and kitchens (see Chapter 15) or repairing leaking appliances or pipes can help lower household humidity. But many individuals also look at dehumidifiers to bring that humidity down, especially with lower floors or basement areas of homes.

Just remember, though, to change the dehumidifier's collector pan of water regularly—to avoid creating new sources for mold on floors or carpets.

Humidifiers

On the flip side, make sure your home is not too dry (below 35 percent relative humidity), which could cause discomfort for your asthmatic child in the form of a dry throat, nose, skin, and lips. In this case, you may want to consider a whole-house humidifier attached to your heating system or a portable room or console unit.

However, make sure you follow the manufacturer's guidelines carefully for use and continuous maintenance of the humidifier. If too much moisture is added to the air, the growth of biological organisms, including dust mites or mold, could be encouraged.

Recent studies by the EPA and the Consumer Product Safety Commission have shown that ultrasonic and impeller (or "cool mist") humidifiers can disperse microorganisms and minerals from their water tanks into indoor air. Two other portable humidifiers (evaporative and steam vaporizer) can allow for growth of microorganisms if they are equipped with a tank that holds standing water, but they generally disperse less, if any, of the pollutants into the air.

Both government agencies note, though, that only limited information currently is available on the growth and dispersal of microorganisms and minerals by home humidifiers.

 Essential

To avoid microorganism growth—and possible lung irritations among children susceptible to certain types of airborne pollutants—the EPA recommends that you strictly adhere to manufacturer recommendations regarding changing water and cleaning the humidifier. Also, be cautious about any spills on furniture or carpeting, which could generate more mold.

The EPA also recommends cleaning portable humidifiers every third day—emptying the tank and using a brush or other scrubber to clean it. In the absence of specific recommendations, cleaning is suggested for all humidifier surfaces that come in contact with water with a 3 percent solution of hydrogen peroxide.

When cleaning and maintaining console and forced-air (furnace-mounted) humidifiers, also carefully follow manufacturer directions. In particular, if a humidifier contains a tank, do not allow water to stand in the tank for extended periods of time, which could also cause a mold problem.

Vacuum Cleaners

One of the best ways to remove allergens from your home is vacuuming—from bare floors to carpeted floors to furniture. When it comes to your child with asthma, effective vacuuming can be a first line of defense.

Many new and effective—but sometimes higher-priced—vacuums are on the market today that can do a top job removing possible allergens from your home. But if some of those tools are out of your price range, there are steps you can take to make the best out of your current vacuuming system or a less expensive system.

Choose Your Model

When looking for a model that will help cut down on allergens, consider not only the efficiency of the filters used but also the machine design as well—machines that get deep down into carpeting. At the top of the line, vacuums with HEPA filters, generally found on upright vacuums, are certified to filter 98 percent of dust particles and have sealed construction that prevents dust and debris from returning to the air.

Other vacuums have similar but less expensive filter systems that work well in vacuuming dust and allergens while preventing them from leaking back into your house. Check publications such as *Consumer Reports* to compare prices and the efficiency of the models.

And, remember that most filters usually require cleaning or replacement on a periodic basis to enable the vacuums to perform at their best.

Bags or Bagless?

Another important factor to consider when using a vacuum is whether they have bags or are bagless. Sometimes with bagless models, you could end up accidentally throwing dust and allergens back into the air when you clean the vacuum.

When using bags, remember to fill the vacuum bags only half way up to ensure that you get the maximum suction power from your vacuum. By avoiding overfilling, you can help limit the amount of dust and debris that leaks out when your remove the bags. Also consider using double-thickness bags—instead of single-thickness bags—to cut down on dust emissions.

To avoid the bag and bagless debate, some families have chosen to use the central vacuum method that automatically cleans floors in a home through a central system. When using this system, the central vacuum bag is usually located outside of the house, such as in the garage, and is usually changed a few times a year.

Vacuum Effectively

To get the most out of vacuuming carpets—while removing allergens—resist the temptation to quickly run through this job. Instead, remember to vacuum slowly over an area several times to carefully draw out the dirt and debris.

For tiled or wooden floors, take several other precautions if you use a vacuum. First, remember to disconnect or shut off the beater brush because it could end up kicking the dust, dirt, and debris (and potential asthma triggers) back up into the air—where you don't want it. As an alternative, also consider using attachments that just suck up the dirt.

Many vacuums have special attachments and brushes designed particularly for cleaning furniture, including mattresses. Attachments are often included with vacuums to clean draperies and curtains as well. These attachments can also be useful in tackling the hidden parts of your home—under furniture, along baseboards, along hanging light fixtures and ceiling fans, on entrance rugs, and in corners.

Fact

Don't forget that dust and dirt are not only on the floor. A commonly overlooked area when vacuuming is upholstered furniture. While vacuuming can't totally eliminate house dust mites and other asthma triggers, it can lower their population.

Pesticides and Pest Repellants

Cockroaches are found everywhere—even in the cleanest of neighborhoods and homes. While there are many things you can do to eliminate cockroaches—ranging from sealing up food to immediately wiping up spills (see Chapter 15)—you sometimes want something stronger to make sure they stay away from your home. But chemical pesticide sprays on the market could end up irritating your child's lungs as well.

Essential

To address a pest problem, think "integrated pest management"—a strategy that requires a number of steps to achieve the goal of pest control using the least toxic alternatives. Cleaning up areas in your home is a start, followed by sealing up areas from which insects and other animals may be entering your home.

If pest problems continue after you have tried nontoxic alternatives, move up the ladder of toxicity starting with the least toxic alternatives. This can include using boric acid, a common, inexpensive household powder that becomes an insect stomach poison when ingested by household pests. Try using solid poison baits or traps before using pesticide sprays.

Also, silica gels and diatomaceous earth, which are found in hardware or retail stores, may be used. They ultimately dehydrate pests. But, remember to carefully follow directions—especially when used around children.

Also available in hardware and home supply stores are insect and rodent baits containing nonvolatile chemical pesticides made with essential oils, such as garlic, pepper extracts, and citrus oil, among others.

If all else fails, request professional pest specialists, including those with many major pest control companies, who practice the concept of integrated pest management.

Other Cleaning Products

While you may be working to remove dust, dirt, and allergens from your home that could trigger your child's asthma, you may also be unwittingly introducing household products that could be bothering your child's lungs as well.

Alert!

Some products, such as air fresheners, toilet bowl cleaners, mothballs, and other deodorizing products, may contain volatile organic compounds that may cause modest reductions in lung function, according to research from National Institute of Environmental Health Sciences.

Also, powdered carpet fresheners sometimes may trigger asthma and allergy symptoms—in addition to frequently clogging filters on vacuums, resulting in more frequent filter changes.

When shopping for cleaning products, keep a few thoughts in mind so you don't purchase a product that could hinder your efforts to keep a safe home environment for your asthmatic child:

- Read labels carefully before purchasing all household chemicals, along with beauty and health products.
- Avoid using air fragrance or deodorizer sprays, wicks, or other devices. To freshen the air, clean up the odor source and ventilate (such as running bathroom or kitchen exhaust fans).
- Avoid using household chemicals around children, pets, or food.
- Consider using simple cleaners (such as a 5 percent solution of bleach and a small amount of detergent) to clean things such as moldy surfaces in a shower or under a sink.

Also, just because a product is labeled "natural" does not mean that it is safe. Always read the label to make sure you know what you are getting and to minimize potential health risks.

Asthma-Friendly Products

To help take the guesswork out of selecting products that are appropriate for families with members who are asthmatic, the Asthma and Allergy Foundation of America and the Asthma Society of Canada have teamed up in separate programs with a product testing company to certify if various products are "asthma friendly."

For a range of products being introduced to the retail market—from mattress covers to toys, pillows, vacuums, paint, air filtration products, flooring, and window coverings—the company, Allergy Standards Ltd., uses scientific testing to determine if the products qualify for a label indicating it has been verified to be asthma friendly. The label also carries customized instructions on how to maintain the item in what is considered "a low-allergen state."

CHAPTER 17

When You're Away

Whether your child is going to camp, visiting grandparents, or enjoying a sleepover at a friend's house, getting away from home and school can be fun. But accompanying your child are possible challenges posed by her asthma. While she may feel fine before leaving home, a different environment with potentially new asthma triggers could mean trouble. To avoid unwanted surprises, take time to plan ahead. An ounce of prevention and preparation—in terms of good communication, up-to-date asthma action plans, and filled prescriptions—can mean a ton of fun later.

Visiting at a Friend's House

Your child probably doesn't want to be left out of many of the fun activities his friends are doing—play dates, birthday parties, or just hanging out. But a new or unfamiliar environment could hold some unforeseen problems that could trigger his asthma—spoiling what should have been an enjoyable time. A little planning ahead of time, though, might enable you to avoid this unpleasant scenario.

Open Communication

A successful visit can start with some communication. Alert your child's friends' parents or supervising adult about his asthma—using his asthma action plan.

The plan, developed with his health care provider, provides written instructions about monitoring asthma and includes the child's asthma triggers, names of medications, peak flow zones, warning signs of worsening asthma, handling an emergency, and how you could be reached. (See Chapter 2.)

Help answer any questions before the visit, such as how to administer medication, what to expect from the medicine, what symptoms may signal a problem, and what to do if your child does not improve after using his quick-relief medication.

 ## *Essential*

You also can do some fact-finding yourself: for instance, determine if there are pets (that your child may be allergic to) or if a smoker is on the premises. If this would be a problem for your child, you might have to suggest an alternative—such as a play date at your house or another activity in a location (such as the playground or the movies)—where those triggers could be avoided.

Consider pretreatment with a quick-acting medication before he goes to the friend's house—if you have concerns about some potential triggers. This pretreatment also should be spelled out in your child's asthma action plan.

A Sleepover

If it's a sleepover at a friend's house, the same rules apply with talking to a parent or adult coordinating the event. Make sure they know what to do if her symptoms (listed on her asthma action plan) emerge or an emergency occurs. Review with them how she uses her inhaler. And, let the person in charge know where you can be reached at any time.

But, you need to talk about critical issues, too, with your child such as when she can take her medications, and what she should do if she is having difficulty breathing.

Since no house is entirely dust-free, she may want to take precautions such a placing a mat on the floor beneath his sleeping bag or maybe avoiding the inevitable pillow fight or jumping on the couch that could release clouds of dust.

In the Good Old Summertime

When school lets out for the year, it may be no more teachers and no more books. But, your child may run into trouble with his asthma if he fails to adjust or follow his routine schedule used for managing his asthma. Often with vacations, camp, swimming pool time, and other leisure activities, regular use of his medications and monitoring of his symptoms may fall by the wayside—setting the stage for problems with his asthma.

Alert!

At the beginning of summer, you and your child should make up a new schedule that will ensure she gets her asthma medication in a timely fashion every day and that she carefully monitors her symptoms.

This new summertime schedule should include both time at home and away during the summer months. Different time cues should be set up—perhaps at breakfast or bedtime—to help your child to remember to use medication or his peak flow monitor.

Off to Camp

Summer camp—both day and sleep-away—can have many wonderful things: swimming, boating, hiking, and, of course, roasting marshmallows. But it can have other things, too, in terms of asthma triggers such as molds, dust mites, animal dander, and pollens that aren't so fun.

While many parents think they are preparing their asthmatic child for a safe camp experience by sending along a bag of medications, they still may fall short in alerting camp staff about her asthma, what special precautions should be taken, and what to do in case there is an asthma emergency.

Alert!

Sometimes, parents may think that checking off "asthma" on the camp medical release form may be enough. But an asthma action plan is needed here to help manage and control the child's asthma during the camp stay. This should be on file with the camp nurse, and made available to camp counselors working with your child.

Having an asthma action plan on file with the camp becomes particularly important for children whose asthma occurs and worsens after exercise and vigorous activities. In this case, pretreatment with a quick-acting bronchodilator and warm-up exercises are important steps in preventing exercise-induced asthma symptoms.

In regard to inhalers, parents should check with the camp administrator on the camp's policy of permitting children to keep their quick-relief medication with them at all times. Also, check on the distance of the nearest emergency room or emergency services—just in case.

While many children with asthma enjoy going to camp with old and new friends, some children with more severe asthma might be more comfortable going to camps specially designed with them in mind. The American Lung Association (*www.lungusa.org*) and the Consortium on Children's Asthma Camps (*www.asthmacamps.org*) list many local camp programs that help children learn how to manage their asthma better, while participating in the usual camping activities.

Prepare for the Road

Before taking a trip, you and your child should take several important steps to make sure you are prepared for a smooth journey ahead:

- **Medical checkup.** If your child hasn't seen his health care provider in a while and he is going on a lengthy trip, it would be helpful to have a medical exam to see if his asthma is being managed well and to refill medications.
- **Asthma action plan.** Make sure to bring along the latest version.
- **Devices.** He should have all of his devices, including his peak flow meter or nebulizer with him.
- **Emergency information.** Learn from your health care provider whom to call in case an emergency occurs. Also, emergency medications along with instructions on how to use them may be advisable.
- **Insurance coverage.** Depending on where you are traveling to, check to see if your insurance carrier covers the areas to which your child is going or if out-of-plan health care services are available.

Just remember that bad surprises don't take a vacation, so try to anticipate problems before they happen.

Travel and Medications

When getting ready to travel, keep in mind that you also should pay special attention to your child's medications—particularly where they are stored and stowed and how they are labeled.

Alert!

> Make sure your child takes extra medication with him on a trip—at least one and a half times more than you estimate he'll need—just in case he is delayed or uses more medication than initially anticipated because of an asthma flare-up.

The medications should be kept in the original containers they came in and labeled with your child's name, the medication, the prescriber, and the dose. Also, learn the generic names of the medications—particularly if you are going to another country: Oftentimes medications are sold under different brand names from those purchased in the United States.

Keep the medications close by and accessible at all times during the trip. In a car, place the medications up with the passengers rather than in a suitcase in the trunk in order to avoid extreme temperatures. Also, keep medications in carry-on luggage when boarding a plane to make sure they are not accidentally lost in transit.

Challenges of Flying

When it comes to flying, asthmatic children have several special concerns. First, it is getting on the plane—with medications and related devices—in an era of increasing security restrictions. Next is the act of flying in the plane with pressurized air.

Airport Carry-Ons

The federal Transportation Safety Administration (TSA) now requires that all medications in any form or type—including inhalers, tablets, and pills—be screened when passing airport security checkpoints. All medications must contain the original labels with the child's name on them so they are identifiable.

Medication and related supplies, such as spacers, are normally X-rayed. However, TSA now permits the option of requesting a visual inspection of your medication and associated supplies. However, you must request a visual inspection before the screening process begins.

To take advantage of this option, you must have the medication, devices, and supplies separated from your other property in a separate pouch/bag when approaching the security officer at the walk-through metal detector. These medications and supplies do not have to be put in the same zip-top quart bags that passengers use to hold other small carry-on items.

 **Essential**

To prevent contamination or damage to medication and devices, you may be asked at the airport security checkpoint to display, handle, and repack them during the visual inspection process. Any medication or associated supplies that cannot be cleared visually must be submitted for X-ray screening.

Nebulizers will need to be packed into checked-in luggage. For convenience, you may want to consider a smaller, portable nebulizer or a metered-dose inhaler with a spacer—if your child's medication is available in that form. Check with your health care provider about your options.

You can check for the latest updated information on taking medications and devices through a screening at *www.tsa.gov*.

On Board

Recycled air, like that found on an airplane, can be dry and irritating to an asthmatic child. The air also has less oxygen, meaning it is thinner. It is important that your child's asthma be under control before boarding a plane so her symptoms are not further aggravated once she is in the air. If she is having difficulty controlling an asthma flare-up, consider canceling until she improves.

To combat dry air inside the airplane, consider having your child use a nasal saline solution and encourage her to drink plenty of water. (Just remember, though, about restrictions on carrying liquids through security; additional beverages can be purchased after passing through the security checkpoint.)

Staying in Comfort

Smoke-free rooms—and now even entirely smoke-free buildings— have become more common in the lodging and resort business over the past few years as customers have requested them. This has made it easier for families with an asthmatic child to find comfortable accommodations without worrying about secondhand smoke— imbedded in carpets, fabrics, and furnishings—possibly triggering an asthma flare-up.

A New Look

A new trend among the larger hotel companies also may be helpful to your child: They have developed "allergy resistant" rooms for guests sensitive to dust, molds, and chemicals. These are rooms that have been gutted and then retrofitted with environmentally friendly products and materials.

These rooms have been designed to eliminate items that contribute to poor indoor air quality. This meant replacing standard carpeting with hardwood flooring, which is easier to clean and minimizes dust; coating door hardware, plumbing fixtures, and other frequently touched surfaces with an antimicrobial agent to eliminate germs; using paint, adhesives, coatings, and furniture free of volatile organic compounds and other off-gases; and using wallpaper that is perforated to prevent moisture from getting trapped and creating mold.

Also, air-purification systems in each room collect 99 percent of particles and gases. A monitoring system is used to maintain proper levels for odors, gases, carbon monoxide, carbon dioxide, humidity, and temperature—reducing the amount of dust mites and mold. These rooms, though, usually have a premium price attached to them.

Taking Your Own Precautions

While planning your stay at a hotels or other lodgings away from home, be wary of potential asthma triggers such as concentrations of dust mites and molds in carpeting, bedding, mattresses, and upholstered furniture, along with fumes from cleaning products.

To avoid some of these problems, the American Academy of Allergy, Asthma and Immunology has compiled a list of points you can consider when staying in a hotel:

- Ask when you are making reservations if allergy-proof rooms and/or nonsmoking rooms are available.
- If your child has a sensitivity to molds, request a sunny room away from any indoor pool area.
- If your child is allergic to animal danders, inquire about the hotel's pet policy. If pets stay at the hotel, ask for a room that is designated as pet-free.
- If your child's asthma symptoms are triggered by dust mites, consider bringing your own pillows and bedding, and dust-proof or zippered covers for pillows and mattresses during your stay. Also, check to see if the hotel offers synthetic pillows.

- Consider using the air conditioner instead of opening the windows to circulate the air through the room; request that filters be changed, if possible.
- Avoid using a hotel room's closet or dresser drawers if there is a sensitivity to mold.

These tips can be applied as well when staying in other places such as cottages or cabins in woods or near a beach. Take additional steps to make sure the buildings are thoroughly cleaned and aired-out before you arrive to help reduce dust mite and mold concentrations.

Also, if you're being a little more rustic—camping out in tents— remember to air them out before using them again. Also, air out sleeping mats and sleeping bags. If possible, do not use campfires to cook, but instead use self-heating camp stoves.

Watch Out for Triggers

The joy of getting away is to see new sites and enjoy new experiences. The drawback is those experiences might involve exposure to asthma triggers that were not anticipated in some of the most unexpected places.

Family and Friends

While it's great to see familiar faces, sometimes when families or friends host, there might be triggers present—say secondhand smoke or indoor pets—that could cause trouble for your child's asthma symptoms. If it is not possible to work around them, consider staying at a nearby hotel (and explain the problem to them).

Scenic Spots

With flowers in bloom, this might be a great time to visit a favorite location—but not such a great idea if your child has asthma and pollen is one of his triggers. Check with several Internet sites such as *www.aaaai.org/nab* or *www.pollen.com* to see what the mold and pollen levels are before you go. If levels are too high, you might want to go another time.

Also, be aware of areas when pollen levels are high much of the year—much of it from grasses. For instance, Hawaii has grass pollination year round, while many of the Southern states typically have the longest pollination period—around ten to eleven months throughout the year. Ask your health care provider about the appropriate use of antihistamine medications for allergies, in addition to your regular asthma medications.

Cruises

Sailing into a tropical port of call can be exciting. However, meeting up with dust mites, pollen, and mold there may not be. These allergens also could be heavier on river cruises as well. On extended cruises, find out about the availability of medical care. Let medical personnel on the ship know if your child will need any assistance with her asthma during the trip.

Beaches

If you want to stay away from pollens, consider a trip to a beach where the winds blow in from the water. But, be careful of other triggers such as the "red tide toxins"—blooms of an ocean algae concentrated along the coast that produce highly potent aerosolized toxins that affect individuals with asthma. Since these blooms are localized, find another beach without them. Also, if your child has eczema, an allergic skin condition found among many individuals with asthma, be cautious of sun exposure because it can make it worse.

Traveling Abroad

When traveling to another country, make sure that medications are labeled with your child's name and medication. You should have an asthma action plan or letter from your health care providers describing your child's asthma and medicines. This could help you with airport security or customs.

If your child is using a nebulizer, make sure you have the correct plug adapters because the electrical outlet may vary from country to country.

Also, in a new area, familiar yourself with the nearest hospitals and find out how to contact emergency services—just in case.

Activities and Exercise

Generally, if your child's asthma has been well-controlled, he should be able to do most activities on a trip such as sightseeing, biking, or swimming. However, remind him to use techniques—such as warm-ups and premedication with his quick-relief inhaler—to avoid exercise-induced asthma.

Also, if he is traveling to higher elevations from a lower elevation, his asthma should be manageable at higher altitude—but make sure he or you discuss any management strategies beforehand with his health care provider.

Also, encourage your child to have fun with a buddy when involved in any of these activities—just in case he needs any assistance. And, of course, remind him (if he is carrying an inhaler with him when at school) to continue to do so when away.

Other Away-from-Home Tips

Keep in mind these other tips to make your child's time away from home a healthy and pleasurable one:

- If you cross several time zones, take into consideration the time differences so your child's medication dosage schedules remain constant.
- When traveling by car, close your windows and turn on the air conditioning or ventilation instead—to keep out molds and pollens.

- To avoid excess air pollution when driving, consider travel in early morning or late evening when the air quality is better and heavy traffic can be avoided.
- If your child uses a nebulizer, you may want to think about a portable nebulizer that plugs into your car's cigarette lighter or uses a portable battery pack.

Just remember that taking simple steps can mean less worry about your child's asthma symptoms—no matter what journey she is taking.

CHAPTER 18

Emergency Care and Hospitalizations

Hospitalization is not a normal part of having asthma. While spending time in a hospital to treat asthma symptoms can happen, in many cases, it should not have to happen with proper treatment and guidance provided to parents by health care providers. But this often does not occur—leaving parents in the dark about what they should do to prevent this from happening. However, steps are there to help you make sure your child stays out of the hospital for asthma—for a long time.

Hospitalization Trends

Asthma hospitalizations now represent about 3 percent of all hospitalizations among children, according to the Centers for Disease Control and Prevention's National Hospital Discharge Survey. In numbers, this means twenty-seven hospitalizations for asthma per 10,000 children for a total of 198,000 hospitalizations nationwide a year. This makes it the third leading cause of hospitalization in the country for children.

High But Steady Rates

These national statistics, based on data from 2004, provide some measure of good news: From 1980 through the mid-1990s, asthma hospitalization rates for children from infancy through seventeen years of age climbed steadily upward. However, by the late 1990s, these rates flattened out, although at historically high levels. Unfortunately, behind these numbers is some sobering news: While the hospitalization rates are holding steady, the types of pediatric asthma cases now being seen in hospitals are more severe than ever.

Potential Prevented Cases

Between 15 to 54 percent of all annual pediatric asthma hospitalizations in the United States (about 29,000 to 106,000 cases) could have been averted, according to a study performed at a Boston Medical Center of children admitted for asthma treatment. Also, an estimated $161 million to $581 million could be saved annually with several preventive steps.

The study, which surveyed parents, primary care health care providers, and inpatient attending physicians, found that many of the hospitalizations could have been avoided with better education about the child's condition, medication use, the need for follow-up care, and the importance of avoiding known disease triggers.

 **Fact**

Adolescents and families who failed to contact their primary care health care providers prior to a visit to the hospital were at greatest risk for hospitalization. Specifically, no phone call to a health care provider prior to a hospital visit translated into a two times greater chance for a preventable hospitalization. Also, children older than age eleven were twice as likely as younger children to experience a preventable hospitalization.

Knowledge Is Power

These statistics show that the number of cases of children hospitalized for asthma episodes does not appear to be going down as it should—despite the availability of safe and effective treatments to stop and control asthma. But, it may not have to be that way—especially if parents and children become more knowledgeable about what asthma is and realize that it can be managed.

 **Question?**

Should you be worried that your asthmatic child could end up hospitalized?
It depends. Thousands of children's hospitalizations actually could be avoided each year if parents were better educated by pediatric providers about their child's asthma and were more proactive about follow-up visits, according to researchers at the Medical College of Wisconsin.

Research findings suggest that inadequate education of parents about their child's condition can contribute to the child being hospitalized for an illness that could have been prevented. Both health care provider groups and parents agreed on this assessment.

Medication Questions Dominate

Parents of the children in the Wisconsin study said the top reason for avoidable hospitalizations was their lack of adherence to medication-related issues such as including instructions on proper dosages, dose frequency, treatment duration, and how to obtain needed refills easily.

To avoid this, the researchers suggested that parents should review the following with their child's health care providers:

- Every medication's name and purpose
- The medication's dosage and dose frequency
- How to give the medication to a child
- How long to take the medications
- How to refill the medications
- Whom to call if the child runs out of the medication

Parents in the study also acknowledged that they did not take appropriate preventive measures to keep their children out of the hospital. This included helping children with asthma avoid triggers such as cigarette smoke and dust.

Follow-Up Visits

Another link to avoidable hospitalizations was the delay or lack of follow-up visits. Parents in the study cited this reason far less than the health care providers. This suggests that parents need to be better educated on the need for and importance of follow-up visits, the researchers said.

In addition, they pointed out that health care providers and parents needed to work together on recommending and scheduling future visits, so the child's condition is continuously monitored after hospitalizations.

Missed Medications

Sometimes, even those children who consider their asthma to be under control can end up in the hospital emergency department with an asthma flare-up. Exposure to high levels of allergens (molds, pollens) or irritants (wood smoke, ozone), a particularly difficult virus, not keeping up with immunizations, or not taking medication as prescribed all can trigger asthma symptoms—and lead to seeking emergency care.

Inhaled Corticosteroids

Many of these hospitalizations for asthma, though, may be the result of not taking prescribed daily inhaled corticosteroid medications that are recommended to control airway inflammation, according to one study.

In the study, the overall adherence to inhaled steroids was found to be about 50 percent. Those patients who missed one out of four doses of their prescribed inhaled steroid were found to have doubled their risk of being hospitalized.

Approximately 60 percent of hospitalizations could have been prevented if the patients had taken their inhaled medications as directed.

Reliance on Quick-Relief Medications

Sometimes children may not be taking their inhaled corticosteroids all the time because they have found they can get relief—albeit temporary—from using their quick-relief medications when symptoms flare up.

Alert!

Flare-ups are triggered by inflammation of the airways, which require daily medication. When the quick-acting medications wear off, the natural instinct is to use more. However, during that period, symptoms that are due to inflammation may have been getting worse throughout their airways for the past several hours.

If you notice your child using her quick-relief inhaler repeatedly during the day, find out when she last used her long-term control medication. And, monitor her symptoms and determine what they indicate on her asthma action plan.

Prednisone—Now?

The oral corticosteroid, prednisone, is used to decrease swelling and inflammation of the airways that can lead to an asthma flare-up. Oral corticosteroids also have been linked with serious side effects when they are used long-term; these side effects, though, usually have not been cited with shorter-term use.

When use of prednisone may be indicated for an impending flare-up, you may be tempted to try to wait as long as possible to use it. However, as the inflammation continues, it may become harder to reverse. Using the prednisone sooner—rather than later—could avoid a possible trip to the emergency room—and ironically a week of prednisone to reverse inflammation.

Of course, always check with your health care provider if a flare-up seems imminent and review exactly what symptoms indicate the need to start a medication such as prednisone. But remember to start as soon as appropriate to get it under control, before it becomes more serious.

Be Prepared

The best way to deal with an asthma emergency is to prepare for it. Then if you ever need to handle an emergency you are more likely to remain calm and know exactly what to do, increasing the likelihood of a positive outcome.

 Essential

As a start, speak with your health care providers about which hospitals they would select when an asthma emergency arises. Sometimes, health care providers have admitting privileges or arrangements at certain hospitals, which means yours could be available to provide your child care.

Select a Hospital

The first step is identifying the hospital and emergency department that is near you and able to handle a pediatric emergency. This should be listed on your child's asthma action plan.

While all hospital emergency rooms should be able to provide the basic asthma treatment, some smaller community hospitals may not have as many inpatient pediatric services or units available. Some of these services may be available at larger regional facilities or children's hospitals.

Ready to Go

If an emergency occurs, you might find it helpful to have a list of items ready to go to the hospital. This will include your child's asthma action plan so medications and information about your child's asthma can be reviewed.

In addition to your insurance card, bring along your child's actual asthma medications; any asthma devices such as inhalers, spacers, or nebulizers; peak flow meter records; a favorite toy or book of your child; and any overnight essentials such as clothes or toiletries—just in case you need to stay the night.

What an Emergency Looks Like

Sometime, it might happen: Your child might be having an emergency. Here are some of the signs that you should look for that indicate his symptoms are getting worse (and which should be listed on your child's asthma action plan):

- He is sweating.
- He is breathing so hard that he has difficulty speaking.
- He is using his abdominal muscles to breathe out and skin is denting in around his ribs with breathing.
- He is showing a bluish color around his lips and fingernails.
- His nostrils are beginning to widen when breathing in.

- He is continuing to wheeze, breathe hard, or cough—even after the rescue medications have been given.

Now is the time to follow the directions on his asthma action plan that outline how to handle an asthma attack. Remember that it's better to seek medical care earlier rather than later during an asthma attack.

At the Emergency Room

If your child's asthma flare-up ends up bringing you to the emergency room, she will first be assessed to determine how severe her illness is. She will be checked for her vital signs, which include her temperature, pulse, breathing rates, and blood pressure. A triage nurse will listen to your child's chest to determine wheezing or air movement.

 Essential

In the treatment area, a peak flow meter reading should be taken to determine air flow. A quick-relief bronchodilator, such as albuterol, most likely will be administered by a metered-dose inhaler or a nebulizer. Generally, the doses will be higher and more frequent than those used at home—which could make your child somewhat jittery.

Additional oxygen may be given—either as a precaution or a response to a low reading from the device called a pulse oximeter on her finger. Sometimes the low oxygen is a response to the airways being plugged with mucus, which could lead to collapse of part of a lung.

Oral steroids (such as prednisone) may be given to reduce lung inflammation and help severe asthma symptoms within a few hours.

After these medications are given, the child will need to be observed for several hours to see how she is doing and how she responds to the medication.

If her condition is better, she will be discharged—with more albuterol to use as she needs it—and a short course of oral corticosteroids or other medications.

When she returns home, she should continue to use her regular medication. However, she should contact her health care provider about getting an appointment. An emergency room visit indicates that it might be time to re-examine her asthma action plan.

When Hospitalization Happens

If your child fails to respond to treatment, a hospital stay might be in order. This might mean being discharged to another room upstairs or to "overnight" rooms attached to the emergency room that are for shorter stays. Most individuals hospitalized because of asthma symptoms stay about twenty-four to forty-eight hours.

Again, the doses of asthma medication might be higher and more frequent than the ones used at home. These treatments initially will be given closer together and then spaced apart—moving to a pattern that can be followed at home.

Hospital Team

In the hospital, you will meet many health care providers, aside from physicians, who will be assisting with your child's care such as nurse practitioners, physician assistants, and respiratory therapists. They also can provide asthma assessment and monitoring, managing asthma over the long term, and controlling various factors that can increase asthma severity.

Social workers and case managers may also work with you to discuss appropriate services and review what equipment might be needed at discharge. Dietitians can be helpful in discussing food allergy concerns.

A team approach has been found to work well at hospitals in providing asthma care. Each member should be able to answer your questions and review your child's management plan.

The ICU

Sometimes, if a child fails to respond to current treatments, she may be transferred to the hospital's intensive care unit (ICU). Here, asthma care could include continuous treatments with albuterol and intravenous medicines.

A child would be placed in the ICU if her airways are severely obstructed and she has difficulty removing gases such as carbon dioxide from her lungs. A build-up of these gases could cause the child to become drowsy—spending even less energy on breathing. This would make the waste gas levels rise even further—causing the child to stop breathing. In this case, a child would need to be placed on a ventilator.

While in the Hospital

Being in the hospital can be a confusing and anxious time. While there, remember that you and your child have the right and responsibility to understand and question the care that your child is given.

Of course, those taking care of your child are well-trained medical professionals, but sometimes mistakes happen—perhaps a prescription is read incorrectly or a health care provider's order for a test is forgotten.

Alert!

Patient safety mistakes happen thousands of times a day across the country. If you notice something that confuses you or just doesn't seem to make sense to you, speak up. It's not disrespectful or rude, and it can help both you and your child understand or prevent any further problems.

The Joint Commission, a private group that accredits hospitals and health care organizations, has developed a list of your rights as a patient or as a legal guardian or advocate of a patient (in this case, your child). This list includes your right (as your child's guardian) to:

- Be informed about the care your child will receive.
- Get information about care in your language.
- Know the names of the caregivers providing your care.
- Get an up-to-date list of all your child's medications.
- Be listened to.
- Have pain treated.
- Be treated with courtesy and respect.
- Make decisions about your child's care, including refusing care.
- Have safe care.
- Know when something goes wrong with your child's care.

The campaign also suggests other questions to ask such as: How often will your health care provider see you during the stay; can you get a copy of your child's medical record and test results; what happens if something goes wrong during treatment; what is informed consent; and to whom do you speak if a problem arises during a hospital stay? More information about the "Speak Up" program is available at *www.jointcommission.org*.

The Hospital Discharge

The discharge should be planned far in advance of leaving the hospital. Your child's health care provider should arrange for a follow-up visit soon after the discharge date.

Preparing for Home

Oral corticosteroids are likely to be continued for a few more days—until the inflammation is reduced. Quick-relief medications can be continued, roughly at the rate of one dose every four hours. Your child should also continue with his long-term controller medication.

Also during this period, it is important that your child avoid triggers such as tobacco smoke, wood smoke, or perfumes because his airways are inflamed and sore.

Following a severe flare-up and time spent at the hospital, your child should be encouraged to rest and avoid physical activity for a short time. You and your provider should discuss when he should return to school or daycare.

Discharge Summaries

At the time of discharge, you may want to request a discharge summary that you could carry to your first post-discharge visit to your child's health care provider.

A study from Emory University on discharge summaries found that primary care providers often did not receive adequate patient information from hospital-based health care providers following a hospital discharge. These discharge summaries often lacked important information such as diagnostic test results, treatments provided, discharge medications, test results pending at discharge, patient or family counselling, or follow-up plans, the researchers said.

However, the discharge summary will not be dictated or completed until the child has left the hospital, so requesting it before leaving is not reasonable. Asking for a written summary of tests performed and treatments given as well as discharge medications is a reasonable request, and many hospitals do this routinely. You can also request that a copy of the discharge summary be sent to you when it is completed.

Someday, computerized electronic records transmitted from the hospitals to the primary care providers could address this need—when the technology becomes more common and privacy/safety issues can be assured. But for now, the researchers suggested creating computer-generated discharge summaries on paper that patients, acting as couriers, could deliver to their health care providers. This could vastly shorten the delivery time of discharge communications.

When Hospital Visits Increase

The time of the year when hospitalizations or trips to the emergency department are most likely to increase for asthmatic children is in the late summer and early fall—or around when school begins for most children.

 **Fact**

> One of the top reasons for emergency department visits in September is the increased exposure to colds and flu, which can be easily passed from child to child during the school day—triggering asthma episodes.

In a study at a New York medical center, pediatric asthma emergency department visits jumped after Labor Day—especially for children who were in elementary school. The rates for visiting the emergency department also were up for preschool students and older students, but the rates for adult asthma patients remained steady.

To avoid colds and flu when returning back to school, experts recommend old-fashioned hand washing and hand sanitizing to keep germs and viruses off hands.

Returning to school also means exposure for children to indoor air pollutants—such as dust, molds, and aerosols—in the schools that can trigger asthma symptoms among children as well. (Also see Chapter 11.) Parents should ensure that their child's asthma management plan is updated, and medications are refilled. If necessary, a visit with your primary care provider should be scheduled prior to the start of school.

This should serve as a reminder to give teachers, nurses, and coaches your child's updated asthma action plan—plus any medications to the school nurse or designated staff member—to get her off to a good start in the new school year while avoiding trips to the hospital.

CHAPTER 19

Exercise and Fitness

With growing concern about childhood obesity, new emphasis has been placed on improving kids' fitness through exercise. But when you have an asthmatic child, some questions seem to nag at you such as: Will asthma interfere with her participation in sports, or what can be taken to make sure she remains safe when exercising? It is important to keep in mind is that with proper medical care, treatment before exercise, and physical conditioning, your child can participate in most of the physical activities she loves—from the playground to the school gym to the softball field.

The Truth about Asthma and Exercise

Many opportunities are available for children—from hiking to biking to playing baseball—to burn calories and keep them strong. Your child, in most instances, does not have to avoid many of these activities because of asthma.

Instead, you can help your child take steps to control asthma symptoms while letting him participate in—and not avoid—physical activities that he enjoys with his friends, teammates, and classmates. In the process, he can gain a sense of accomplishment, well-being, and increased self-esteem.

 **Fact**

Recent research has shown that children with asthma are more likely to be overweight or obese—possibly related in part to engaging in less exercise than other children their age without asthma. Social and economic backgrounds were not seen as a factor with these differences. Ongoing research has also been looking at whether obesity can be considered a risk factor for developing asthma.

Just as asthma severity varies from child to child, the reaction of a child with asthma to exercise will vary as well—depending on the type of exercise, the vigorousness of the exercise, the season of the year, air temperature and humidity, and location of activity. Most children who have a history of asthma will show symptoms of exercise-induced asthma when engaged in various physical activities.

Oftentimes, exercise in which a child is constantly in motion— maybe running or jumping—will cause symptoms for those whose asthma is not well controlled. Sometimes, children will show symptoms only when they exercise.

The good news is that today's treatments can successfully control asthma so that your child can participate in physical activities much of the time. But as a parent, there's still more work to be done—in particular, communicating with teachers, coaches, and other instructors to help them understand what asthma is and what the needs of your child are.

It is important to work with your health care provider to develop the asthma management plan and exercise guidelines that will help your child when exercising. This plan should be shared with those instructors and coaches that your child is working with in the school or sports team settings.

At times, it may be necessary that your child have some modifications to planned exercise, such as varying the type, length, location (indoors or outdoors), or frequency of activity. But make sure your child is part of the action and not sitting behind on the bench or left in the library. The goal should be lifelong physical fitness and a better quality of life.

Exercise-Induced Asthma

The exact cause of exercise-induced asthma is not clear. But exercise-induced asthma, which also may be referred to as exercise-induced bronchospasms or exercise-induced bronchoconstriction, appears to be related to strenuous or continuous exercise or physical exertion—oftentimes performed in cool, dry weather.

Ninety percent of children with chronic asthma are likely to encounter symptoms when exercising. However, other children without chronic asthma appear to develop symptoms only when they exercise. Forty percent of those children may have allergic rhinitis, but 9 percent with exercise-induced asthma have no history of allergy or asthma at all.

Symptoms

The symptoms of exercise-induced asthma usually will begin within five to ten minutes after beginning to exercise, or within five to ten minutes after a brief exercise period has stopped. After about twenty to thirty minutes, your child will begin to feel better.

Children with exercise-induced asthma are sensitive to sudden changes in temperature and humidity. The symptoms often appear worse with cold and dry air rather than with warm, humid air.

Question?

Why does cooler air trigger breathing problems during exercise?
A child—while exercising—breathes faster and harder through her mouth so she can pull more air into her lungs. But the air that comes through her mouth has not been filtered, warmed, or humidified through her nose. This means the air that she breathes is cooler and drier than normal.

With mouth breathing, air is moistened to about 60 to 70 percent relative humidity, while nose-breathing warms and saturates air to about 80 to 90 percent humidity before reaching the lungs. For the child with asthma, her extra-sensitive airways react to the cooler air, with muscle bands around the airways contracting. This narrows the airways, making it more difficult to breathe, resulting in symptoms that can include:

- Coughing
- Tightening of the chest
- Wheezing
- Unusual fatigue while exercising
- Prolonged shortness of breath when exercising

With children, who may not know how to recognize exercise-induced asthma, their symptoms might be somewhat harder to detect. For instance, they may complain to you about: chest congestion, discomfort, or pain; a sensitivity to cold air that is accompanied by coughing when moving from outdoors to indoors; a general feeling of being out of shape or winded; comments about tiring easily or low energy; dizziness; frequent colds; stomach aches; frequent throat clearing; and observations that they can't keep up with their friends when running or playing.

Parents concerned about these symptoms should ask their health care provider about what treatments are available.

 **Fact**

Warmer outside air, however, may not always protect against exercise-induced asthma. Pollens and molds are present when children play and exercise outside during warmer weather, especially in the late summer. During extended dry periods or drought, these pollens and molds could dramatically escalate and increase the chance that your child could experience breathing difficulties while exercising.

Diagnosis of Exercise-Induced Asthma

While the symptoms exhibited by a child during exercise may point to exercise-induced asthma, the condition should be diagnosed by a health care provider. This diagnosis will be based on medical history, a physical exam, a simple lung function test, and response to treatment. However, diagnosing this condition is not always simple.

When the diagnosis is unclear, a medical professional can confirm it through an in-office visit by using breathing tests at rest and after exercise, for instance, using a treadmill or cycle for about six to eight minutes. Both before and several times after the test, the child breathes into a spirometer, a type of breathing machine that measures the ability to breathe out. A decrease of about 12 to 15 percent of the volume of air blown out could indicate possible exercise-induced asthma.

A test also can be conducted on the field following a six- to eight-minute "free run" or after participation in a sport or activity that appears related to respiratory symptoms. Again, airflow is measured before and after exercise ends. While a portable spirometer can be used, a peak flow meter can be tried as well to measure a decrease in airflow.

It is important to correctly diagnose exercise-induced asthma among children because in some cases it might be another medical condition that requires a different medical treatment.

Alert!

Researchers have found that what was thought to be exercise-induced asthma in children may have causes other than asthma. While asthma is the top cause of exercise-induced asthma, some children without other asthma symptoms had other conditions such as poor physical conditioning, cardiac disease, or muscle disorders.

Another condition is vocal cord dysfunction (VCD), a disorder in which vocal cords do not open as fully as they should when breathing. Sometimes VCD and asthma may co-exist in athletes. The results need to be confirmed through further workups and testing.

If exercise-induced asthma is misdiagnosed, the child will find that a prescribed routine treatment—such as use of a short-acting inhaler before exercise—does not provide benefits that she wants during exercise. This could mean frustration for you and your child in terms of getting the proper treatment, along with use of unnecessary medication.

Treatment, Control, and Conditioning

A number of different approaches using medication, training, and conditioning are available to help your child prepare for—and hopefully halt—symptoms related to exercise-induced asthma. These steps are implemented before, during, and after the physical activity.

Getting Ready to Exercise

Researchers have found that as many as half of all individuals who control their asthma with inhaled medications can still show signs of exercise-induced asthma. But there are several pre-exercise steps your child can consider to control his asthma symptoms when participating in sports or other vigorous activities. In addition, short-term or long-term medications can be prescribed by his health care provider that can make breathing easier when exercising.

These steps include:

- Using a short-acting inhaler fifteen minutes before exercising.
- Warming up for between six to ten minutes before starting an exercise program to help lessen chest tightness that occurs after exertion.
- Drinking plenty of fluids before, during, and after the activity.
- Stopping exercising immediately if symptoms occur.
- Covering up the mouth and nose with a scarf or ski mask in colder weather.
- Moving indoors to practice during colder weather.
- Taking time to cool down at the end of a strenuous exercise by stretching and jogging to help prevent air in the lungs from changing too quickly from warm to cold.

These short-acting drugs can also be used to relieve symptoms related to exercise-induced asthma after they occur. Longer-acting bronchodilator sprays, such as salmeterol and formoterol, have been found effective. They can also be used thirty minutes before exercise, and can last from ten to twelve hours. (Their protective effect, though, will last for less than eight hours with continued use.)

Essential

> About five to thirty minutes before exercise, your health care provider may recommend inhaling a short-acting bronchodilator spray, always with a spacer, which includes albuterol, pirbuterol, levalbuterol, or terbutaline. They have been found to be effective in 80 to 90 percent of patients, act quickly, and last between four to six hours. Cromolyn sodium or nedocromil sodium also may be recommended as a pretreatment five to thirty minutes before exercise.

Continuing Care

If your child continues to have symptoms even with pretreatment, you should discuss with your health care provider whether a daily anti-inflammatory medicine is appropriate. Recurring symptoms may mean that inflammation is present in the child's airways and that even stronger medications (such as inhaled steroids or leukotriene inhibitors in pill form) might be needed.

Your child should remember also to restrict her exercising if she has a viral infection, if temperatures are extremely low outside where she is playing or practicing, or if pollen and air pollution levels are high (and she has seasonal allergies). During these times, her airways could be more sensitive and symptoms could occur more readily.

Continue to remind your child that appropriate treatment will let her get the most from her exercise programs. In addition, it will help her maintain an active lifestyle that will benefit her as she grows older.

Conditioned for Success

While medication may help your child, you still might want to look at another area: physical conditioning. Oftentimes, children may limit their physical activity and exercise because of their asthma.

As a consequence, they have not developed as much of the muscle strength or physical stamina needed to fully participate in various sports or exercises.

Alert!

If your child begins to experience asthma symptoms during exercise, she should stop and re-use the inhaled medication used prior to the exercise. If the symptoms go away, she can resume. However, if her symptoms return, she should stop the activity and repeat her quick-relief medication. Your health care provider should be consulted for further advice.

Recent research has suggested that physical training—relying on exercises to build muscle and endurance—could assist children in strengthening their bodies, along with their breathing. The actual body of study on physical conditioning for asthma patients still is small, but involvement in fitness activities was shown to be related to fewer health care provider visits and school absences than before starting exercise routines.

Conditioning exercise usually should be performed about three to five times per week for at least thirty minutes. Talk with your child's health care provider about how much exercise your child should strive for to get better conditioning.

What Exercises Work

For children diagnosed with exercise-induced asthma, some activities may be easier for them to participate in than others. Sports or activities that involve short, intermittent bursts of exertion—such as baseball, kickball, karate, golf, short-term track and field events, surfing, aerobics, volleyball, gymnastics, walking, hiking, and wrestling—are generally better tolerated. Even the practice of yoga, which uses both stretching, breathing, and meditation techniques, may provide benefits for the child with asthma.

 **Fact**

Swimming has proven to be a popular sport among children with asthma because it is conducted in an environment that is warm and humid, can be done year-round, and builds upper body strength. However, ongoing research is looking at whether swimming sometimes could aggravate asthma due to swimmers' exposure to chlorine byproducts in the air and the water.

On the other hand, activities that involve longer periods of exertion and movement—such as soccer, long-distance or marathon running, basketball, and field hockey—may be less well tolerated by the child. In addition, cold weather sports that require constant motion—such as ice skating, ice hockey, and cross-country skiing— could also be challenging. However, with proper training and treatment, children with asthma can still participate in these sports.

One sport that has generated much discussion in recent years is scuba diving. Until a few years ago, the general thought was that no asthmatics should be permitted to dive because of concerns about air flow obstruction. But with great strides in management of asthma— due to new medications—and with the recognition that there are varying degrees of asthma, new recommendations have emerged that asthmatics can scuba dive, provided their medical condition is carefully evaluated by a medical professional before a dive.

Essential

> When children engage in unscheduled physical activity, such as playing on the playground or participating in a game of pickup basketball, they may not have their medications with them. In these instances, a simple long-acting regimen given at home might be more effective than short-acting drugs that must be administered in a timely fashion for the child with exercise-induced asthma.

Another fun kid sport—horseback riding—can be considered, but only after consulting with your health care provider. Riding horses could prove problematic for children with animal-related allergies.

Banned or Okay Medication

If your child becomes more actively involved in organized sports, questions are likely to come up regarding whether the asthma medication being used is legal or banned during competition.

The broad answer lies not in whether the medication is medically necessary, but rather if it can be determined to be performance-enhancing—giving an athlete what would be considered an unfair competitive advantage.

Since several organizations may have oversight on this determination, the athlete using asthma medications should check with his coaches, health care provider, and appropriate athletic authority to learn the status of the medications and what actions need to be taken ahead of time.

Various athletic organizations differ on what is banned or allowed in terms of asthma medication used by athletes during competition. For instance, the United States Olympic Committee follows International Olympic Committee guidelines for testing. While many amateur athletic organizations have also adopted these guidelines regarding drug testing at sports events, they are not universal.

Asthma and Physical Education

For children with asthma, physical education classes can sometimes be intimidating. What if they can't run very far? Will the other kids laugh at them when they take their medication? Will their teacher scold or belittle them because they are not participating? The list can go on. But a number of actions can be taken to make sure the child with asthma gets to participate as much as possible in her physical education classes and other recreational school activities.

 **Essential**

To help avoid problems in school associated with physical education, parents should make sure that a copy of the child's asthma management plan is available to physical education teachers and coaches, with their roles clearly identified in helping to manage your child's asthma.

Asthma Management Plan

Supporting your child's efforts to follow her asthma management plan is an important step to keep her participating in physical education activities at her school. Your child needs sensitivity and understanding from both her teachers and other students in dealing with her asthma. If your child is teased about her asthma, she may avoid using her medication when she needs it or may skip her physical education class. Or if she is told to "tough it out" in a physical education class, she may risk health problems or just give up entirely.

If peer pressure is a problem, parents can suggest that the school use an asthma awareness curriculum (developed by the National

Heart, Lung, and Blood Institute) that teaches children from kindergarten to sixth grade about asthma and how they can offer support to children rather than barriers.

Working with Teachers and Coaches

At school or perhaps on a sports team, your child could encounter questions from teachers or coaches when he declines to participate in an exercise or sport because of asthma symptoms. While it is important that teachers and coaches respect the child's report of his own condition, it also is important that you keep lines of communication open with them.

 **Alert!**

If your child is asking on a regular basis to be excused from physical education class or recess, a real physical problem may be present that needs to be addressed. Or maybe your child could use additional assistance and support from his teacher or coach that would let him become a more active participant.

Teachers and coaches can play important roles by talking with your child and learning his concerns about asthma and exercise. They should be able to reassure him they understand his condition and have a shared understanding about the conditions that require activity modifications or medications. They should respect his limits.

To improve the experience of your child with asthma, find out if his teachers and coaches are doing the following:

- Including adequate warm-up and cool-down periods with the activity.

- Consulting with either you or your child's asthma management plan on the type, length, and frequency of any limitation.
- Observing for asthma symptoms (such as wheezing, coughing, or chest tightness).
- Encouraging the child to monitor his peak flow if he uses a peak flow meter.
- Monitoring the surrounding environment—and consider a temporary change of location—for potential allergens and irritants, such as a recently mowed field or pollen; poor air quality; extreme weather conditions; or possible interior conditions that could promote asthma symptoms, such as a refinished gym floor.
- Making exercise modifications when needed (such as permitting a child to walk or walk/run if running is scheduled).
- Keeping a child involved if temporarily unable to participate. (For instance, asking a student to be a scorekeeper, timer, or equipment handler until he returns for full participation.)

Teachers and coaches should recognize symptoms of exercise-induced asthma, and be ready to take action if it occurs. You should make sure that your child's asthma plan and the school's emergency plan are easily accessible so that they know what to do and take appropriate action if your child shows the following symptoms while exercising: coughing, wheezing, pain or chest tightness that may last several minutes to an hour or more. They should know that these symptoms are very different from breathlessness and deep, rapid breathing usually seen after an aerobic exercise that quickly returns to normal in children without asthma symptoms.

Once the child stops the activity that is causing symptoms, the asthma management plan should be followed. Assistance should be provided with medication, if necessary.

Teachers and coaches should observe if an emergency is occurring and if it's necessary to call for medical help. The symptoms indicating an emergency are: The child is hunched over with shoulders lifted—struggling to breathe; the child has difficulty completing a sentence and takes breaths between words; and the child's lips or fingernails turn blue.

Alert!

Also keep in mind how environmental factors on the school playing fields might trigger—and even worsen—your child's exercise-induced asthma symptoms. For instance, insecticides, pesticides, fertilizers, and herbicides used to maintain playing fields might cause symptoms to appear. Paints and other decorative materials that enhance the appearance of playing fields could trigger symptoms as well.

Access to Medication

Many children with asthma require two different medications: one that they can use for daily control and prevention, and the other to treat and relieve symptoms. Generally, the longer-acting bronchodilator sprays can last up to twelve hours—precluding the use of the shorter-acting sprays.

However, short-term inhaled medication still could be needed by your child—sometimes about fifteen minutes before physical education class or recess. In this instance, if accessing the medication is difficult during the school day or is inconvenient or embarrassing, your child may get discouraged and fail to use the inhaler as needed. Then, her asthma could get worse and her exercise and physical activities could be unnecessarily restricted.

Most states now have passed legislation that does permit children to carry their daily inhalers with them at all times at appropriate ages. (See Chapter 11.)

Monitoring Peak Flow

Aside from watching for symptoms, your child can use a peak flow meter to monitor for signs of exercise-induced asthma. The peak flow meter is a hand-held device that measures how fast air is blown out of the lungs: The peak flow number will drop when your child's lungs are congested. A sharp drop in the peak flow number may signal that extra medicine or a brief rest during exercise is needed.

 **Fact**

A peak flow meter can be an objective way to make decisions about participation in sports or physical education class. Sometimes, teachers or coaches may not fully understand the impact of asthma on an athlete: Some may prohibit an athlete from participating while others may push for them to keep up with their peers. A peak flow meter can help take away some the confusion.

CHAPTER 20

Self-Management and Record Keeping

A s the old adage goes, you can lead a horse to water, but you can't make it drink. In a way, the same concept appears linked with asthma management. While many new asthma advancements have been emerging, many children are still having trouble successfully managing their asthma. Even among those children who are controlling their symptoms most of the time, a little room for improvement is still there. Through self-management, patient education, and personal record keeping, you might see some changes in asthma management in the near future.

Managing Change

For years, the Boston-based Institute for Healthcare Improvement (IHI) has worked with health care organizations on new and different ways to provide quality health care. One of the ideas behind its work is that quality is a two-way street—change needs to be made by both health care providers and patients.

This includes dealing with chronic conditions such as asthma. In order to achieve what IHI calls breakthrough levels of improvement for individuals with asthma, several areas of change are needed including:

- **Self-management.** Effective self-management is very different from telling patients what to do, according to IHI. Instead, patients should have a central role in determining their care—one specifically that encourages a sense of responsibility for their own health.

- **Decision support.** Treatment decisions need to be based on explicit, proven guidelines supported by at least one defining study.
- **Delivery system design.** The delivery of patient care requires not only determining what care is needed, but clarifying other roles and tasks to ensure a patient gets the care. It also means making sure that all the providers who take care of patients have centralized and current information about a patient's status.

While these levels of change are important for health care providers, in a way they're also very important for you—as the parent of a child with asthma.

Of course, relying on your asthma team—which includes your health care provider—is important in getting off to the right start in managing asthma. But, when you are away from the health care provider's office, it's important that you know the value of self-managing —knowing what the guidelines are and knowing what your child's own medical information is—to help him successfully address his asthma symptoms.

Self-Management Education

While skillful and caring medical care is critical in improving asthma outcomes, it needs to be combined with self-management education, according to the National Asthma Education and Prevention Program (NAEPP) guidelines on asthma.

Essential

In order to improve outcomes and support quality care, all patients—including children—need to participate actively in their care. This means using strategies and taking aim at minimizing exposure to causes of asthma symptoms and making adjustments to better manage this chronic disease.

Studies have found that the benefits of educating individuals in self-management skills are related to: improved self-assessments, improved medication use, reduced visits to emergency departments and hospitals, decreased health costs related to asthma, reduced health symptoms, and improved overall health status.

Asthma Action Plan Plus Daily Management

Self-monitoring is critical to effective self-management of asthma, according to the NAEPP guidelines. Probably this is best emphasized through the creation of individualized asthma action plans that are based on factors such as asthma severity and your child's ability to perceive blocked airflow. (Also see Chapter 2.)

The written asthma action plan can help indicate what your child—or those who care for her—should do to take care of asthma symptoms in terms of medication or contacting health care professionals in case of emergency. This includes using peak flow monitoring, symptom monitoring, or both to prevent asthma symptoms. The plan is important because it can improve the communications between you, your child, and your health care provider.

However, ongoing studies also have pointed to adding daily management strategies for asthma as well to this plan. With a daily management plan, your child can monitor her symptoms—either with a peak flow meter or through acute symptoms—and consider related self-adjustments for medications and instructions for daily treatment.

An Ongoing Partnership

Rather than just accepting a quick educational session on asthma, forging a strong and ongoing partnership with your child's health care provider can help emphasize the important aspects of asthma self-management.

 **Fact**

One study found that this therapeutic relationship—where both you and your child should feel comfortable when speaking with your provider about questions or concerns— could improve quality of life, promote better symptom control, and increase lung function, particularly among those with moderate to severe asthma.

Developing this level of communication is designed to provide you and your child with a basic knowledge about asthma and to promote self-management skills in several basic areas. These include:

- How to detect differences between normal airways and asthmatic airways.
- How medications—including long-term control medications and quick-relief medications—work and how their use fits in with daily treatment.
- How to use inhalers (with your child demonstrating), how to use spacers and nebulizers, how to assess symptoms (with or without using peak-flow meters), and how to detect if asthma symptoms are flaring up.
- How to avoid indoor and outdoor asthma triggers.

This partnership should emphasize that education is continuous and that education sometimes takes a while to master. Ongoing research has shown that it can even take as much as six months to a year for the impact of education to become evident.

Goals of Self-Management

An important aspect of self-management is discussing and meeting goals important to you and your child in terms of controlling and managing his asthma. These can be combined with general goals proposed by your provider and can include:

- Requiring no or fewer visits to a hospital or emergency department.
- Not missing days at school because of asthma.
- Choosing to participate in any activity, including sports-related or other vigorous activities, through asthma treatment.
- Becoming more symptom-free—particularly during the night.
- Having top lung function all day.
- Finding satisfaction with current asthma care.
- Reducing the use of quick-relief medications.

These types of goals should be incorporated into your child's treatment and listed in his asthma action plan. They can be divided into short-term and long-term goals, and should be reviewed during each office visit to see if they are being met.

For example, perhaps your child's asthma does not seem to be controlled well with his daily inhaled corticosteroid. After meeting with his health care provider, it might become evident that he is not using his metered-dose inhaler properly and therefore was not getting the medicine he needed every day.

A short-term goal might be to improve the technique of using the inhaler and writing down how it is controlling his asthma each day. If this ends up not working, perhaps a new dosage or a new medication might be needed.

If the goals have side effects—perhaps the medication leaves a bad aftertaste or is causing a sore throat—these should be discussed with your provider on how that is preventing your child from meeting his goals. Adjustments or solutions should be proposed to help meet those goals.

Barriers to Self-Management

Sometimes the barriers to self-management may inadvertently come from those we know and love and who live around us. While we want the best for our children, we still may listen to parents, other relatives, friends, or others in our communities who provide us with well-intentioned advice on treating and managing asthma that may conflict with what your medical professionals may be saying to you.

Asthma-Related Beliefs

The identification of asthma as a disease goes back centuries. This means that attitudes and perceptions about asthma go back centuries as well.

In some minority communities, for instance, asthma has been viewed as a condition in which you treat the symptoms when they arise—rather than manage the condition itself. This means that at times a lower level of asthma control may be accepted because these communities may not be aware of the impact that appropriate (and newer) asthma management may have on their lives.

This could make compliance with a daily long-term controller medication to prevent airway inflammation more difficult and may lead to poorer asthma outcomes. In addition, lack of symptoms on certain days in some communities may mean that someone's asthma is actually okay when it's not. The idea that long-term medications need to be taken every single day—even when symptoms are absent—may have a hard time gaining acceptance.

 **Fact**

> One study found that a "no symptoms, no asthma" belief could be associated with a likelihood of using an inhaled corticosteroid one-third less times when asthma symptoms were not present. Better clarification of what long-term controller medication does and why it is needed every day could more effectively address some of those community views.

But each community can be different. One study noted that living in an "ethnic enclave"—which had a high percentage of foreign-born residents—appeared to be good for children's health, with far fewer children having asthma and respiratory symptoms compared to the national rate.

Cultural and Ethnic Perspectives

Sometimes it may seem that health care providers come from one world and patients from another in terms of cultural beliefs. While a provider may see asthma as something to treat with medication and avoidance of triggers, other cultures and ethnic groups may have a different set of parameters.

This doesn't mean one group is right or wrong. In fact, you may be familiar with some of these ideas. But, it does mean that health care providers should make attempts to understand an individual's cultural viewpoint and values to ensure better ongoing management of asthma.

For instance, many Latinos may make distinctions among illnesses as being "hot" or "cold." Rather than dismissing this belief, your provider—as a part of the therapeutic relationship—can consider maybe incorporating a hot drink such as tea when taking a medication.

Similarly, if a preparation or home remedy is being taken by a child with asthma that could be harmful, the provider should step in to provide advice and suggest an alternative. Some of these home remedies, such as herbs, for instance, might contain ingredients that could replicate properties in a medication, which could cause serious complications.

Language Barriers

Any communication with a health care provider should be done in a language you understand well. Some providers in the past have relied on children to interpret for their parents when an interpreter is not available. However, this is risky when medical terminology and medication usage is discussed.

Alert!

If you are a parent of a child with asthma—and you are uncomfortable conversing in the language(s) spoke by the health care provider—a medical interpreter who is familiar with the language and the medical terminology should be present during those office visits.

Good communication has been found to correspond to better compliance. For instance, several studies among Hispanic parents and children found that the language barrier was a leading risk factor for having inadequate asthma therapy for their children.

Getting Great Care

While guidelines have been available for years on managing pediatric asthma, a large gap has existed between what are considered best practices to provide quality care and the actual care provided to children.

To get a better handle on this issue, the federal Agency for Healthcare Research and Quality (AHRQ) combed through more than 3,800 articles in the published literature to get answers related to both pediatric and adult asthma.

It looked at four primary types of outcomes that were related to: measures of clinical status (e.g., asthma symptoms), functional status (e.g., days lost from school), health services utilization (e.g., hospital admissions), and adhering to guidelines (e.g., numbers of patients given prescriptions for inhaled corticosteroids).

This was crossed with types of quality improvement strategies, which included components of patient education, self-monitoring or self-management, and provider education. After sorting through the information, AHRQ found that:

- Young children with asthma benefit the most from quality improvement strategies that also include their parents or caregivers at some point of the process.
- School-based programs, which included patient education programs, reported "statistically significant improvements" in outcomes of care for children with asthma.
- The small number of educational programs aimed at teens— even those taught by peer teachers, health care providers, and nurse educators—did not show significant changes in asthma outcomes for most of the studies.
- Although only a small number of studies were available, expanding the usual asthma care with additional specialty asthma clinics staffed by specialty-trained nurses and phar- macists improved care—particularly with the increased use of inhaled corticosteroids and improved clinical outcomes.

Education for parents and caregivers of asthmatic children about asthma triggers in their homes and better asthma control on the home front were found to be effective in the many studies AHRQ scanned on the National Cooperative Inner-City Asthma Study, sponsored through the National Institutes of Health.

After the parents and caregivers were provided training in areas such as asthma triggers (e.g., dust mites, cockroaches) and environmental controls (e.g., vacuum cleaning, clean air filters), the number of symptom-free days rose while days lost from school and the number of asthma symptoms declined.

Record Keeping: Asthma Diary

Just like you may write numbers in your checkbook register to remind yourself of how much you've spent or deposited, you or your child should consider using an asthma diary to record items such as peak flow readings or symptoms. (See Chapter 10.)

It can become a very valuable tool in self-management—showing what medicine was taken and when or if peak flow rates fluctuated over the course of weeks and months. It can also note if you had to contact your health professional or seek emergency care.

It also can help pinpoint trouble spots. Perhaps your child visited a friend who has cats or rode in the car of an aunt who smokes, and the diary indicates a drop in her peak flow rate or additional use of a quick-relief medication. These may be signs of possible triggers that she may have to avoid.

 Essential

It's helpful to pick two points in the day—usually morning and evening—to record data in an asthma diary. It can be done in any number of ways—in a notebook, on a calendar, on a sheet of paper, or even on a computerized spreadsheet.

Also, free interactive diaries are becoming available on the Internet to keep track of symptoms, medicines, and quality of life. For instance, the National Jewish Medical and Research Center (*www.njm.org*) in Denver offers "My Asthma Diary" to patients and other consumers that includes graphs to chart progress in controlling asthma. It also provides up-to-date information on asthma treatment and research. The interactive diary closely follows the NAEPP guidelines.

Record Keeping: Personal Health Records

The health care services that your child needs today may seem more fragmented than ever. Perhaps there are recent visits to a primary care health care provider or specialist, new prescriptions, or maybe test results. But what about your child's visit to that other health care provider two years ago when you had a different health plan or lived in another part of the country?

Question?

Why do you need your child's personal health records?
While living with asthma means looking ahead and setting goals, it also means looking at past medical history—maybe to detect patterns, to review medicines that did or did not work, to note when emergency department visits were necessary, or to examine when quick-relief medications were being refilled.

You might have a stack of records that you keep in a drawer or carry around with you. For instance, you may have a notebook with dividers that helps keep all your records in one spot and easy to grab as you go out the door for a health care provider visit.

But when a real asthma emergency occurs, will you have the records you need with the important information? To help, new personal health records—both online and offline—are becoming available for free or low-cost that you can have when you most need them.

Rights to Your Records

When your child has a chronic condition such as asthma, it becomes very important to create her personal health record (PHR) that shows all her health-related information including her health care provider visits, medications, emergency visits, and other pertinent medical information. (You might find this information helpful for you and other family members as well.)

Alert!

If an emergency should arise, you'll know that you can have fast access to your child's health information so that he can receive appropriate care. While many think that an emergency room can obtain their medical information quickly, this is not currently the case with the current state of health information technology.

Under the federal Health Insurance Portability and Accountability Act, patients are allowed to view and obtain copies of their health information documents. You'll need to request and sign an "authorization for the release of information" form from the medical provider to receive the data.

You can view or receive entire copies of your records, or you can request a shorter summary of the information. Most providers will charge for copies—so a summary may be less expensive. However, the fee charged by a medical provider can only include the cost of copying (with supplies and labor included in the cost), plus postage if you ask for the copies to be mailed.

Keeping a PHR

You have a choice in how you can maintain your PHRs. The simplest is keeping a file folder or binder with paper copies. But other options include compiling electronic files on your computer. This information can be transferred to computer disks or to a portable USB drive key that you can carry with you.

Internet-based services also are available that you may access from your computer and where you can store and retrieve your PHR information. Some of these services can assist you with collecting the information you need from health care providers.

Also, some insurers, employers, and various health care providers now are offering PHRs as a part of their health care services.

Some online PHR tools are available for free and others may require purchase or a subscription fee. To learn what options are available, the American Health Information Management Association (AHIMA), an industry group, has created a Web site (*www .myphr.com*) to research options and decide what could work for you. (AHIMA does not make, sell, or endorse any of the PHR products.)

AHIMA notes on its Web site that each supplier has various policies and practices on how they may use data they are storing. If you use electronic PHRs, you are urged to study the policies and procedures to make sure you understand how your personal health information will be used and protected. These policies include privacy and security, the ability of users to access their information, and control over accessibility by others.

One free service is iHealthRecord, a secure and confidential PHR that includes interactive programs to explain medical conditions and medications. With this PHR, you can decide which of your health care providers will have access to your record, and for what period of time. The PHR also can be accessed by hospitals and emergency departments—with your permission—in case of a medical emergency. See *www.ihealthrecord.org* for more information.

Web Sites for Parents of Children with Asthma

Air Quality Indexes

www.epa.gov/airnow
Environmental Protection Agency
AIRNow Air Quality Index

www.aaaai.org/nab
National Allergy Bureau of the
American Academy of Allergy,
Asthma and Immunology's
Aeroallergen Network

www.pollen.com
Local pollen reports and
allergy forecasts

Asthma Action Plans (Sample Forms)

nrc.uchsc.edu
From National Resource Center for
Health and Safety in Child Care

*www.noattacks.org/Asthma-
ActionCardStudent.pdf*
From Joint U.S. Environmental
Protection Agency and Asthma
and Allergy Foundation site

*www.nhlbi.nih.gov/health/
dci/Diseases/Asthma/
asthma_actionplan.pdf*
From National Heart, Lung
and Blood Institute

*www.aaaai.org/members/
allied_health/tool_kit/hand-
outs/my_action_plan.pdf*
From American Academy of
Allergy, Asthma and Immunology

*www.lungusa.org/atf/cf/{7A
8D42C2-FCCA-4604-8ADE-
7F5D5E762256}/AAP.PDF*
From American Lung Association

Camps for Children with Asthma

www.asthmacamps.org
Consortium on Children's Asthma
Camps listing of camps

Clinical Trials

www.acrn.org
Asthma Clinical Research Network of the National Heart, Lung and Blood Institute

www.asthmacare.net
Childhood Asthma Research and Education (CARE) Network of the National Heart, Lung and Blood Institute

www.centerwatch.com/ ctrc/aafa/indexnew.html
Asthma and Allergy Foundation of America—Clinical Trials Resource Center

www.clinicaltrials.gov
Provides regularly updated information about federally and privately supported clinical research from National Institutes of Health

www.lungusa.org/site/pp.as p?c=dvLUK9O0E&b=37101
American Lung Association—Asthma Clinical Research Centers

Advocacy and Consumer Health Groups

www.aanma.org
Allergy and Asthma Network/ Mothers of Asthmatics Inc.

www.aafa.org
Asthma and Allergy Foundation of America

www.lungusa.org
American Lung Association site

www.nclnet.org/asthma
National Consumers League site on asthma

www.noah-health.org/en/lung/ conditions/asthma/index.html
New York Online Access to Health (NOAH) provides access to consumer health information on asthma in English and Spanish.

Complimentary and Alternative Medicine

www.nap.edu/catalog. php?record_id=11182#description
2005 book from National Academy of Sciences on Complementary and Alternative Medicine in the United States

www.nlm.nih.gov/medlineplus/druginfo/herb_All.html
National Institutes of Health Medline Plus Directory on Herbs and Supplements

Government Sites

www.cdc.gov/asthma
Centers for Disease Control
and Prevention asthma site

www.epa.gov/asthma
U.S. Environmental Protection Agency asthma site

www.epa.gov/iaq/headstart
Promoting smoke-free homes
for Head Start families

www.nccam.nih.gov
National Center for Complementary and Alternative Medicine of
the National Institutes of Health

*www.niehs.nih.gov/oc/
news/asthma.htm*
National Institute of Environmental Health Sciences of the
National Institutes of Health

www.noattacks.org
Joint U.S. Environmental Protection Agency and Asthma
and Allergy Foundation site

*www.nhlbi.nih.gov/about/
naepp/index.htm*
National Heart, Lung and Blood
Institute's National Asthma Education and Prevention Program

Asthma Guidelines

*www.nhlbi.nih.gov/guide-
lines/asthma/index.htm*
Guidelines for the Diagnosis
and Management of Asthma

*public.nhlbi.nih.gov/newsroom/
home/event-transcripts.aspx*
Transcript of telebriefing announc-
ing the 2007 asthma guidelines

Health Plan Report Cards

www.hprc.ncqa.org
National Committee for
Quality Care annual health
plan report cards

Insurance and Coverage

www.ahip.org
America's Health Insurance Plans

www.insurekidsnow.gov
State Children's Health
Insurance Program

www.naic.org
National Association of Insurance Commissioners

Medical Organizations

www.aafp.org
American Academy of
Family Practice

www.aap.org
American Academy of Pediatrics

www.aarc.org
American Association
of Respiratory Care

www.acaai.org
American College of Allergy,
Asthma and Immunonology

www.chestnet.org
American College of
Chest Physicians

www.thoracic.org
American Thoracic Society

www.nasn.org
National Association
of School Nurses

Pharmaceutical Assistance

www.kids.pparx.org
Provides information on public
and private assistance programs
available to help children in need

www.rxassist.org
Pharmaceutical access infor-
mation center created by
Volunteers in Health Care

School-Related Sites

www.lungusa.org/afsi
Asthma-Friendly Schools Initiative

www.schoolasthmaallergy.com
Tools and information to assist
those caring for school-aged children with asthma and allergies

*www.epa.gov/cleanschoolbus/
antiidling.htm*
U.S. Environmental Protection site on school bus idling

Appendix B
Glossary

Albuterol

The generic name of a quick-relief asthma medication (also see beta2-agonist).

Allergic asthma

Asthma accompanied by allergies. Reactions such as wheezing and coughing are triggered by such allergens as mold spores, animal dander, or contents found in household dust. (Also known as atopic or extrinsic asthma.)

Allergic rhinitis

Often called "hay fever," allergic rhinitis can be caused by outdoor allergens (pollens, molds) and indoor allergens (animal dander, indoor molds, dust mites). Ongoing research has cited evidence that allergic rhinitis and asthma are linked—suggesting the idea of "one airway, one disease."

Allergen

A substance that triggers an allergic reaction. These include dust mites, animal dander, mold, and cockroaches.

Allergist

A physician with special training in allergies.

Alveoli

Tiny air sacs where oxygen is transferred into your lungs and carbon dioxide waste enters the airways in order to be exhaled out.

Asthma

A chronic, inflammatory disorder of the airways characterized by symptoms such as wheezing, breathing difficulties, coughing, and chest tightness. People with asthma have very sensitive airways that are constantly on the verge of overreacting to asthma triggers.

Asthma action plan

A written plan that tells people with asthma, or those who care for them, how to take care of asthma symptoms. This includes how to prevent symptoms, and what to do if symptoms are severe. This plan should be developed together with a health care provider and family members. When used properly, the plan can help people control their asthma.

Atopic asthma

Asthma that is triggered by allergens. (Also see allergic asthma.)

Beta2-agonists

Asthma drugs that relax the muscles around the bronchial tubes. Two types are used: The long-acting type is taken every day to prevent symptoms, often in combination with a steroid. The short-acting type is used for quick relief of symptoms.

Bronchial tubes

Airways in the lungs. One major branch going into each lung.

Bronchioles
Smallest airways in the lungs.

Bronchoconstriction
When the muscles encircling the airways constrict tighter and tighter, pinching the airways closed.

Bronchodilators
Drugs that relax the muscles around the airways, thus opening the airways up. Some bronchodilators are used for quick relief of symptoms during an asthma attack. Others are taken every day to prevent symptoms.

Controllers
Anti-inflammatory medication used by individuals with asthma to control asthma symptoms and keep airways open.

Corticosteroids
Used for long-term daily control of asthma to prevent inflammation. They are most frequently inhaled by using a metered-dose inhaler, dry powder inhaler, or nebulizer. Oral corticosteroids are primarily used for short-term treatment and to slow inflammation that could lead to an asthma flare-up.

Cromolyn
An anti-inflammatory drug that may be used on a daily basis to prevent symptoms of asthma.

Cough-variant asthma
Also called hidden asthma, where the only symptom of asthma is coughing. It possibly may represent early stages of persistent asthma.

Dry powder inhaler
A small device similar to a metered-dose inhaler, but where the drug is in powder form.

Exercise-induced asthma
Asthma that occurs during or following vigorous activity.

Forced expiratory volume (FEV)
Measures of how much air can be emptied from lungs.

Gastroesophageal reflux disease (GERD)
A major asthma trigger. Occurs when stomach acid and undigested food wash back into the esophagus, causing airways to contract. (Also called acid reflux disease, or heartburn.)

Immunoglobulin E (IgE)
An antibody that is part of the immune system that reacts against allergens.

Immunotherapy
A process of injecting shots containing an allergen to help build up the immune system's tolerance to that allergen.

Inhaled corticosteroids
Daily anti-inflammatory medication that is available in metered-dose inhaler, dry powder inhaler, or nebulizer forms.

Leukotriene modifiers
Control drugs used orally for patients with mild to moderate persistent asthma. For mild asthma, they are sometimes used as an alternative to inhaled steroids; for moderate asthma, they may be used as a supplement to inhaled steroids in place of long-acting beta2-agonists.

Metered-dose inhaler (MDI)
Device that lets individual with asthma inhale a specific amount of medicine (a "metered dose").

Mold

An indoor and outdoor trigger for asthma.

Nebulizer

A device that creates a mist out of an asthma drug, which makes it easier to breathe the drug into the lungs.

Nedocromil sodium

An inhaled medication that may be used on a daily basis to treat inflammation in the airways and prevent asthma attacks.

Nocturnal asthma

Asthma symptoms often occurring at night that can cause awakening from sleep.

Non-allergic asthma

Asthma not caused by allergens. It can include irritants that aggravate the nose, throat, or airways. These irritants include cigarette smoke, strong odors or smells, wood smoke, household cleaners, or environmental pollutants. (Also referred to as nonallergic, non-atopic, or instrinsic asthma.)

Peak flow

A measurement (using a peak flow meter) of how well air can be blown out of the lungs. It can show if airways are open normally or if they are closing.

Peak flow meter

A hand-held device used to determine peak flow of lungs.

Pollen

Allergen that can trigger allergy or asthma symptoms.

Rescue drug

A quick-relief medication that works quickly to address asthma symptoms.

Sensitization

When the body's immune system identifies an allergen as an invader, it produces antibodies against it that begins an allergic reaction.

Sinusitis

Inflammation or infection of one or more sinuses, which are located behind the nose and eyes.

Spacer

Tube that connects with metered-dose inhaler to help deliver medication (also called a holding chamber).

Spirometry

Instrument used to diagnose asthma in children generally older than five years. It measures the maximum volume an individual can exhale after taking in a breath.

Theophylline

A drug sometimes used to help control mild asthma, especially to prevent nighttime symptoms.

Trigger

That which can cause asthma symptoms to flare up. Can include allergens, irritants such as tobacco smoke or air pollutants, exercise, medications, or respiratory tract infections.

Vocal cord dysfunction

A disorder in which vocal cords do not open as fully as they should when breathing. Sometimes the symptoms may be misidentified as exercise-induced asthma.

Guidelines: Classifying Severity and Control

CLASSIFYING ASTHMA SEVERITY IN CHILDREN 0–4 YEARS OF AGE

Classifying severity in children who are not currently taking long–term control medication.

Components of Severity		Classification of Asthma Severity (Children 0–4 years of age)			
			Persistent		
		Intermittent	Mild	Moderate	Severe
Impairment	Symptoms	≤2 days/week	>2 days/week but not daily	Daily	Throughout the day
	Nighttime awakenings	0	1–2x/month	3–4x/month	>1x/week
	Short–acting beta2–agonist use for symptom control (not pre-vention of EIB)	≤2 days/week	>2 days/week but not daily	Daily	Several times per day
	Interference with normal activity	None	Minor limitation	Some limitation	Extremely limited
Risk	Exacerba-tions requiring oral systemic corticosteroids	0–1/year	≥2 exacerbations in 6 months requir-ing oral steroids, or ≥4 wheezing episodes/1 year lasting >1 day AND risk factors for persistent asthma		
		Consider severity and interval since last exacerbation. Frequency and severity may fluctuate over time.			
		Exacerbations of any severity may occur in patients in any severity category			

Charts courtesy of the National Asthma Education and Prevention Program 2007 Guidelines for the Diagnosis and Management of Asthma.

CLASSIFYING ASTHMA SEVERITY IN CHILDREN 5–11 YEARS OF AGE

Classifying severity in children who are not currently taking long–term control medication.

Components of Severity		Classification of Asthma Severity (Children 5–11 years of age)			
				Persistent	
		Intermittent	Mild	Moderate	Severe
Impairment	Symptoms	≤2 days/week	>2 days/week but not daily	Daily	Throughout the day
	Nighttime awakenings	<2x/month	3–4x/month	1x/week but not nightly	Often 7x/week
	Short–acting beta2–agonist use for symptom control (not pre-vention of EIB)	≤2 days/week	>2 days/week but not daily	Daily	Several times per day
	Interference with normal activity	None	Minor limitation	Some limitation	Extremely limited
	Lung Function	Normal FEV$_1$ between exacerbations $\cdot$FEV$_1$ >80% predicted $\cdot$FEV$_1$/FVC > 85%	$\cdot$ FEV$_1$ >80% predicted $\cdot$ FEV$_1$/FVC > 80%	$\cdot$ FEV$_1$ = 60–80% predicted $\cdot$ FEV$_1$/FVC = 75–80%	$\cdot$ FEV$_1$ <60% predicted $\cdot$ FEV$_1$/FVC <75%
Risk	Exacerba-tions requiring oral systemic corticosteroids	0–1/year	≥2 in 1 year		
		Consider severity and interval since last exacerba-tion. Frequency and severity may fluctuate over time for patients in any severity category.			
		Relative annual risk of exacerbations may be related to FEV$_1$			

CLASSIFYING ASTHMA SEVERITY IN YOUTHS ≥ 12 YEARS OF AGE AND ADULTS
Classifying severity for patients who are not currently taking long–term control medications.

Components of Severity		Classification of Asthma Severity (Youths >12 years of age and adults)			
			Persistent		
		Intermittent	Mild	Moderate	Severe
Impairment **Normal FEV₁/FVC:** 8–19 yr 85% 20–39 yr 80% 40–59 yr 75% 60–80 yr 70%	Symptoms	≤2 days/week	>2 days/ week but not daily	Daily	Throughout the day
	Nighttime awakenings	<2x/month	3–4x/month	1x/week but not nightly	Often 7x/week
	Short–acting beta2–agonist use for symptom control (not prevention of EIB)	≤2 days/week	>2 days/ week but not > 1x/day	Daily	Several times per day
	Interference with normal activity	None	Minor limitation	Some limitation	Extremely limited
	Lung Function	Normal FEV₁ between exacerbations •FEV₁ >80% predicted •FEV₁/FVC normal	• FEV₁ >80% predicted • FEV₁/FVC normal	• FEV₁ > 60% bu < but predicted FEV₁/FVC reduced 5%	• FEV₁ <60% predicted • FEV₁/FVC reduced 5%
Risk	Exacerbations requiring oral systemic corticosteroids	0–1/year	≥2/year		
		Consider severity and interval since last exacerbation. Frequency and severity may fluctuate over time for patients in any severity category.			
		Relative annual risk of exacerbations may be related to FEV₁			

ASSESSING ASTHMA CONTROL IN CHILDREN 0–4 YEARS OF AGE

Components of Control		Classification of Asthma Control (Children 0–4 years of age)		
		Well Controlled	Not Well Controlled	Very Poorly Controlled
Impairment	Symptoms	≤2 days/week	>2 days/week	Throughout the day
	Nighttime awakenings	1x/month	>1x/month	>1x/week
	Interference with normal activity	None	Some limitation	Extremely limited
	Short–acting beta2–agonist use for symptom control (not prevention of EIB)	≤2 days/week	>2 days/week	Several times per day
Risk	Exacerbations requiring oral systemic corticosteroids	0–1/year	2–3/year	>3/year
	Treatment–related adverse effects	Medication side effects can vary in intensity from none to very troublesome and worrisome. The level of intensity does not correlate to specific levels of control but should be considered in the overall assessment of risk.		

ASSESSING ASTHMA CONTROL IN CHILDREN 5–11 YEARS OF AGE

Components of Control		Classification of Asthma Control (Children 5–11 years of age)		
		Well Controlled	Not Well Controlled	Very Poorly Controlled
Impairment	Symptoms	≤2 days/week but not more than once on each day	>2 days/week or multiple times on <2 days/week	Throughout the day
	Nighttime awakenings	<1x/month	>2x/month	>2x/week
	Interference with normal activity	None	Some limitation	Extremely limited
	Short–acting beta2–agonist use for symptom control (not pre-vention of EIB)	≤2 days/week	>2 days/week	Several times per day
	Lung Function •FEV$_1$ or peak flow •FEV$_1$/FVC	>80% predicted personal best >80%	60–80% predicted/ personal best 75–80%	<60% predicted/ personal best <75%
Risk	Exacerba-tions requiring oral systemic corticosteroids	0–1/year	>2/year (see note)	
		Consider severity and interval since last exacerbation		
	Reduction in lung growth	Evaluation requires long–term followup		
	Treatment–related adverse effects	Medication side effects can vary in intensity from none to very troublesome and worrisome. The level of inten-sity does not correlate to specific levels of control but should be considered in the overall assessment of risk.		

ASSESSING ASTHMA CONTROL IN YOUTHS ≥12 YEARS OF AGE AND ADULTS

Components of Control		Classification of Asthma Control Youths ≥ 12 years of age and adults		
		Well Controlled	Not Well Controlled	Very Poorly Controlled
Impairment	Symptoms	≤2 days/week	1–3x/week	>4x/week
	Nighttime awakenings	≤2x/month	1–3x/week	>4x/week
	Interference with normal activity	None	Some limitation	Extremely limited
	Short-acting beta2-agonist use for symptom control (not pre-vention of EIB)	≤2 days/week	>2 days/week	Several times per day
	EV₁ or peak flow	>80% predicted/ personal best	60–80% predicted/ personal best	<60% predicted/ personal best
Risk	Validated Questionnaires ATAQ ACQ ACT	0 <0.75 >20	1-2 ≥1.5 16-19	3-4 N/A ≤15
	Exacerbations	0-1/year	≥2/year (see note)	
		Consider severity and interval since last exacerbation		
	Progressive loss of lung function	Evaluation requires long–term follow-up		
	Treatment–related adverse effects	Medication side effects can vary in intensity from none to very troublesome and worrisome. The level of intensity does not correlate to specific levels of control but should be considered in the overall assessment of risk.		

Index